Last Exit from Bridgeton

Bridgeton Cross in the 1930s. In this busy scene, a policeman directs the traffic, a practice which survived into the 1950s. Many of the buildings survive. Timpson's Shoe Shop can be glimpsed between the trams.

Last Exit from Bridgeton: an East End childhood remembered

Second Edition

James McKenna

Glasgow
The Grimsay Press
2006

The Grimsay Press
an imprint of
Zeticula
57 St Vincent Crescent
Glasgow
G3 8NQ
Scotland.

http://www.thegrimsaypress.co.uk
admin@thegrimsaypress.co.uk

First published by James McKenna in 2003 in a limited
edition of 364 copies, ISBN 1-8735868-6-8

This Second Edition, with additional contributions and
photographs, first published in 2006

© James McKenna 2003, 2006

*Every effort has been made to trace possible copyright holders and to obtain
their permission for the use of any copyright material. The publishers will
gladly receive information enabling them to rectify any error or omission
for subsequent editions.*

ISBN 1 84530 038 6 Paperback

In memory of
Ellen McKenna
12 June 1906 - 31 July 1982
and
James McKenna
20 September 1906 - 13 February 1984

James McKenna was born in 1947, and lived in the Bridgeton/
Dalmarnock district of Glasgow until 1966, when his family
moved to East Kilbride, where he still lives. He attended school
in the East End; he later attained an Honours History degree
from the University of Strathclyde in 1991.
A growing interest in local history and reminiscence work from
1996 to 1999 - spent partly working on 2000 Glasgow Lives,
a reminiscence project from Glasgow Museums - as well as a
fondly remembered childhood in the East End, motivated the
writing of this book.

Foreword

I lived in Swanston Street in Bridgeton from the age of two until I was thirteen.

James has evoked so many memories of my own childhood and given me a real insight into the history of a part of the world I love dearly.

This is a must read book for anyone with connections to Bridgeton, Glasgow and Scotland, and James should be congratulated on his achievement.

Lorraine Kelly
April 2005.

Preface to the First Edition

Jim McKenna has written a book of memories, which will resonate within the minds of several generations of Brigtonians. He writes of a place now changed beyond all recognition and of a time rapidly being forgotten by its present inhabitants.

There is a comfortable feel to these recollections which I am sure will be shared by those many Brigtonians who remained at home as well as those who have moved to the far corners of the world.

They speak of a simpler, but harder life – one held in common by the many hundreds of thousands who lived through the period he describes. There is no doubt that this book will stir people's own memories – the names of neighbours, shops and streets might vary between individuals, but the routine and events will be familiar.

It is only in recent years that the social history of the ordinary people of the East End of Glasgow is being made explicit and recorded for posterity by the people who underwent that experience. Jim McKenna's book makes a significant contribution to the story of our fathers and mothers who struggled to make us what we are today. I have no hesitation in recommending it to all who have any connection with Bridgeton and would like to know more about their own history.

Gordon Adams, June 2002.

Gordon Adams is the author of *A History of Bridgeton and Dalmarnock* (Hill and Hay Printers: Glasgow, 1990) and *A History of Tollcross and Dalbeth* (Clydeside Press: Glasgow, 1992)

Contents

Contributors Index

List of photographs.

Acknowledgements

In the early days, it was a case of writing or typing out a few hundred words at a time. Sometimes weeks would pass without me putting a single word on paper. By 2000 though, I had begun to spend longer periods on recollecting places, events, etc., from my childhood and was working on the book most days of the week.

It was only by early 2001 though, that I had made the first moves to find a possible publisher. At the same time I had applied for a QNIS Millennium Award Grant to self publish the book, having quite accidentally come across a leaflet on QNIS at a small exhibition in George Square one Sunday afternoon, late in the summer of 2000.

Whilst one or two publishers I had contacted showed some interest in my work, I decided that the route of self-publishing would be the most hopeful one. It was more in hope though than expectation that my application went off to the QNIS offices in Castle Terrace Edinburgh, in the autumn of 2000.

At first I was informed that, although soundly worded and well presented, my application was unlikely to succeed, as it did not quite demonstrate the possible beneficial effects my project would have to the community area with which it was concerned. This was a vital requirement in attaining a grant for the project. However, I was given every encouragement, to slightly re-word my application and to re-submit it.

This I duly did in the early winter of 2000; three-months later, I was duly informed in March 2001 that I had been successful in my application for a grant. Needless to say, I was delighted at this news and from that point on I worked on the book almost every day at some point.

Without this grant, the option of self-publishing would have been a near impossibility and I am indebted to all at QNIS for providing me with this opportunity to produce this book. Most especially though, I am indebted to *Mrs. Jessie Bruce*, the Project Leader, whose initial encouragement, consistent understanding and assistance during our meetings throughout 2002,was invaluable.

Secondly, a special mention to Mr. William (Wull) McArthur of *www.glesga.ukpals.com*. Just after my book became available at the end of January 2003, I became aware of this website through Mr. Bob Currie, one of the contributors to my book.

Since then I have been a member of 'Glesga Pals' and log in on a daily basis. 'Glesga Pals' is a website which reunites Glaswegians scattered all over the world but mainly in places like America, Canada, Australia and England. Members can log in and have a 'blether' with others about the 'old days' and reminisce about people, places and events etc. Many members have been reunited with old school friends through the site. There are also forums on the site for sport, current affairs and even jokes.

I am indebted to Wull and his website, initially for giving my book advertising space – some copies were sold this way – but especially for the assistance the site has given me in obtaining the additional contributors for the reminiscence section of this edition. The majority of the new contributors had their details posted in the

Guestbook section of 'Glesga Pals.' Wull himself is one of these contributors.

A special thank you goes out to *Lorraine Kelly*, presenter of GMTV, who lived in the Bridgeton area in the 1960s and the early 1970s. I only discovered last year that Lorraine had lived in Bridgeton when a child and on contacting her at GMTV she most kindly agreed to write the Foreword to this second edition.

Another special thank you goes to *Willie Miller*, former Aberdeen and Scotland defender, former manager of Aberdeen and now Director of Football with Aberdeen. Willie has introduced the expanded reminiscence section at the back of the book. Willie is also originally from Bridgeton and attended Dalmarnock Primary School in Albany Street.

I would also like to thank *Miss Fiona Hayes*, curator of The People's Palace Museum in Glasgow. Between the summer of 1996 and late 1998, I worked with Fiona at the Open Museum in Glasgow on the *2000 Glasgow Lives Project*. As well as motivating me further, working on this reminiscence project provided me with invaluable experience in compiling information for my book. Fiona provided me with access to the catalogue of photographs held at the Burrell Collection in Pollok Park Glasgow. Thanks also to *Mrs.Winnie Tyrell* at the Burrell for providing the ones I selected and used in this book.

A special big thank you must go to *Mrs. Linda Blair*, who very generously gave of her time to proof-read the whole work for me. Given my sometimes 'dodgy' grammar, I can assure you that this really was a big help to me.

Other mentions must go to the staff of the Glasgow Room at the Mitchell Library in Glasgow, who provided very good service in seeing to my sometimes overwhelming requests for access to directories, newspapers, books etc. Not forgetting too, supplying me with photographs from the 'Virtual Mitchell' collection, which make up the bulk of the photographs included in the book.

In this regard too, my warmest thanks to *Mr. Gordon Adams*, author of two previous books on the East End of Glasgow, who most kindly agreed to provide a foreword for my book.

Thanks are owed to the staff at the Strathclyde Area Genealogy Centre in Glasgow whom I found to be very helpful during my two visits there to consult registers on births, deaths and marriages. Also to the staff at the Glasgow Archives Room based in the Mitchell Library, next to the 'Glasgow Room.'

And finally! My thanks to all of the people who contributed to that section of the book, which included peoples' memories of the area.

They are: Tommy Adams, Margaret Douglas Aitken, Bill Auld, Andy Baird, May Ballantyne, Michael Bell, Martha Best, Alex Brown, Margaret Brown, Cathie Brydson, Mary Cairns, David Cameron, Ronnie Campbell, Ruth Conner, Richard Cooper, Elspeth Crosbie, Andy Crossan, Tommy Crossan, Bob Currie, Margaret Davies Hale, Mrs Docherty, Rachel Dryburgh, Jean Dundas, Tommy Dunn, Eddie Fairman, Donald Findlay, Wilma Flavell, Marion Forte, William Fraser, Paul Gunnion, Mary Hall, Elizabeth Hunter, Les Jackson, Wilma Stirling Johnston, Jack Kennedy, John Kirkwood, Alice Maxwell, Alistair May, Bob May, Tam MacArthur, William MacArthur, Nan McConnell, Bill McGillivary, Myra McGuigan, Frank

McKenna, John McLaughlin, Janette McLean, Jane McMullen, Elizabeth McNeill, Elizabeth Miller, John Oliver, Helen Orr, Linda Pinnock, Eddie Reid, David Reilly, Peter Scott, Claire Tedeschi, Margaret Thomson, Thomas M. Waugh, 'Wee Meg', and Carl Wilson.

Ruby Street, on 4 September 1962, the last day of the Glasgow trams. Dalmarnock Depot, a favourite haunt of mine for 'tram-spotting' is on the left-hand side. Dalmarnock Public Baths and the 'Steamie' ('Wash-house) are near the top end, on the right-hand side.

Photograph Acknowledgements

I have selected photographs which I considered to be the best available to me of places that I remember from the area. There are other locations that I would have liked to have included, but unfortunately no photographs were available.

While some of the photos are dated, the places they represent, and relate to, looked very much as they did at the time I am writing about.

The photographs on pages 42, 44, 48, 52, 54, 56, 62, 69, 71, 91, 100, 110, 130, 143, 175, 209, 233, 247, 277, 308, 310, 327, 330, 332, 333, 342 and 431 are included courtesy of the Glasgow Room in the Mitchell Library - as seen in the Virtual Mitchell collection.

The photographs on pages iv, 9, 202 and 314 are from the Anthony Duda Collection and appear in the book *Old Bridgeton and Calton* by Eric Eunson (Stenlake Publishing: Ochiltree, 1997)

The photographs on pages xxiv, 17 and 67 appear in the book *Old Bridgeton and Calton* by Eric Eunson (Stenlake Publishing: Ochiltree, 1997)

The photographs on pages 40, 46, 94, 106, 115, 127 and 312 are from the Gordon Adams Collection and appear in the book *A History of Bridgeton and Dalmarnock* by Gordon Adams (Hill and Hay Printers: Glasgow, 1990)

The photographs on pages 77, 79 and 238 are from the Burrell Photograph Collection, The Burrell Collection, Glasgow.

I would like to include my thanks to Mrs Marjorie Winters, Headteacher of Dalmarnock Primary School, for providing me with the photo on page 379.

The photographs on page 396 are from Alice Maxwell.

The photographs on pages vii, viii, xxvi, 5, 102, 272 and, 306 are from the author's own collection.

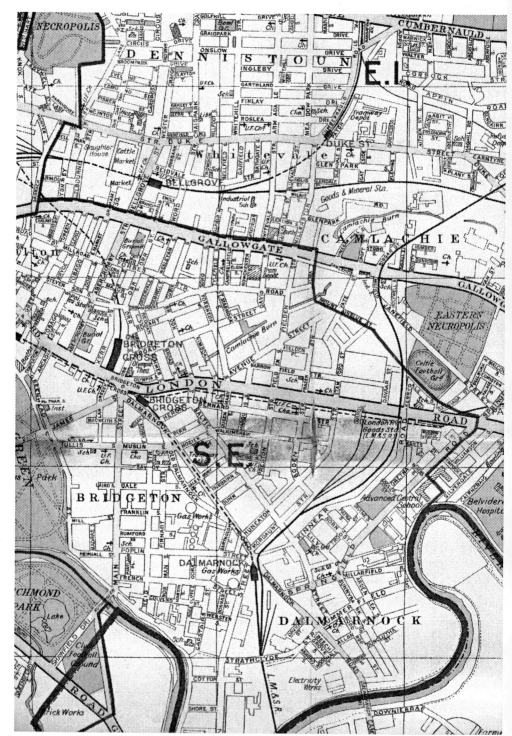

Bridgeton, before I was born

Author's Preface to the First Edition.

I was born at one o'clock in the morning on the thirteenth of September 1947, a Saturday, at Robroyston Hospital, which stood in the North-East side of Glasgow.

Among the items of news making up the front page headlines in the newspapers that far-off day, was a report of a Kilmarnock man who had been a hero when fire broke out on the liner *Reina Del Pacifico* off the coast of Northern Ireland. Fifteen people had died in the blaze. On a somewhat lighter note, it was reported that spectators at Dens Park, Dundee would not be permitted to take bottles into the ground during the League Cup tie, due to be played there that afternoon. This ban had resulted from bottle throwing by spectators attending the previous Saturday's Dundee v Celtic game that had also been played at Dens Park. On the thirteenth, Celtic were playing Third Lanark at Cathkin Park, and the 'bully wee' Clyde were playing Hearts at Shawfield.

You could go to the 'Plaza' ballroom at Eglinton Toll that Saturday evening for six shillings (30p) with the hall closing at eleven o'clock. On the cinema scene, Robert Ryan, (a lifelong favourite of mine) was starring in a film called *Trail Street* at the Bedford cinema in Eglinton Street, in the South-side of the city, and not far from the aforementioned 'Plaza' ballroom. At Green's Playhouse in Renfield Street, Alexis Smith, a lovely redhead – who was to become another big favourite of mine, through watching a lot of her old films on television – was starring in *Stallion Road,* a film that incidentally, also starred a future American President - a certain Ronald Reagan. A film called *Waterloo Road,* starring John Mills and Alistair Sim, was billed to commence the following week at the Regent in Renfield Street.

My birthday is recorded in the *Evening Times* at the beginning of the following week. I notice also that I share my birthday with a fellow Brigtonian of the same name, James McKenna, whose parents lived in Poplin Street, just off Main Street in Bridgeton and close to Shawfield Park. This was where Clyde at that time played their home games. This boy had also been born in Robroyston Hospital.

I seem to have been born on what we Glasgow folk would say was a 'nice day.' The weather forecast for the thirteenth of September was "fair with scattered showers," not that I would be too concerned, mind you!

It is quite fascinating really when you compare and contrast things such as the newspapers of that era with those of today. Both the *Daily Record* and the *Evening Times* were a mere eight pages in length. The *Daily Record* cost one old penny, while the *Evening Times* was a bit dearer, at three old halfpennies.

Author's Introduction.

It was the summer of 1991. I had just graduated from the University of Strathclyde just a few months short of my forty-fourth birthday, with an Honours degree in Modern History and Politics. I had at last fully capitalised on an interest in both of these subjects that I had had for many years. In the case of History, most probably one which, if at the time latent, had been with me since childhood. At that point though, I had little or no interest of any kind specifically in local history.

I had, throughout my years of college and university study, made countless visits to the Mitchell Library in Glasgow, especially to the Glasgow Room on the fifth floor of the building. So much so, that I used to jokingly refer to it as my 'office.' Over a period of time and most especially during the course of my third and fourth years of study for my degree, I would usually have a five or ten minute break from my reading. During this break, I would wander around looking at the books on the shelves of the Glasgow Room. I would usually have commenced my afternoon or evening of studies in either the Social Sciences department on the second floor, or the History department which at that time, was the adjoining room on floor five. Nowadays, the Glasgow archives department is where the History department was at that time, and the History department and the Glasgow Room, are merged into one single unit.

As it was, I increasingly looked forward to reading these books in the short time that was available to me. While my studies obviously came first, I found that in the short term as it were, at least these books in the Glasgow Room were more interesting and certainly far less tiring than the political theories of Thomas Hobbes or Edmund Burke. Even the works of AJP Taylor, on say the two World Wars, which, amongst others had been most probably the initial reason for my visit to the library, were temporarily discarded.

By the time the summer of 1992 came around and with me still drawing dole money, having found no regular full time employment, I found myself with much spare time on my hands. It was at this point that I became an avid reader of many of the Local History autobiographies written by Glasgow-born folk. These were about their childhood and in particular, the areas of the city in which they grew up; what it was like, memories of shops in the area, picture halls, dance halls and much, much more.

Over a period of time, I came to read some really interesting stories about life as it used to be in different areas of the city, through the personal experiences of these writers. There were some really enjoyable memories from Glaswegians who grew up in areas of the city such as Govan, Govanhill, Partick, Maryhill, and the Gorbals, but also in other areas like Anderston, and the West-End. I began to realise just how little had been written with regard to the East End and in particular the Dalmarnock area of Bridgeton where I grew up. I had lived in this area from 1947 when I was born, until 1966.

I decided there and then that this 'gap', regarding reminiscences of the area in which I grew up and still fondly remember to this day, could, with a bit of effort and much time, be filled. This could be done, I decided, by myself with my own memories of the first eighteen and a half years of my life, as spent in Dalmarnock Road SE, as it was then referred to in the street directories of the time. It is now referred to in directories etc., as Glasgow G40.

Everyone remembers their roots; things such as your first memories, going to school, where you played and who you played with, are indelibly imprinted more or less for the rest of your life in your mind. At various times and in varying degrees, these memories come to the surface during the course of your life. Things also, like your first home, the environment and the local area of your childhood, special family occasions and other things like your first job on leaving school, are all there. The happy times, the not so happy times, and the downright sad times. They are all there just waiting to be recalled, once more to be tapped into and, by extension, to be broadcast to anyone interested enough to read about growing up in the city through the memories and the experiences of one of life's fellow travellers. Hopefully this book may stimulate and provoke comparisons, contrasts or whatever, from contemporaries, most especially fellow East Enders and former Brigtonians everywhere. Also, I hope it may interest present day dwellers in that particular area of the East End, and perhaps also the younger generation in the area.

I plan this story to be seen by the reader as a true, honest commentary on everyday life as experienced by a former Brigtonian who grew up in the area some forty years ago. I also have included some additional comment at times throughout the book, on the area as it is in the present day.

This book is not intended to serve as a history of the particular area of the city with which it is concerned - that has been done already by another author. Rather, my own book is intended to serve as a fond recall of childhood and youth in that area and what life was like in a working class home, in a working class area of the city. I say 'fond recall' as even if there were times when life did not seem all that great the good times DID outnumber the bad times. Everyone has a story to tell. Everyone has his or her own special memories of growing up. In this book I hope that in some modest way, I can contribute to the growing collection of reminiscence works available to the Glasgow public as we enter the new Millennium. At the same time, I would like to think that my story would encourage other similarly minded people to put their memories into print.

Further motivation to write this book was provided by my experiences while working as part of the *2000 Glasgow Lives* project between 1996 and 1999. This project is run by the Open Museum in Glasgow and is intended to be a permanent Oral History collection of the memories of Glasgow-born people or, people who have spent part of their life to date, in the city. My own taped memories are included in the collection.

Author's Introduction to the Second Edition

This book was originally published at the end of January 2003. There were 364 copies printed by Clydeside Press, Glasgow. The book proved very popular and all copies were sold in a relatively short period of time. Not though without a hard slog on the part of myself – visiting libraries, book stores, answering the many e-mail enquiries, and some telephone calls about my book that materialized after its publication. I also of course had to keep accounts regarding sales of the book as well as making out invoices and delivery notes etc, for sales of the book.

All of this was of course worth the effort required; seeing your work in print and knowing that people are interested in it is one very good feeling. People have told me how it brought back memories of the area to them and that they really enjoyed the trip down memory lane. It was this, perhaps more than anything else, that gave me a lot of satisfaction. I set out with the idea of doing just that, of rekindling peoples' memories of Bridgeton-Dalmarnock in past times; when people who had read the book were telling me that it had recalled so many memories, I realized that my book had served its main purpose.

I decided to write this second edition because I enjoyed completing the original book so much. Heartened further by the popularity of the book I decided that I had to do it again.

I had little or nothing to add to my own story. I think I have almost exhausted my memories of growing up in Glasgow's East End, but I have made one or two additions and some small amendments too. The main additions to the original book are by far to be found in the **People's Memories** of the area near the end of the book. Here I have doubled the number of contributors, from thirty to sixty. Unlike the first edition where all of the contributions came from one-to-one interviews, reminiscence meetings and the occasional written recall, all of the additional contributions in this edition were obtained 'on line' mainly from the 'Glesga Pals' website to which I refer in the acknowledgements. These contributions have been a valuable asset to the original book and I am most grateful to these contributors.

I still get enquiries about the original edition and I am hoping that this new edition will prove just as popular.

James McKenna,
July, 2006

1

Awakenings

It is a most intriguing thing when a person attempts to recall their very first conscious memory however unclear and probably, at least slightly inaccurate that memory may be. It is in effect, your very first conscious memory of being alive in a certain place, and, if your memory is really good, at a certain time too. It is the first point from which you can trace your own existence and your own part in the great scheme of things called 'being'. Most certainly, writing a book such as this, based on your very own recollections, does prompt the writer to put all his or her efforts into focusing on that first memory. And, any memory strong enough to have stayed fixed in your mind decades later, is surely a more-than-suitable starting point when launching seriously into memories of your childhood.

To pin down one particular memory or recall of a person, place, event or whatever, as being the first recall of your life, is of course difficult, perhaps in some, many or even most cases, very difficult, but certainly by no means impossible.

Different people will, of course, have greatly differing first memories. As a child you are 'aware' of things around you from a very early age, even if these cannot be understood or fully comprehended. Most of these memories are though quickly forgotten. Your first durable, lasting memory is likely to be of some significant event in your early life - like your very first day at school, or in some cases, a person may remember as a child being frightened by some long ago incident or even of a strong curiosity about something. Other childhood memories can be of a place visited, perhaps on a regular basis or, maybe on just one special occasion. Another one can be memories of a particular person; usually these will be happy ones - perhaps of a relative, a grand parent etc.

In my own experience of Oral History, these childhood memories are often pre-school. Quite a lot of people have recalled simple things, like playing in the backcourts of the tenement buildings they lived in. Or, playing in the streets, (the streets being a lot less busy with traffic in past eras.) Although perhaps most people's early memories are of a pre-school nature, they can of course, be from schooldays too. I have heard it said that some people have claimed to "remember" things from as far back as when they were only one or two years of age. If this is indeed true, it surely must be a tiny minority only who can say this with any degree of certainty, as I think most people's earliest memories would start from about three or four years of age.

In my own particular case – and at a distance of almost half a century – I too find it somewhat difficult to say, with absolute certainty, exactly what my very first memory of my life is. I have no recollection of playing in the backcourts or in the street in my very early years. I also have no definite recollection of being out with my parents during this period. Not that there would be any lack of opportunities or playing 'facilities.' At that time Dalmarnock was an area full of tenements, backcourts, parks and quiet side streets, off the main roads, where children could play all day and every day. They could play in a much safer and friendlier environment, in what was a much more innocent era than the present one and where people for the most part, felt much more generally secure, than they do in the present day. My generation was, to a degree, free from the dangers which lurk the city streets in the early part of the twenty-first century.

I think though, that my very first memory is of approaching the 'close' mouth, of the tenement building where we lived, one winter morning about noon, with my mother, and hearing from one of our neighbours, Mrs. Miller that King George V1 had died. That would be in January 1952, and, even with the passing of all these years, it is clear in my mind to this day. As this was about seven months before I commenced my schooling, this is clearly a pre school memory.

I do recall one other time being with my mother and my father and getting my photo taken - not something that I was ever too fond of. This was in premises near Bridgeton Cross, at the corner of London Road and Kerr Street on the right hand side of London Road, as you look westward to Calton and Glasgow Cross. The area where this photographer was has changed very little to this day, though the actual premises are long gone. (From my research I found that the photographer's premises were called *The State Studios*, which was at number 581 London Road. These premises are now occupied by an Indian 'takeaway.')

I think, though I cannot be certain, that this memory dates from after I had started school.

From a glance at the photo, which I still have at home to this day, I would say that I was about five or six years old at the time it was taken. I wonder if it was for anything special? According to the smile on my face I must have enjoyed the occasion, whatever it was.

Right next to The State Studios, at number 583 London Road, there was a dentist, Grimson's. I have a very vague memory of being in here with my mother one late afternoon or early evening "keeping the place" as it were for my father who had made an appointment for after he had finished work. This may have been a pre-school memory but I am not sure. 583 London Road was a 'close' and as well as the dentist, there were tenants living there. That is still the case in the present day.

My next memory is far clearer. It is of my first day at school; the Primary School in question being Springfield Primary, which was, then situated in Connal Street with part of it winding round into nearby Lily Street, just off the main Springfield Road. This would be in August of 1952 when I would be a month or less short of my fifth birthday. I have little recall of actually being inside the premises on that very first day but I do most certainly remember assembling in the playground at the Connal Street entrance; all the mothers were there, including my own mother, with their children.

One of these other mums was a Mrs. Connor, with her son, also called Jim. I can clearly remember her saying to my mother "I know you." Well, they soon did know each other because, for about the next decade or so, Jim and myself were pals and

4

A class photo at Springfield Road Primary in the smaller of the two boys' playgrounds, which I think was taken about 1954. I am fifth from the left in the back row between a girl whose name I cannot remember and a boy whose first name was Bernard but whose surname somehow escapes me.

5

we would all go on holiday together, or maybe go just for a day down the coast to Ayr or Largs, perhaps Saltcoats. Jim Connor at that time lived in Millerfield Road, near Springfield Road. He later moved with his parents, and younger brother Robert, to Arden and later to Barlanark, so I did not go to the same Secondary school as he did. His parents later moved back to Greenhead Street in Bridgeton. Later on I think Jim lived in either Poplin Street or French Street, both just off Main Street, also in Bridgeton. This was after he got married. We lost touch sometime in the late 1960s and I have no idea where he is or what he is doing now. I've always remembered that he is nine days older than I am.

Yes, back to that first day at school. The Korean War was into its third year. Winston Churchill was still Prime Minister of Britain and wee Jim McKenna was entering the State education system. Was I nervous on that first day? I honestly cannot remember for sure, I don't think I was crying though, well that's my story and I am sticking to it. This was to be my place of learning until the summer of 1959 when I would leave Springfield Primary just short of being twelve years of age, to attend Riverside Senior Secondary only a few hundred yards to the North up the main Springfield Road, on the right hand side. I will return to memories of my schooldays in much more detail in later chapters.

2

Oor Hoose.

I lived with my parents at number 337 Dalmarnock Road in the Bridgeton area of Glasgow's East End. My parents had moved in there in 1945, the year of their marriage. I came along two years later. We lived on the North side of the main Dalmarnock Road, between Nuneaton Street to the left, (as you looked face on at the tenement building) and Mordaunt Street to the right.

At that time the area was a lively, bustling, hive of activity sort of place with people coming and going all the time. As well as the shops, the area was full of factories, mills and all sorts of other industrial activity, during an era in which the majority of people still generally worked in manual occupations. Certainly that was the case in the part of the area where I grew up.

There were plenty of shops too. You did not have to go far for the necessities of everyday life; there were many small and not-so-small shops around the immediate locality where we lived, catering for your every need. From my recollections, Dalmarnock Road was always busy during the daytime. There were always plenty of people moving about, with the tramcars still running up until 1962. Plenty of buses too; it was indeed one busy area.

What a contrast with the area as it is in the present day. Almost all the old tenement buildings have long since been demolished, and the original ones, which remain, at the Bridgeton Cross end of Dalmarnock Road, have all been modernised. The tenement block where we lived was demolished in the mid 1970s. An empty space, with a few small industrial premises in the background in Nuneaton Street, now dominates the spot where we lived.

The empty spaces in the area as a whole though, have become fewer over the years as new homes have been built. Some attractive looking new houses have been built over the last fifteen years or so in the middle part of Dalmarnock Road. The side streets off Dalmarnock Road are almost unrecognisable from forty years ago. Most of the new houses in the area are in places like Ruby Street – where the old tramcar depot used to stand – and Heron Street, and the many other adjoining little streets. Sometimes when I happen to be walking through, I do find it quite difficult to picture the area as I knew it when I was a boy.

Our first home at number 337 was on the first floor of the tenement block. There were nine tenants in all, three in each of the three floors. There were no living quarters on the ground floor. I can't remember them being called flats in those days, always tenements. We lived in the middle home on the first floor.

It was a 'single end', which meant that there was only one room within the household, so this room served as a living room, kitchen, and bedroom all in one. The other two homes on either side of us were two-apartments; each had a short hall, or 'lobby' as it was often called, separating the two main rooms – a bedroom and a living room which would double as kitchen. This set up with a single-end between the two two-apartments was the same on all three floors and I think would be typical of the immediate area as a whole.

Dalmarnock Road in 1912. I lived with my parents some forty years later in the tenement buildings on the right-hand side of the photo just past Mordaunt Street, in the middle block. All that remains of this long ago scene is the then Caledonian Restaurant building (later Taylor Brothers the undertakers) and the railway wall next to it. The other railway wall, at the far end on the other side of the road at the corner of Nuneaton Street also still exists in the present day. This scene though remained virtually unchanged until the mid 1970s.

9

We lived in that first home till I think about 1954, when we moved up to a two-apartment on the second floor on the right hand side as you went up the stairs. I have only very vague memories of that first home. Not surprising really, as I was very young when we lived there. I do remember one day though, my mother tending to some illness or injury I had at the time and she sat me down on a chair near the window. This could actually be another pre-school memory, though I cannot be certain.

The house was very small and I think the bed where I slept with my parents was near the door as you came in from the stairway. The washing and cooking facilities were at the other end of the room near the window, which looked out on to Dalmarnock Road. I cannot remember us having a radio, or a 'wireless' as it was more commonly referred to in those days, though we may have had but I have just forgotten about. We certainly did not have a television set at that time. That came along a few years later.

When we moved upstairs to our new home, our washing and cooking facilities were all in the smaller of the two rooms. This room looked out into the backcourts, facing north. The imposing red brick wall of the 'Plaza' picture house dominated the 'scenery'. This cinema had its front entrance in Nuneaton Street. From our window you could also see the tops of the tenement buildings in Nuneaton Street and on the other side you could see the buildings in Mordaunt Street. There was a little dairy shop, which you could see from the window, in Mordaunt Street, McKay's at number 14. I recall being in here quite often for milk.

And the Orange Halls, which were at that time in Mordaunt Street too.

I slept with my parents in this room for a little while. Then, as I got older, I moved into the larger of the two rooms, which looked directly on to Dalmarnock Road. I have no recollection though, of our 'flitting' upstairs or of being in our new home for the first time.

As I grew older and more especially when I reached my mid-teens, I came to spend a lot of my time in this larger room, especially in the evenings. I had acquired a portable radio and used to spend hour after hour simply listening to the great music of the early and mid 1960s; Cliff Richard, Billy Fury, Adam Faith, the Beatles and all that, not forgetting the one and only Elvis Presley of course.

This was long before the days of Radio Clyde, and my favourite station at that time was Radio Luxembourg. I can clearly recall listening to Luxembourg DJ's such as Jack Jackson, Sam Costa, Barry Aldis and a certain guy called Jimmy Saville, long before we had to refer to him as Sir Jimmy. Especially in the summer, I would listen while in my bed, to the great sounds coming out of this magic wee thing called 'the tranny,' - transistor radio. I would often still be listening in at two o'clock in the morning, especially at the weekends; there was no early rise the next day.

Another big favourite of mine around this time, was the Sunday programme *Pick of the Pops,* which came on, I think, at 4pm and finished at 6pm. This would be on the old Light Programme of the BBC, and a while before the days of Radio 1 etc. I seldom missed this programme – it was simply a must for a music fan like myself. Alan Freeman's famous catchphrase with which he opened the programme was "Hi there, pop pickers" and he would then play the top twenty records of the day.

It is often said that most people can remember where they were when the news came through of the assassination of the American President John F. Kennedy on November 22 1963. I can most certainly recall where I was; I was in that room listening to my 'tranny.' I think it would be just after six that Friday evening when my father came through from the other room to tell me that Kennedy had been killed. My parents had heard of the shooting on the telly in the other room. Strange I did not hear about it on the radio, now that I think about it.

Looking back, I can remember that in this room, there was a fireplace in the centre of the wall across from my bed. I cannot recall ever seeing this fireplace actually being used. Perhaps though it was used when we had visitors, especially at New Year time and probably also on some long ago cold winter evenings that I have forgotten about. Just along from this was what was called a 'recess,' - a space where an extra bed could be put. I don't think we ever used it for that purpose though, it was used in the main as a storage area. Next to my bed just beside the door to the small hall, was a large wardrobe and on the other side of my bed, near the window, sat a large organ, which I never learned to play properly at all. I recall many 'practice sessions' at that organ with my parents on Sunday afternoons, but the sounds emanating from my attempts to play the thing should have got me arrested for disturbing the peace and quiet of a Sabbath afternoon, I was that bad. Finally, right next to the window and beside the fireplace, was a cupboard where various odds and ends and everyday type of things were stored.

The other room was the smaller of the two but was much more the centre of everyday activity as it were. From the sink beside the window at one end, to my parents' bed at the other end, right in the corner, there was not very much space at all. We used to have all our meals on a small table beside the wall near the door. This door led out onto the small hall and to the outside door of the house. In the hall or the 'lobby' was the coalbunker. Our little coal fire was right in the centre of the room between the bed and the window.

When you think back, it is quite amazing how even three people could manage in such a small room, especially when you remember that this room doubled up as the main living room and the kitchen and was also where my parents slept, not forgetting all the washing etc that would also be done in here. Looking back though I cannot recall us having any major problems, and manage we most certainly did.

More space would be taken up by two large armchairs, one where my mother sat and the other one used by my father. Also, on the opposite side of the room, facing the fireplace, there was a set of drawers, where the old 'wireless' sat. When we got our first television set, in 1957, it was placed on a stool next to the drawers. I remember, as a boy, taking a cushion from either of the two armchairs when my parents weren't looking and propping it up against the bottom of one of the armchairs, my mother's I think. I would then spread myself across the floor while watching my favourite programmes on the telly. This I did just about every evening, I think for a few years, after we first got the TV set installed. It was my favourite spot, especially on Monday evenings, when programmes like *Wagon Train* were on.

There were many other programmes that were big favourites of mine around this time. I always used to look forward to adventures like *Robin Hood* and *William Tell* ; in the winter when football after school was not possible, I would rush home from school to see these. There were others, such as *Rawhide,* another western, the one with the catchy theme song and a very young Clint Eastwood. Then there were the dramas like *No Hiding Place, Boyd QC* and of course good old Jack Warner in *Dixon of Dock Green*. All of us liked the quiz programmes such as *Double Your Money, Take your Pick* and *Spot the Tune*. My mother simply loved *Coronation Street*, and I think that we were still living in Dalmarnock Road when that other soap *Crossroads* first appeared on our screens. I also used to enjoy the comedies such as *Hancock's Half-Hour* and *The Army Game.* In the latter, Michael Medwin and the late Alfie Bass were particular favourites of mine. Another programme that all three of us 'never missed' as it were, was *I Love Lucy,* on Sunday evenings starring the late Lucille Ball and Desi Arnaz. We would all be crowded round the 'little box' at 'number 337' to see that one. Sunday evening as I recall, always had "good TV" as shortly after 'Lucy' the variety show *Sunday*

Night at the London Palladium would be on and later still *Armchair Theatre, which* more often than not gave us a really good play.

Looking back at these dramas and comedies some forty years later through the medium of the Cable channels, a lot of them have aged rather badly, but at the time they were really something. For most people at that time, television was still something of a novelty and it was only from about the late 1950s that the manual classes began to acquire a set, usually rented. Seen in that context, it is hardly surprising that what we would consider nowadays as 'dated' and 'old hat', was all the rage at the time. Television had been around for about twenty years up till then but had largely been the preserve of the middle classes.

I remember at that time that if a football match on BBC was on at the same time as Coronation Street on Scottish Television, my mother and father would sometimes have a 'tiff' over who should get preference. I think it was usually resolved by taking turn about as it were, but not always. Thanks to that modern wonder, the video recorder, such a thing would never happen in the present day, and my mother could have watched her 'soap' late at night after the football. At that time of course, live football on television was something of a 'special occasion' with nowhere near the coverage of the game that we have in the present day. In some ways it was more of a treat then, something you eagerly looked forward to for days, a real live football game in your living room, Wal! In the present day with saturation the norm, much of the novelty value has diminished and live football is taken for granted. It is even harder to believe too, that until 1964, there were only two channels and they both went off the air about 11pm. Nowadays most channels in the multi–channel packages from Satellite and Cable, are 24 hours, round the clock affairs.

Another pastime of mine, around this time, was simply sitting looking out of the window. 'Hanging' out it (complete with cushions 'transferred' from the easy-chairs to make it easier on the arms) would perhaps be a more apt term in the circumstances. In those days everyone, or so it seemed, opened their windows and sometimes for hours on end would watch the world go by. In my own case I used to spend hours as a boy just watching the tramcars, in particular, going along Dalmarnock Road from the vantage point of the window in the large room. I used to enjoy looking to my right down Dalmarnock Road from the window. Providing it was not foggy you could see the trams in the distance coming along Dalmarnock Road to where we lived. You could see them turning at the bend at Heron Street close to Bridgeton Cross; I used to enjoy guessing what number the tram would be before it reached where we lived.

I would sometimes note the number of the tram as it went towards Farme Cross or Burnside where the numbers 26 and 18 respectively terminated before beginning their journeys in the opposite direction to Scotstoun and Partick respectively. I would also sometimes jot down the serial numbers of the trams and look for them coming back down on their return journey. I used to spend hours at the window just watching the trams when I was a boy. The simple pleasures of childhood.

A June 1962 scene showing Dalmarnock Road near Bridgeton Cross. The tramcar would soon be a museum piece, the trams being taken off the road completely three months later. Tenement buildings in London Road can be seen in the background.

When I think back to that period in the late 1950s and the first part of the 1960s, the practice of looking out your window was widespread. Certainly it was in the area of which I am writing, and I have no reason to believe it was any different in other parts of Glasgow.

I can remember during the summer especially, there was one couple who lived directly opposite us on the other side of Dalmarnock Road who seemed to look out of their window all of their waking hours. I can picture this couple in my mind all these years later. The woman was a big stocky sort of woman and her husband a smaller, rather frail looking chap. I never did know their names but my mother knew the woman through meeting her at the shops etc. I remember my mother speaking to her a few times when I was there. She was one of those characters who never missed a trick. She knew all and everything that was going on in the area, as I recall my mother telling my father and me. She was what you would call a 'busybody' though she was harmless, and as I remember, really quite friendly – one of the 'characters' of the area. When you think of it, perhaps it is not surprising that she never missed anything, given the amount of time she and her other half spent at that window.

It could be quite funny at times really. My mother could have been speaking to Mrs. Miller next door on the stairs for ages, then a few minutes after going indoors she would probably see the Millers 'hanging' out of their window to the left of us as you looked out into Dalmarnock Road. Then the conversation would immediately start up again. It wasn't planned or anything like that; you just went to the window. If the neighbours happened to be looking out of their window too, you usually started talking to them. That is the way people lived then. It was part of everyday life.

In the summer my parents used to enjoy watching the Orange Walk parades pass along Dalmarnock Road. These were, for the most part, during July and August; most people in the area would watch them as they made their way from the Orange Halls in Mordaunt Street (at number 36), to Bridgeton Cross and beyond. Then late in the day again, when they returned in the opposite direction from their destination - perhaps the city-centre or even further afield. Although my father had gone to a Roman Catholic school, he used to enjoy the bands. Both my parents liked the bands in these parades, simply for the music as it were. It certainly had nothing at all to do with the sectarianism associated with them.

In fact, I remember we also used to watch the parade of the children from the Sacred Heart Roman Catholic School in Old Dalmarnock Road down near Bridgeton Cross. I remember that this procession, as my mother always called it, used to pass along Dalmarnock Road going eastward, once a year, in early May. All the children would be dressed in their best clothes, rather appropriately I think, as the parade was always on a Sunday. My mother, who had gone to a Protestant school, used to particularly enjoy this annual event, just as her favourite in the Orange Walk was always the accordion band. She truly loved that.

The custom of 'hanging' out your window is largely a thing of the past. Most of the old tenement buildings in Glasgow are long gone anyway and their modern day equivalents, the flats are, for many reasons, not conducive to the old custom. For a start, most of the blocks of flats are higher than the old tenement buildings were and it would be a pretty dangerous business. In fact even in the old tenement buildings I can remember looking directly down on to the street below and on occasion feeling a bit queasy. We were only on the second floor too, or, 'two stairs up' as it was more commonly, if somewhat misleadingly, referred to.

In those days of course people lived much a more simple existence than they do in the present. In the late 1950s, the spread of television sets was still in its early days and most people still made do with the 'wireless' and other more basic pastimes within the household. People in those days would play cards, play the piano, or just simply sit and talk amongst themselves to while away the time. And of course they would also go to their windows and spend hours there. Nowadays with almost every household having at least one television set, and with a large majority also possessing a video recorder, the pastimes of the present generation are greatly changed from those of forty years ago. The spread of video games and other modern pastimes has further changed the old habits. If you rarely see people 'hanging' out of their windows these days, it is not simply because most of the old tenement buildings cease to exist, but owing in no small part to the changed lifestyles of people in general as we enter the new century.

As I mentioned, space (or the lack of it) was

never a big problem. I certainly cannot recall this ever being so. It was probably not even considered to be a problem. You just accepted things as they were and took each and every day as it arrived. If something 'better' came along, then so be it but our wee family was happy and contented in our own wee modest hoose. We were not rich by any means, not by any stretch of the imagination. Thanks though to my mother's careful budgeting and 'balancing of the books,' (she would have made a superb Chancellor of the Exchequer me thinks) we were never short of the basics and necessities of daily life. There were usually always too, a few minor luxuries to be enjoyed along the way, especially at weekends. It is often said that thirty or forty years ago people were a lot more contented with their 'lot' than people in the present day are. I would certainly go along with that.

3

Everybody needs good neighbours.

I remember number 337 as a place where we had good, friendly neighbours. Everybody knew each other or at least knew who it was that lived in a particular house.

It is most difficult to say with any reasonable degree of certainty, whether the rosy picture painted of the 'good old days' community spirit and friendly neighbours, was a fact of life. Perhaps such a rather idyllic situation is largely a myth or at least increasingly exaggerated with the passage of each decade or so. I would from my own experience, tend to believe that for the most part, neighbours were indeed much more in contact with one another on a day to day basis during the period I am referring to here, than what would appear to be the case these days.

In making a judgment on this though, many variables have to be taken into consideration. It is not an open and shut case that can be argued either way without first taking due account of these variables. Probably the most obvious of these was the physical layout of the old tenement buildings. Where we lived, as I have said, there were three tenants on each floor and this would probably be par for most of the tenement buildings all over the city. So, people were in close proximity to one another physically; this, together with the wider social context in which people lived their everyday lives, was, most arguably conducive to the fostering of a genuine spirit of concern for each other, and for the flourishing of friendly relations. This was before the days of the multi-storey buildings, which sprang up in the 1960s, and long before the modern day scourges of drugs and increasing incidences of serious crime. All of these things, but others too, have tended to break the bond that existed in the old tenement buildings. In the modern equivalent of the tenement, the 'flat', it would seem that people are, or feel much more isolated than was the case with those who experienced the old tenements. It has to be remembered also though, that people, talking about the past, will see things according to the conditions etc. they experienced in the immediate environment in which they lived. Also, whether a person was and is an outgoing person by nature or whether they tended to keep to themselves in the course of their daily life will, one way or the other, colour their views about the past. In short, the subjective element in oral history and reminiscence is very much to the fore.

It must not be forgotten though, that as a child, you undoubtedly see things from a very different angle from that of a grown-up. When in childhood the world is a much more innocent, friendly place, you simply are not aware, at an early age, of the problems and the dangers of everyday life as experienced by adults. Taking this into consideration though, what I recall from my own childhood and my experience of everyday life at that stage of my life, leads me to draw some firm conclusions. I would definitely take the view that the children of the present generation face many more potential dangers and problems than was the case with my generation.

As a boy and after that as a teenager, I could see from everyday observation and experience, that there was indeed closeness between neighbours in those days. In the course of my reminiscence work, many of the senior citizens I have spoken with are adamant in varying degrees of certainty that this closeness does not exist in the present day. Or, if it does still survive, then it is most certainly not nearly as strong or as widespread as it was in previous generations. This is applicable to the city of Glasgow as a whole and is in no way exclusive to the area where I grew up and with which this book is concerned.

The most common reasons given for this loss of neighbourhood friendliness is crime, fear of crime, drugs, and changed working patterns - more shift-working etc.

Even all these years on, I can remember most if not all of our fellow residents at number 337. On entering the close mouth from the street, the main features of the ground floor, where there were no houses, was the entrance itself. This led straight to the stairs. To the right, just at the beginning of the stairs, there was a door, which I can never remember seeing open but which would lead into Mann's, the newsagents, at number 339. It may have been used as a storeroom. To the left of the stairs was a small passageway that led directly into the backcourt and on the left-hand side, right at the point where the backcourt began, there was another door. This one too, I cannot ever remember seeing being used for anything, though it was I think, the back entrance to Frew's the greengrocers at number 335. Again this was probably used as storeroom. Frew's incidentally had at one time been called The Western Fruit Company.

On the first floor, on the right hand side as you went up the stairs, lived a Mr. and Mrs. Lind who –to a boy like myself – looked 'old' but were probably only in their fifties or thereabouts. They had two daughters who lived there with them. We lived in the centre house on that floor originally and when we moved upstairs, a Mrs Green replaced us in our wee single end. Mrs. Green had previously lived at number 343 just along the road and as she was on her own, the single end would have suited her. I think she was still there when we left the area in 1966 and may even have been still living there just before the entire block of tenements was demolished, in the mid 1970s.

On the other side of us on that floor, lived a Mr. and Mrs. Kerr, an elderly couple. After Mr. Kerr died, round about 1959 I think, Mrs. Kerr moved out to East Kilbride where her daughter lived. After we moved to East Kilbride, I remember my mother renewing her friendship with Mrs. Kerr.

When we moved upstairs to the second floor, beside us in the single end on that floor, were a Mr. and Mrs. Calvert, a young couple. They had replaced the Johnstons, who had moved to number 343. Later on, another young couple, the McLatchies, moved in there. The Calverts later moved to Castlemilk - at that time a new housing scheme. It was one of a number, during this period, which were being developed to cater for the 'overspill.' This was a term used in reference to the large-scale relocation of people from the tenements to the suburbs and the housing schemes such as Drumchapel and Easterhouse, as well as Castlemilk. I recall that the Calverts did not settle in Castlemilk and returned in a very short space of time. They too ended up at number 343, which was the next close to us as you went towards Mordaunt Street. When we left in 1966, a Miss Logan, a woman on her own, had replaced the McLatchies in the single end. I recall that at about this time, the McLatchies had a shop in Farmeloan Road Rutherglen, just around the corner from Main Street. I cannot remember who had lived in our new home previously, though from my research I think it probably was a family called McGregor, of whom I have no recollection at all from the time when we lived downstairs.

When I think back on it, moving upstairs must have been something akin to entering new territory for me. As a boy of about seven at the time, it is quite possible that I had never been up the stairs before we 'flitted' there. It is equally possible though, that due to a natural childhood curiosity, I had been upstairs before that time but have just forgotten about it.

Directly across from us on the second floor, lived the Millers - a couple at that time probably somewhere in their fifties - or perhaps a bit younger. They had a son called Eddie, who I think lived there most of the time that we were there. I recall that Mr. Miller and his son were both Celtic supporters; I remember seeing them on a number of occasions either going to a match or coming down Mordaunt Street into Dalmarnock Road with their Celtic scarves on, returning from a game at Celtic Park. In the late 1950s and early 1960s, Celtic were going through a prolonged 'lean' spell and many a time I can recall my father saying to me that he had just been speaking to Mr. Miller, coming from a game and moaning about another poor showing by his team.

The Millers were the neighbours we were closest to, both in terms of physical proximity and in terms of speaking to them on a regular basis. My mother and Mrs. Miller would often be 'blethering' outside of the tenement doors, in the closemouth, or even on the pavement in Dalmarnock Road.

On the top floor and directly above us, lived old Mr. Pattison who was on his own. The McCrackens, of whom, unlike the other neighbours at 337, I have little or no recall, occupied the single end on the top floor. On the other side of the third floor lived a woman called Catherine McCorriston, along with a man called Willie Porterfield. Both were middle aged. Willie worked as a toilet attendant down at Bridgeton Cross. I can still in my mind's eye, picture both of these people. Cathy as we called her, was a little woman. Willie was a bit taller, with glasses. They were both quite friendly and I can remember, as I got older, sometimes talking to Willie about football, if I met him on the stairs. I still to this day don't know what team he supported. I don't know what relation these two were to one another. I don't think they were man and wife – you just did not ask about things like that in those days when you were growing up. In fact you did not even call people by their first name – it was always Mr. or Mrs. something-or-other.

One particular thing stands out in my mind about the two people I have just mentioned. They had a large collie type dog called Roy, which I often saw Willie out walking with in Dalmarnock Road.

We would often hear Roy barking, sometimes quite loudly too (perhaps that's why I never ventured up the stairs out of my own immediate environment when I was very young.) Anyway one day when I came home from school my mother told me that Roy was dead. Apparently Cathy had come in and found the dog dead behind the door. Funny how small, unimportant things like that stick in your memory?

When old Mr. Pattison died, which would be around 1960, a young couple, the Martins, moved in above us. They were very friendly; though you could quite often hear them playing loud music on their record player at weekends, long before the days of cassette recorders and Hi Fi systems. In those days if the neighbours got *too* noisy, you would usually just get a hold of a bit of wood or something, perhaps a brush, and knock on the ceiling, or on the wall if the noise was coming from the side. Occasionally, there might be a few bumps on the ceiling too. I can remember on occasion, my parents doing this late at night when our neighbours perhaps got a bit noisy. I can't ever remember though, us having any serious or prolonged trouble in this regard with our neighbours in those days and it was never a regular occurrence as I recall. Usually the knock on ceiling did the trick and things would quieten down again. This was, of course, decades before the 'neighbours from hell' term became an almost everyday expression; I cannot imagine that the 'chap on the ceiling' would still be as effective today as it was in those days. At least the noise emanated from good music in those days, so you didn't mind too much. Not that my dad would have agreed with that; he hated most pop music.

I remember speaking to Mr. Martin a few times when I passed him on the stairs. My family got on well with them. Mr. Martin was Rangers daft and I remember he used to rub it in when Rangers beat Celtic - at that time they did that just about every other time the two sides played each other. He was a good guy though.

4

Neighbours: Afterthoughts.

Looking back on these far off days, life at number 337 was for the most part a period of my life, which I will always remember fondly. Even allowing for the far more innocent perception one has of things when a child, the happy memories I have of that environment by far outnumber the not-so-happy ones. So, if indeed it is true that in past generations neighbours were indeed a lot closer to one another, then the area where we lived was a good example of this.

As I have related above, the Millers, who lived opposite us, are the family I remember most from that time. I have particularly strong memories of a period during the mid-1950s when the Millers used to invite us into their home to watch television, usually on a Tuesday or Wednesday evening if I remember correctly. I have one very clear memory of my father and I watching a Rangers v AC Milan European cup- tie in the Millers' living room. As. I remember it Rangers lost, 1-4. My mother may have been there too, although she was never a football fan. This would be in 1956 I think, as we did not get our television set until 1957. Probably only a minority of people had television sets in those days and I remember it was a real treat for us to watch television in the Millers' home. Certainly for me, it was a whole new world. I can also recall us seeing other programmes on occasions in the Millers. One that particularly stands out in my mind is *The Three Musketeers*, which for some reason or other, seemed to be a favourite. I have no memory whatsoever of who the stars were or anything like that. I think *The Count of Monte Cristo* may have been another of the 'regulars' we watched.

What I remember also of those visits to the Millers was that they always had the lights off when the telly was on. It gave you a feeling of being at the cinema, watching a sort of mini-screen. The darkness enhanced the old black-and-white images from the telly. It's actually something that has stayed with me all my life, as I always watch films on the telly with the lights off, particularly in the case of the old black-and white-films where I think it really does enhance the quality of the picture. Also, if I remember correctly, the Millers had a 17-inch screen, which I think was slightly larger than the norm for the period. I think that the standard screen size at the time was 15 inches. This was at a time when TV rental was on the increase and within another decade most families would have a television set in their home.

I fondly remember when we got our own first television set. I can recall going along London Road one day in 1957 with my parents to the 'DER' (Domestic Electric Rentals) shop, which was situated close to Templeton's carpet factory in the Calton, for my parents to sign the papers that would see our television set being delivered to our home. An exciting day for a ten year old. Our very own television set and no more need for us to go to the Millers to watch theirs, highly enjoyable as these visits had been. My parents remained as customers of 'DER' for the rest of their lives.To the present day, I rent my television and video from what used to be called 'DER.' It was some time in the late 1980s that 'Radio Rentals' took over most of the 'DER' chain of shops. In 2000 all the branches were renamed 'Box Clever' as a result of a merger of the few remaining 'DER' shops and the 'Radio Rentals' shops.'

On other occasions during this period, coming home from school, and in the rare instance of my mother not being home from work before I arrived, I would ring the doorbell of the Millers. Mrs. Miller would welcome me in to her house till my mother arrived. After I went to secondary school, if my mother was going to be late home, she would leave the key of our door with Mrs. Miller, and I would collect it there when I came home from school and let myself into our home. The Miller family certainly was very helpful, and always there if you needed them.

When we first moved up to the second floor, an old gentleman called Mr. Pattison lived directly above us. He was on his own. Whether he was a widower or had never married I am not sure. I suspect that he was perhaps a widower. He was a kindly old gentleman who always greeted you on passing on the stairs or outside on the street. As I remember he was always well dressed. He wore a hat and a long dark coat. I have a vague memory of myself and my mother going up in an ambulance to Duke Street with him when he became ill one evening. I think this would be some time in the early 1960s. Perhaps he didn't have any family, but I recall us going up with him in the ambulance. I think it was shortly after this that he died. I recall my mother asking me not to play music on the wireless for a day or so as a mark of respect for Mr. Pattison. He was well liked by all the neighbours. How times have changed. I just can't imagine the same level of respect being given by people nowadays on the death of one of their neighbours.

In the old tenement buildings of that time, there were, of course, no inside toilets - at least not in the poorer areas of the city. On each of the 'landings' as we called them, that is the space halfway up each floor, there was a toilet which of course you had to share with the other two tenants who lived on the same floor as you did. When we moved up to the second floor, the toilet was 'through the wall' just next to our sink in the kitchen-cum-living room.

When you had to go to the toilet, you would listen for the plug being pulled which would signal that the person who was in the toilet was about to leave and you would get ready to make your way down the stairs. Sometimes though, you didn't hear the plug being pulled and you would go down not knowing whether the toilet would be occupied or not. If I remember correctly, the tenants did not have a key of their own for the toilets, one on each of the three landings. I think what happened was that a communal key was hung on a nail just outside the toilet door. When you'd used the toilet, you put it back up on the nail, after locking the door. On reflection, it seems unbelievable almost, that as well as sharing the toilet itself; you had also to share the key too! Many a time I can recall going down to find the door locked and having to go back upstairs and wait. If the key was missing, wholesale panic ensued rather quickly. Not surprising when you think of it, especially on a cold night.

Looking back on those days it is amazing really how the modern generation takes so much for granted. Speak to a youngster about outside toilets and they will not know what you are talking about; when you explain it to them, they will look at you in a disbelieving way. It is really difficult though, to envisage such a long-ago situation. Even those of us, who lived through the period, sometimes wonder how we coped, when you contrast that period with the situation as it is in the present day. Really though, it was just the case that it was the way people lived then. You didn't know any other way and just got on with it. In the course of my work with *2000 Glasgow Lives,* many people whom I interviewed for the project, spoke of the time when they moved from such districts as the Gorbals and Partick, etc., to the new schemes such as Castlemilk and Drumchapel. Some of them spoke of the time of the 'big flit' being the happiest period of their life when they moved into their new home with all the 'mod–cons' and – in particular – an inside toilet.

I can recall that sometimes after the toilet had been used and the cistern flushed, there would be a noise of running water from the cistern and it often went on for quite a while. Sometimes in fact, it would go on throughout the early hours and you would get little, if any sleep. This could go on for a few days until the plumber came and fixed it; it would be all right for a while before the same thing would happen again and the toilet would start 'running,' once more, as my mother called it.

Then of course you had the problems with burst pipes in the winter, 1962 being a particularly good example of this. I cannot recall, though, the toilet ever being out of use for a lengthy period due to burst pipes. I am sure I would have remembered having to make a rather uncomfortable trek all the way down to Bridgeton Cross where the nearest 'proper' public toilets were situated. I do have admittedly though, vague memories of my mother having to get basins and buckets of water from the shops downstairs during times when there was a burst pipe crisis.

As a child I was always somewhat wary of leaving the house to go to the toilet late at night. I recall one particular evening I had been watching a film on television with my parents. It was an old black and white one called *The Spiral Staircase*, which starred George Brent and Dorothy McGuire, and to a child, it was pretty scary. It was late when the film ended and I had to go to the toilet; after watching the creepy George Brent, I felt even more apprehensive than usual on going out the front door and down to the toilet. Just as I was about to open the door, there was this loud noise from the direction of the backcourt and I froze in terror. I never did find out what was the cause of the noise, but it sure scared me.

It may have been a windy night and perhaps some slates had been blown off the roof - this was a frequent occurrence in the old tenement buildings. Every time I see that film on the telly though, I somehow remember that long ago night in Bridgeton.

When you look back at the layout of the old tenement buildings with their outside toilets especially, it is really not hard to see why the stories of 'closeness' between the neighbours are very much in vogue. With the toilets being where they were, the chances were that you would more than likely meet someone on the stairs on your way up and down to the landing. Unlike today, you never passed anyone without some sort of greeting to them or from them to you.

Some of the people I have spoken to in connection with *2000 Glasgow Lives* recalled that in the old tenement buildings there was usually, in each close, some unofficial 'caretaker' who reported faults and things like that to the landlords so that things ran smoothly in every day life. This was usually one of the neighbours who themselves lived in the same close. This person would also, it seems, have been responsible for reporting any trouble caused by noisy neighbours etc., and also to make sure that all the neighbours took their turn of cleaning the stairs.

This cleaning of the stairs was usually done on a weekly basis. Someone on each of the floors would take their turn of brushing and washing their own particular area of the flights of stairs. I can remember my mother doing these tasks. Many times I saw her down on her hands and knees with a bucket and cloths. Doing the stairs was a much more arduous task in those days. I have only a very vague recollection though, of there being this 'caretaker' person present. I certainly cannot remember who it was that filled that role in our close. I cannot remember there being any serious disputes over whose turn of the stairs it was etc. I think what was done was that you would hang a thread bobbin or something similar on the door handle of the person whose turn it was and when they had completed the task, they in turn would hang it round the next door and so on.

On each landing there was a window, which looked directly into the backcourts below, and it was on these landings that us children seemed to congregate when it was raining and therefore couldn't play outside. Most of my fellow playmates from the area though, came from Number 343. I cannot recall any of my pals coming from number 337 itself; indeed few if any children at all lived at 337. Sometimes some of the kids we knew from around the corner, from both Nuneaton Street and Mordaunt Street, would come up our close. I can even remember on occasion there would be a few from Springfield Road which has its junction with Dalmarnock Road about a couple of hundred yards from where our house was. I shall say a lot more about playing in the backcourts and in the streets in later chapters.

5

Going to the Shops.

Dalmarnock Road stretches from Bridgeton Cross to Dalmarnock Bridge just before you reach Farme Cross in Rutherglen. At the point where it meets the bridge, it becomes Dalmarnock Road, Rutherglen, so the stretch of Dalmarnock Road that is actually within the city of Glasgow boundary, is a relatively short one.

In the late 1950s and throughout the 1960s, this area was a haven of shops. There were shops of every kind in Dalmarnock Road and in the side streets leading off the main road too, as well as the very busy area around Bridgeton Cross where Dalmarnock Road, Main Street, and James Street all meet.

The area at the cross is still a busy area. The shops have changed greatly though. Apart from the buildings in the part of Dalmarnock Road nearest the cross, which have largely remained intact, most of the others in Main Street and James Street having long since gone, have been replaced entirely by modern buildings and new shops. The further up Dalmarnock Road you go, away from Bridgeton Cross, towards where we lived, the fewer shops there are. In fact, apart from a few shops on the south side of Dalmarnock Road just past the junction with Springfield Road, I cannot think of any shops at all away from the Bridgeton Cross part of the road.

This is in complete contrast to the way the area was some forty years ago. At that time there were shops on both sides of Dalmarnock Road, all the way from Bridgeton cross right up to Dalmarnock Power Station, just before you crossed the bridge into Rutherglen. The Power Station, which has long since closed, was one of the biggest employers in the area at the time. Only a few rows of bricks, a lot of trees and much empty space around remain as signs that it was ever there. One building that does survive though, is the church at 231 Dalmarnock Road. At the time that I am writing about, it was named Bridgeton Congregational Church. It is now called Bridgeton Church.

The shop I remember being in most often was Mann's the newsagent, just to the left as you went out the close mouth into the main road. My memories of being in this shop are mainly associated with going there for the evening newspapers. At that time there were three evening newspapers published in Glasgow: The 'Evening Times', which is of course still with us, the 'Evening Citizen' which I remember well, and the 'Evening News' which I only have very vague memories of. The latter two of these newspapers are no longer published.

Another thing that I always got, from Mann's, was the children's comics of the day, such as the 'Beano,' the 'Dandy' and the 'Hotspur' to name a few. These comics all had their assorted characters, such as 'Desperate Dan,' 'Korky the Cat' and 'Dennis the Menace', again to name merely a few. I used to read these in the morning before setting out for school. I may even have looked at them before I started primary school. Another pre-school memory? I wonder!

Main Street, near Bridgeton Cross again and an undated photo showing a cluster of shops on the right-hand side that I remember well from my childhood. All of this part of Main Street has since been rebuilt. New shops and houses now dominate the spot

I recall that the Manns, who owned the shop, lived in Playfair Street, which is just off the other side of Dalmarnock Road, across from where we lived. The shop also sold sweets, crisps, etc, so I was most probably in there every day from Monday to Saturday for one thing or the other. As I recall, Mr. Mann was a tall thin man and his wife a friendly woman who wore glasses. I remember when Mr. Mann died, sometime in the late 1950s or the early 1960s, there was a large turnout for his funeral, as he was well known and popular in the local area.

At the other side of the close mouth as you went out, there was Frew's the greengrocers. I can remember being in here a lot too for fruit and vegetables for my mother. I can remember most of the shops in the area, especially in the immediate area where we lived, as I would often 'go the messages' for my mother when I came in from school, especially as I got older. Further down from Frew's there was Drummond's the chemists, at numbers 329 to 331.

I can remember being in this shop on occasion for various odds and ends. I think Drummond's is still a going concern, in the pharmacy business, although the particular shop I refer to here is, of course, no longer in existence. The entire block of shops and tenements there, including our own, having been long since demolished.

There were one or two other shops near our close, next to close number 343 - Kerr's which I think was a clothiers, and right at the corner of Dalmarnock Road and Mordaunt Street, was a public house. This was McPherson's and I can recall on a few occasions going in there as a

Definitely my favourite stopping off place on Saturday morning shopping trips with my mother all those years ago was the City Bakeries shop at 579 London road, just along from Bridgeton Cross. The photo dates from 1939

boy with my pals, with empty beer bottles we had collected, to try and get a few pennies on them. I cannot remember if we ever got any money for them or if we got chased out, but I do recall a strong childhood curiosity as to what these places were like and what sort of people went into them. There was also a public house at the corner of Nuneaton Street and Dalmarnock Road; this one was called the 'Plaza Bar.'

On the other side of the road from us, at number 262, there was Caldwell's the bakers, which I went to sometimes for cakes for our tea. I think Friday was the main day for this. We always got wee 'treats' like cakes, buns, etc, at the weekends. I always looked forward to these treats. Next to Caldwell's was Mallard's the drapers at 258. This was a busy shop. I cannot recall ever being in here, though its possible I was there with my mother on occasion. Above here and extending right to the corner of Playfair Street, was a pawnbroker; in fact the entrance was actually in Playfair Street, at number 3. This also seemed to be a busy place most of the time. During that era, pawnbrokers were much more in vogue than they are today, which is a bit surprising really when you think that the 1950s in this country were considered to be a time of relative affluence, following the rationing etc. in the years immediately following the Second World War.

Also across the road from us based at number 264 Dalmarnock Road, was a doctor's surgery. It was to this practice that we went when we needed to see the doctor. This was long before the days when you had to make an appointment two or

The United Co-op Baking Society Shop at 27-29 Main Street in 1926. Thirty years later this was a regular port of call of mine along with my mother on Saturday mornings.

three days in advance before seeing the doctor. In those days you simply went along to the waiting room at the surgery and waited your turn until one of the doctors was free to see you.

As a child I suffered a lot from colds as well as the other usual childhood troubles such as chickenpox etc. and I recall being in the waiting room of that surgery a number of times. It was a small room with two doors in opposite corners; these were the entrances to the doctors' rooms. There were usually two doctors on call; a Doctor McKechnie and a Doctor Mackay. If I remember correctly, it was Doctor McKechnie that we saw most often. He was our favourite. He also made visits to our home on a few occasions when my mother was unwell. I remember also that there was a small middle-aged woman who acted as a sort of receptionist. You would give your name to her when you went into the waiting room; when the doctor was free, she would shout your name out and you would go in to see the doctor.

There were also houses on the other side of the road from us, above the shops; all of these, too, are long since demolished. Although just around the corner on one side of Playfair Street, some of the original tenements still survive. These are the only ones that I am aware of that are still standing in this part of the area, from the time when we lived there.

Next to the doctor's surgery, going towards the corner with Swanston Street, was Rinn's the barbers. It was to Rinn's, at number 268, that I went when I needed a haircut. I cannot recall going to any other barbers during this period. I can clearly remember this shop all these years

This 1960s photo shows Dalmarnock Road at its junction with Pirn Street. Crombie's licensed grocers can be seen on the far left and Mackintosh's sweet shop in the centre of the picture.

later. It was quite a small shop with a few chairs for customers waiting. There were I think, two, sometimes three barbers working there. The "main man" as it were, was a chap called Tommy. I think he was the manager. It was Tommy that I got to cut my hair most of the time. I remember he used to say to me afterwards "That's a lot better looking, you'll get a 'click' (meaning a girl friend) the night." He was a good laugh. I always felt a lot better after a haircut. I would return in good spirits across the road to my home. I recall also that Rinn's, at that time, ran a fleet of single decker buses for outings etc. You would often see them around the area, most especially at weekends. I don't know what became of them.

Next to the barbers and the last shop before you reached the corner of Swanston Street, was Taylor Brothers, the undertakers at number 274, who are still in business in other parts of Glasgow. The actual building where Taylor Brothers were based at that time is the only one still in existence out of all the shops that I have referred to here. I am not sure what the premises are used for these days as there is no name on the outside.

On the other side of Dalmarnock Road as you passed Playfair Street, there were other shops. I remember also that there was a post office, to which I went on a regular basis, mainly for stamps and postal orders etc. for my mother. This was at number 256. This place was always very busy as I recall and being tiny, it could be a bit uncomfortable at times as you waited in a queue.

Here, at number 250, there was also a small café, Tedeschi's. I recall going here with my pals sometimes, as I got older. All of these shops too,

This is the then (no date given) Premier Cafe at number 282 Main Street. I knew it as Crolla's Cafe in the late 1950s and early 1960s when I regularly went there with my mother and grandmother to 'cool off' on hot summer days.

were demolished over the years. Then, just along the road at the corner of Bartholomew Street, there was a bank - the National Bank of Scotland, at number 240. About eleven years ago, this was converted into a public house and it remains so till the present time. Just along from here, right at the corner with Playfair Street, was another bank, the Clydesdale and North of Scotland. All of these shops I remember well. There were always plenty of them open at most times of the day and some were also open into the evening, so you would not go short of the basic necessities of life. All you needed for everyday survival was available to you in the immediate area and I think this would be typical of most of the manual class areas of the city at that time.

There were always plenty of corner shops, and from my talks with some people who lived in other areas of the city during my reminiscence interviews for *2000 Glasgow Lives,* this would seem to be confirmed. On speaking to people who had originally lived in areas such as Govanhill in the south side before moving to Castlemilk in the mid 1950s, I discovered that their main complaint was the lack of shops in Castlemilk. In its early days, many of the people it seemed, had to make trips on a regular basis, back to the very areas they had only recently 'flitted' from, even for the basic necessities.

Certainly from my own recollections of the East End at that time, there was no need to go out of the immediate locality for the basics. You only went into the city-centre, or 'into town' as we called it, when you needed to buy clothes, shoes and the like. In fact, a trip into the centre of Glasgow was a rare occasion. Even when you needed things like a new pair of shoes, there were shops like Timpson's down at Bridgeton Cross at 1 Main Street, as well as a good selection of tailors and clothing shops nearby. And, if you needed household goods, you could go to such places as the large Eastern Co-op Society store at 40-70 Westmuir Street, up near Parkhead Cross, ten minutes or less on the tram or bus.

So rare in fact, were visits to the city-centre, that when I did go 'into town' with my mother, it was, for a small boy, like entering a whole new exciting world. When we did go into the city-centre, it was usually after I had come home from school. I would look forward to the trip all day, often being distracted from my lessons at primary school, by the prospect of the treat in store for me later that day. I would daydream of visits to such places as the old Lewis's store in Argyle Street and the original Woolworth's shop across the road on the other side of Argyle Street.

6

Going to the Shops -again.

As you walked down Dalmarnock Road in the direction of Bridgeton Cross, there were many other shops that I recall visiting on an almost daily basis. One in particular sticks out in my mind. I have been a film fan for as long as I can remember and as I got a bit older, in the late 1950s, I began to put names to faces. One face, which was becoming familiar to me around that time, was that of James Stewart. Well, there was this newsagent shop, which was about half way between Nuneaton Street and Dunn Street - Duncan's; at number 291 I think it was. I always thought the man who served behind the counter and who was I think the owner of the shop, was the double of James Stewart. I think my parents must have agreed with me on this as we always used to refer to this shop as 'Jimmy Stewart's shop.'

Come to think of it, I thought at the time that his wife who also served behind the counter, looked a bit like Doris Day. Perhaps I had been watching too many films, even in those days. Close to this shop, there was Curley's at number 283, which sold cooked meats. I think I was in this shop on a daily basis too. I certainly can recall going there for things like Spam, veal, and tongues, of either the lunch or ox variety.

These were among my favourites and in fact still are to the present day, although you don't see Spam in the shops much these days. Another big favourite of mine at that time, were the small jars of what

This is Curley's Shop which sold cooked meats and which I visited often, especially in the late afternoon after school. Alongside Curley's is Greenlees Shoe Shop. These shops were in Dalmarnock Road between Dunn Street and Nuneaton Street. The photo is from July 1932.

was called 'minced chicken' which I think we used to buy in Curley's shop too. Nowadays this is referred to as chicken spread but somehow I don't think it is as good as it was then. It seemed to be a lot tastier in those days and I remember I always used to enjoy it on my 'pieces' when I started work, in 1963. Right alongside Curley's was Greenlees shoe shop. Just along from this again, at number 293, was the Avonbank Dairy and Turner's butcher at 311 to which I sometimes used to go during the week.

Other shops around this area that I remember well were Nicol Mair's Bakers at number 239 Dalmarnock Road and between Fairbairn and Dunn Streets and close to this, Cochrane the grocer at 245. Then there was Marinelli's café just past Ruby Street at number 191, not forgetting also MacLachlan's dairy at 239 Dunn Street, another "haunt" of mine for milk and other odds and ends.

There were also many sweet shops in the area. I have always had a sweet tooth and, like most children, I was 'into' sweets from an early age. There were sweet shops all throughout the area, both on the main roads and in the side streets. I can remember that my favourites were Jelly Beans and Sherbet Limes, but also others like Soor Plooms and Liquorice Allsorts. In fact if I remember correctly, the latter was always a favourite when I went to the cinema with my mother on a Saturday evening.

In those days you could get two ounces of sweet - today the minimum weight of a portion of sweets is a quarter pound. Another favourite was wine gums. I remember when I was still at school; I used to get two ounces of wine gums on

A September 1932 scene and another shop that I remember well. This is Nicol Mair's Bakers at 239 Dalmarnock Road and looking much the same as it did thirty years later.

almost a daily basis, from this wee shop, which used to be in Lily Street, just across from my primary school. I continued to go into this shop for my usual 'two ounces' worth even after I had gone to secondary school, as I sometimes used to pass Lily Street on turning into Springfield Road on my way back to Riverside Secondary ('Rivi') after being home for my lunch. I recall the man who served behind the counter of this shop always kidding me when I went in for my wine gums. He would say "You on the wine again?"

Another one that I remember was Wallace's sweet shop at 83 Tullis Street. I would usually go in here when I had been down at the nearby bowling green at Glasgow Green. Then there was McDonald's at 6 Landressy Street. I would just about drag my mother and my granny in here for sweets on our way back from summer afternoon walks along the Glasgow Green and surrounding area.

Another sweet shop I remember well was the one down in Dalmarnock Road just past the junction with Heron Street. It was a very small shop and it was always this wee elderly woman who served behind the counter; this would be Mackintosh's at 101. I always used to go in here when I was a boy and had been out with my mother and my grandmother. We went walks in the summer, usually from London Road, where my grandmother lived, right along to the Calton and into Glasgow Green. On the way back we would walk up part of Dalmarnock Road before turning into Ruby Street or Dunn Street on our way back to my grandmother's home which was situated in a tenement building, at 850 London Road, between Dunn Street and Marquis Street.

Shops in Heron Street, c. 1928. Many Bridgeton people referred to this part as 'Wee Heron Street'. it stretched from London Road to the junction with Bernard and Baltic streets. 'Big Heron Street' ran from this junction to Dalmarnock Road. The spot today is almost unrecognisable.

(The latter street is no longer still in existence - the area where my grandmother lived is almost unrecognisable from forty years ago, much more so even than is the case with Dalmarnock Road.) As we turned into Dalmarnock Road, I never missed the opportunity to go in to that wee shop for sweets. Yet another was McClure's, just past the swing park at the corner with Dunn Street. I think it was mainly a newsagents. And I must not forget Fairbairn's sweet shop at number 287. This was an absolute paradise for us 'sweet tooth' kids. As I recall, it was literally packed with sweets, all over the place, a bit like Maxwell's sweet shop at 1 Bridgeton Cross.

Another big thing for us kids, at that time, were the bubble gum machines. You used to see these outside most of the sweet shops in those days. You would put an old penny in the small slot at the side or the top of the machine and your bubble gum would be delivered to you at an opening at the bottom of the machine. The one I remember most was a machine that was just round the corner from our home – it may have belonged to the café opposite – in Nuneaton Street. It was just outside the 'Plaza' picture hall and close to Milne's fish shop at 359 Nuneaton Street where I sometimes went on a Friday for fresh fish, when we were having a change from fish suppers.

I used to like the 'sweaty-cigarettes', which you could get at that time and were very popular with children. You could get them in packets of five or ten I think. Basically they were thin strips of confectionery, white, with a red tip to give the appearance of a real cigarette. I think the main reason I liked them – apart of course from the taste – was that when you bought a packet of these sweets, you would get a small photograph of a famous British football player of the period. Names which stick in my mind are Ivor Allchurch, who was a Welsh internationalist, Tom Finney, the great Preston North End and England winger of the period, and Jackie Mudie, who I think had been born in South Africa but was a Scottish international centre forward at that time. So it would appear that 'cross nationality' in football is not an exclusively modern phenomena. I can recall having these and many others in my collection of football cards at this time. You would save these up and you would attempt to get the full collection, which I think was usually fifty or a hundred. I cannot ever remember getting a full series of these; you would always be short of this one or the other one. You would go about with one of these sweet-cigarettes sticking out of your mouth, imagining you were Jimmy Cagney, Edward G. Robinson or some other 'tough guy' of the period. You still see some bubble gum and chewing gum machines in the present day. But the sweet cigarettes went off the market long ago.

Then there was the 'penny tray' in a lot of the sweet shops at that time. This was literally a tray with every sweet on display costing one penny, hence the name. A big favourite in the penny tray was the 'penny dainty,' a big block of solid caramel with a green and white wrapper.

Yet another favourite sweet of mine as a boy was Spangles, a square sweet, which came in a pack of assorted flavours. Spangles faded from the scene a long time ago. I used to go through packet after packet of these when I went down for the newspapers. They were too much of a temptation to resist.

The mention of newspapers leads me on to a wee shop that was in Nuneaton Street. Mann's shop was closed on a Sunday so we got our newspapers from this other shop at 336 Nuneaton Street, Houston's. It was usually my job on a Sunday morning to go round and get the newspapers from here. I think we used to get about three or four in those days and looking back wonder where we found the time to read them all. We certainly got the 'Sunday Post', the 'News of The World' too I think, and perhaps also the 'Sunday Mail'. I also vaguely remember another Sunday paper from that time, called the 'Empire News'. I don't remember much about this paper. It may have been some sort of supplement to one of the other papers, long before such things became commonplace, or it could have been a sports publication. My father and I used to really look forward to the sports pages on a Sunday, especially if there had been a lot happening on the football front the previous day. I think as the years passed, we got the papers delivered to our home on a Sunday as I don't remember still going round to that shop as I grew older.

As well as the photos you got with the 'sweetie-cigarettes', which I remember from about the time I was at primary school, a bit later on I became an avid collector of foreign stamps. Most of the newsagents in the area sold these, but the one I most particularly remember, in this regard, was the aforementioned Houston's in Nuneaton Street. I would be round here on most days of the week looking for more stamps for my collection. These stamps could be purchased singly but I used to buy them in packets. I think you could get a dozen or more for a shilling or so. You would then place them in your album using the gummed 'hinges', which you bought separately in small packets. The stamps would go on the appropriate page, i.e. the country from where the stamp originated. The countries would be listed in alphabetical order in the album. For some, you would have a few full pages of stamps but for others, none at all or very few. My pals and I used to swop our stamps but even then, some were almost impossible to get hold of, or so it seemed. For some reason, stamps from Afghanistan were very hard to come by. This was a hobby which occupied me for a few years before gradually ceasing to be an attraction.

It was a similar story with football programmes. At one time I had a few hundred, from the continent as well as from Britain. The programmes would be advertised in the football magazines of the day and you would send down to England for them. I remember that if the programmes had arrived by the morning post, my mother would hide them from me because if they were there when I came in from school, I would spend ages going through them before having my lunch or dinner and my mother's good cooking would have been wasted. Smart thinking on the part of my mother, to hide them or to say that they hadn't arrived, until I had finished my meal. Many grown-up people now make a hobby of collecting football programmes. At the time I am writing about, I think that it was mainly youngsters who did. I don't know what became of my collection but after a few years, like the stamps, the programmes fell by the wayside.

At that time in Glasgow there were plenty of cafés and fish and chip shops in Glasgow. A lot of these, which were situated in the areas where there was a large concentration of tenement buildings, have disappeared with the tenements themselves. In the Dalmarnock and Bridgeton areas when we lived there, a plethora of these establishments existed. If not quite one on every street corner, then certainly pretty close to it. The cafés and the fish and chip shops were almost exclusively owned by Italian immigrants to this country, as the Italian population in Scotland had increased from the 1920's, particularly due to the political upheavals in their homeland and most especially after the Fascist take-over by Mussolini in October 1922.

I recall that there was a café in Nuneaton Street at that time, Matonti's at number 354, which I think, became a Crolla's café in about 1962. There was one too in Mordaunt Street, Loreto's at 13-15. As well as being additional places where I could buy my favourite sweets, I also used to buy bottle after bottle of 'ginger' in these shops. We all liked 'ginger', or as it was sometimes called, 'pop,' in the family. My particular favourite was Limeade. I could and would drink bottle after bottle of this. In those days you used to get a few pence back on the empty bottles when you returned them to the shop. I have fond memories of going round, usually to the café in Nuneaton Street right across from the 'Plaza' picture hall, and getting a few shillings back on the empties. You would usually wait till you had at least half

Another favourite cafe of my childhood. This is Peter Rossi's at 320 London Road in Calton near Glasgow Green. This photo was taken in August 1936.

a dozen, so that the return on them would be greater. It was hardly worth your while going round to the shop with just one or two. When you got the money from the person behind the counter, you felt 'rich', with all those pennies in your pocket. My other favourites at that time were Orange and also Lemonade. I still like them to this day, though you don't see Limeade much at all in the present day, or if you do, it is a watered down version - quite literally – of its equivalent in past times.

Of course, I fondly recall the fish and chip shops. Perhaps in fact, even more than the cafés. There were many small fish and chip shops in the area at that time. One I particularly remember was Petrie's, which was in Nuneaton Street, number 325, just before you reached the corner with Baltic Street. I would often go round here in the evenings during the week – mainly for chips I think. In those days you could get a sixpenny bag of chips. You would go into the shop and say "sixpence worth please" and whoever was serving behind the counter, would know what you meant.

A big favourite of both my parents, and myself, was fritters. At that time you could get them in all the fish and chip shops. Nowadays you don't see them very often at all; more's the pity. They were always very tasty and we used to get them regularly, out of Petrie's shop. I can't remember just how much they cost, but you always seemed to get plenty for your money. They were probably quite cheap though, as most everyday things were at that time. I also vaguely recall that there was another fish and chip shop on the other side of Nuneaton Street, so we probably got our evening supper out of there too, though I only very vaguely recall ever being in this other shop. This would be Palombo's, at number 308.

On a Friday evening we usually had a special treat, a few fish suppers. For this I would go along to another fish and chip shop, which was in Baltic Street - De Rosa's at number 205 and on the right hand side of the street as you walked along in the direction of Bridgeton Cross, near the junction with Ruby Street. Baltic Street as it then was, ran parallel with Dalmarnock Road. This shop was always crowded when I went along on a Friday. The queue would be almost out to the street and you could wait for up to half an hour for your order. It was a slightly bigger shop than Petrie's. Petrie's was on the small side, but most of these shops were in varying degrees small. The man, the owner I think, was a man of medium height, and balding. He had one or two female assistants behind the counter; he certainly needed them on Fridays. I still recall to this day, waiting in that queue on Friday evenings and the sheer joy when the waiting was over and I finally got served. It was always worth the wait, as the food we got out of that shop was delicious. We usually got fish suppers and sometimes a so-called 'special fish supper' which was fish with a different type of batter. Very tasty. This particular shop seemed to do that type of fish as their specialty, and it was very popular. In fact, I think if you wanted a 'special', you had to wait a bit longer. The demand was usually greater than the supply and you had to wait until another batch of them was ready to serve.

You seldom if ever, saw anyone eating his or her food on the street – a sight which is commonplace nowadays. People usually just went round to their local fish and chip shops (you never referred to them as 'chippies' in those days) and brought their food home to consume it there. In the present day it seems to be the done thing to eat your dinner or as we called it, your supper, on the way home. In those days of course, what was on offer, in the fish and chip shops, was a lot less varied than what is on offer today in the modern 'chippies.'

Things like King Ribs and Pizzas were simply unheard of and if you had said you were going for a 'Donner' (Kebab), it would have been thought that you were going out for a walk. How times have changed. In fact I cannot even remember things like Sausage Suppers and Hamburger Suppers being on the menu. It was just plain, good old fish and chips - not forgetting the fritters of course - and how we loved them.

Nowadays there seems to be much more litter on the streets than what there was all those years ago. Most of this is most probably connected directly to the growth of the so-called 'fast food' trade. The term 'fast food' is itself of course, a modern day term. You never heard it being used in the period that I am writing about. In those days in fact, when you got your food from the fish and chip shop, it was always wrapped in newspaper rather than the predominantly plain white wrappers of today. Recently however, I have seen some of city-centre fish and chip shops using a form of newspaper, but this is usually a one-off gimmicky sort of thing, and doesn't last long.

7

Dalmarnock life.

As I have already said, Dalmarnock at that time was a bustling hive of activity. A busy place, especially during the day, but a lively place at night too.

I used to love watching the crowds, which you used to see every evening before teatime, coming out of the many mills, factories, and businesses, that dominated the area at that time. I particularly recall watching the workers crowding on to the buses on their way home in the early evening. The tramcars were still going at the time I am referring to, but at that time there were also the red buses, or, as my father called them, the 'Lanarkshire' buses. This was because most of them were bound for destinations throughout Lanarkshire. I recall watching these buses in Dalmarnock Road quite often, during the evening rush hour. There could often be eight or more of them back to back. They would be bound for places in Lanarkshire such as Wishaw, Eddlewood, and Blantyre, to name only a few. To me, a small boy, these were names of far-away places with strange sounding names. They may have been only around ten miles distant, but they could have been on the other side of the world for all I was concerned.

The largest crowds getting on these buses were to be seen around about half way down Dalmarnock Road. There was a bus stop between Fairbairn Street and Ruby Street and it was here that most of these workers got on the buses.

June 1962 is the date of this Dalmarnock Road scene at the junction with Ruby Street on the left and Dale Street on the right Marinelli's Cafe is on the left at the corner with Ruby Street. Note the old style Evening Times delivery van.

The workers would come down the side streets from Baltic Street where there were a lot of mills at that time.You would get them coming from places like the works of William Arrol, which was situated, in both Baltic Street and Dunn Street. Arrol's works was a large organisation that I remember well. The crowds that boarded the buses in Dalmarnock Road were for the most part women workers from the mills. Up Dalmarnock Road, going past where we lived and on towards Springfield Road, there would be further crowds getting on the buses.

Many of these would be from the large Laird's factory, which was in Carstairs Street, round the corner from Swanston Street. There were more mills and other assorted factories in this area, so you had, during the rush hour, huge crowds of workers converging on Dalmarnock Road from both the north side of the road and the south side.

Another busy time of day in the area generally, was at lunchtime. When I came home from school at this time of day, the area was always very busy with workers out of the factories, during their break. Another large employer was the Gas Works in Old Dalmarnock Road, stretching round the corner into Bartholomew Street. The large gasometers of this place could be seen miles away from the immediate area. Nowadays all that is left of all of this is the Bartholomew Street part, which is still in operation as far as I am aware. The remainder of the works, in Old Dalmarnock Road, has completely gone. A motorway to the south side of the city runs through where it used to be. Parts of the exterior walls of the old Gas Works remain visible.

Workers in Mordaunt Street, c. 1920

A particular favourite haunt for a lot of the workers in the area was the Station Tearooms at 365 Dalmarnock Road, just past Mordaunt Street and near the railway bridge. Certainly it always seemed to be crowded and doing a 'roaring trade'.

As with the tenement buildings of the area, almost all of the old factories and the mills in the area are long gone. Baltic Street, where there was a lot of industry, is today almost unrecognisable from what it was at that time; it is now called Baltic Court.

Looking back on those far off days, I was always curious about the other end of the city and what sort of people lived there. All you knew, as a child, was that in the other side of the city, people lived in "big" houses. As a child though, your everyday life centres on the immediate vicinity of where you live. You may be curious about what else there is in other places, but you rarely; if ever, got the chance, as a child, to see these other places that you saw on the destination boards of trams and buses.

Sometimes I would see a tram with the name Hyndland on it and I would wonder where that was. All I knew was that it was some sort of 'posh' area where the rich people lived. Even a trip into the city-centre seemed like a long journey. On those occasions that I would go into town with my mother, from the moment we boarded the tram at the stop in Dalmarnock Road near Swanston Street, I was fascinated by the journey. As you get older of course, you come to realise that these 'faraway places' are not so far away after all.

The State Studios, London Road, 1939

On Saturday mornings I would always go with my mother down to the shops around Bridgeton Cross and Main Street. This was a weekly ritual for us; I always looked forward to it after a week's hard schooling. We would usually always walk down to the shops, but would sometimes get the tram on the way home, being, by that time, loaded with the weekend 'messages'. I recall going into such shops as Blair's the butchers, which was at 22 Main Street, near where the present day mini shopping centre stands. In Blair's, my mother would buy all the meat that we needed for the Sunday dinner: sausages, beef, steak etc.

On the other side of Main Street there was a baker's shop, at number 27, which I think, was a Co-op shop. I remember that if there was a queue in this shop, and there usually was, I would tell my mother that I was going to Watson's newsagent just along the road at number 21. Here I would seek out my favourite comics etc. Then I would meet my mother as she was coming out of the Co-op. Sometimes we would get our weekend treats of cakes, chocolate biscuits etc. out of the Co-op shop. At other times we would go round to the City Bakeries shop, which was in London Road, (number 579) and alongside *The State Studio* photographers. The part of the building, which housed the City Bakeries shop, is in the present day, the 'Lord of the Isles' public house.

I particularly remember this City Bakeries shop, as it was here that we always got one of our very special weekend treats - my particular favourite, 'jam doughnuts.' Their present day equivalents are pale imitations of the real thing. Another favourite of mine that we also used to buy out of this shop was the cream cookie - a sort of plain bun type thing, but with lashings of cream on the top. No weekend was complete for me, without a jam doughnut or a cream cookie, preferably both. My mother, being the good person she was, never let me down.

Quite often on our way back home up Dalmarnock Road in the tram, we would get off at the Co-op shop which was in the middle of Dalmarnock Road and about half way between Dunn Street and Fairbairn Street on the other side of the road. This was the Eastern Co-op society at number 218. I think we would usually go in here for things that may not have been available down at Bridgeton Cross. But I remember us being in here quite a lot. I can still picture this shop to the present day. It seemed to sell just about every thing – cold meats, biscuits, bread and roll – the lot really. Where this shop stood, there are now some very nice looking houses. Just along from the Co-op shop, there was a newsagent, Fraser's, at number 253, which also sold sweets. So often, while my mother was in the queue at the Co-op, I would be found in this shop looking for my favourite indulgences. The Co-op also had a branch down near Bridgeton Cross at number 34 Dalmarnock Road that we sometimes went to as well.

On one Saturday morning, my mother took me in to this clothes shop in Main Street to get me a new jacket or something like that. I remember the assistant who dealt with us, a youngish man, being rather abrupt and impatient with us. Well, did my mother give him what for? You bet she did! She hurried me out of the shop, vowing never to return. And we never did. I think that this would have been the Caledonian Tailors at numbers 72-74.

There was also this big bank down at 42 Bridgeton Cross – the Glasgow Savings Bank – that I remember being in a few times with my mother, when I was very young. I remember looking in awe at this place, as it seemed bigger than any other place I had seen up till then. It was such a busy looking place, with long queues at various windows along the main counter. Nowadays it's still a crowded place — as a bookmakers – the bank having long since gone. How times change indeed. Right next door to this bank, was Scobie's Barber's shop, a well-known establishment in the area. I think that my father used to go in here sometimes for a haircut.

8

Out and about in the East End.

In the late 1950s and right up until I left the area with my parents in the mid 1960s, I was a regular visitor to the many parks that flourished in the area during that period. The Glasgow Green was by far the place I would visit most often. In particular, the bowling green which was in Greenhead Street; also to the football pitches which were just off King's Drive, just before you cross the bridge over the Clyde and into the south-side of Glasgow.

I have many memories of the bowling-green. In the summer when the football was finished for the season, it really was the close season; the football finished at the end of April and did not start again until the second Saturday in August. I used to go to the bowling green with my father, and on sunny summer days, we would spend hours there just watching the men and women playing bowls. The four separate greens always seemed to be crowded with players. Playing bowls somehow seemed to be a more popular pastime than what it is today. Sometimes, in the late afternoon, my mother would join us there and we would all go home together walking up John Street, across Main Street into Muslin Street, then into Old Dalmarnock Road or Dalmarnock Road itself, and home.

Sometimes I would go to the bowling green with my mother and my grandmother. This would probably be during the school holidays between the end of June and the end of August. Again we would sit there for a few hours, just whiling away the time.

On a few occasions, my father had a game of bowls with one or two of my uncles who were visiting us. This was sometimes during the week and I have a distant memory of my Uncle Bobby from Pollok, perhaps my Uncle Tommy from Priesthill together with my father, playing a game of bowls one gloriously sunny Wednesday evening on the green to the right as you entered the bowling green. My mother, I think, was there too, and although I do not remember for sure it is likely that my dad and my uncles would have gone into the 'Bowlers Rest' public house on the corner of Greenhead Street and Tullis Street after their games while I made my way home with my mother to 'number 337.'

On Sundays, all the year round, my father and I would go to Glasgow Green. In those days the place was absolutely packed with hundreds of people playing football on the many football pitches, in an area stretching from the bridge across the Clyde at Main Street, right across westward, to the other end at Kings Drive, and to the south, going towards Polmadie. It was very rare to see a pitch on the green on a Sunday afternoon in those days, which was empty. I think it was mainly works teams, factories etc. who used the pitches; there may have been some sort of system where you had to book the pitch in advance, perhaps during the week before your game was due. I cannot imagine that all those people came along on a Sunday and simply took 'pot luck.' There would surely have been too many disappointed people.

A 1955 Glasgow Green scene, the former Templeton's carpet factory, one of the largest employers in the area at the time, in the background. It is now a business training centre. When I was a boy I would go walks along this part of the Green during the summer months with my mother and my grandmother.

On the odd occasion when there was a spare goalpost, my father and I would have a kickabout, usually with me going in goal and him taking shots at me, or sometimes, penalty kicks. After a while, if we got tired or fed up, whichever came soonest, we would stop playing and go over and watch one of the games that would still be going on. I think people would still be playing till about three o'clock or perhaps a bit later.

I remember the 'main attraction' as far as these games were concerned, seemed to be at the northern end of the Green, near the end of Greenhead Street. Somehow, at this point, there always seemed to be a bigger crowd watching the game on the pitch right at the very edge of the Green. You always knew it was a 'big' game if the goal nets were being used, as in most of the other games, there would be no net for the ball to hit when a goal was scored by one of the teams. These games would draw a lot of crowds and there would be a lot of shouting and bawling. It was sometimes really good entertainment, and of course, it was all for free.

One particular aspect I remember from these visits to Glasgow Green on Sunday afternoons, was that on some of the pitches, you would see dumb people playing football, gesturing in sign language to one another. They would be there every week - I don't know where they came from, but I can remember my father remarking on them to me as we passed by. One of those things that stick in your mind for no particular reason.

We would usually make our way home between two and three o'clock if I remember correctly. If we thought we were a bit early for Sunday

Another 1955 view of Glasgow Green, this time on the playing fields near Fleshers' Heugh at the eastern end of the Green. This is a scene that I remember well from the late 1950s and early 1960s - though typically a lot busier than was the case on the day this photograph was taken.

dinner, we would sometimes take the long way home, over the bridge at Main Street, and walk alongside the Clyde till we came to Cotton Street. Then we would turn into Swanston Street and on to Dalmarnock Road where a short turn to the left and a crossing of the road, would bring us home. Home - to Sunday dinner that was usually mince and tatties, or stew. I used to hope it was chops. This was my favourite, and home made broth or chicken soup, whatever was on offer. My father and I were always ready for our dinner as we had usually been out the house since before noon. Mother's cooking was always something we looked forward to.

There are other parts of Glasgow Green of which I have fond childhood recall. At the other end of the Green going in the direction of Saltmarket, there was a putting green. During the summer holidays from school, I used to spend hours here with my pals, playing putting. At that time, putting was one of my favourite pastimes; this would be in the early 1960s. You could get on the green and play a round of eighteen holes on the green, for about sixpence in old money. I only had a vague awareness of the actual game of golf but I always took my putting seriously. When my pals and I went on to that green, we thought we were the Jack Nicklaus or the Arnold Palmer of Bridgeton.

Another distant memory I have of the Green is when I used to go there with my mother and grandmother during the week. When we came out of the bowling green, we would sometimes go into this little park, known locally as the 'Daisy Park' which was just along from the bowling green. This was a quiet wee spot where people would just come to sit on a nice summer's day and watch the world go by. In this park, there was, in one corner, a space, at the Eastern end of the park, where people played draughts. It always seemed to be old men who played. There was this giant draughtboard on the ground and the men would move their draughts with some sort of large hooks or something similar. There would also be people standing watching them. Sometimes we would stop for a few minutes and watch the game before going out into Greenhead Street to begin our trek home to where my grandmother lived.

Just off Kings Drive on the other side of the road from where the football pitches were on the Green, there was a swing-park. I can vaguely recall, as a small boy, my mother and my grandmother giving me a push on one of the swings. Part of this is now remembered as the 'Gymnasium' by people who frequented it; there were large poles and bar type structures alongside the swings where the more vigorous could do their various exercises etc. There was also, right next to the swings, what was known locally as the 'sawn (sandy) pond.' This was a small area which was filled with sand, a sort of miniature Saltcoats beach if you like, and you would see the kids playing away for hours here. I can remember making a few sandcastles myself here on occasion. I must have been very young at this time, so this is perhaps another pre-school memory, though not a definite one. I don't know what happened to the 'sawny pond' but it is like many other things in the area, long since gone.

On Sunday afternoons, I would sometimes go with my parents to Richmond Park. This is just across the road from Shawfield Stadium. It has changed very little over the last forty years, though I don't think it is nearly as crowded with people as it was during the period with which I am concerned here. This is perhaps not surprising, when you think of the vast changes that have taken place, not only in the Bridgeton and Dalmarnock areas, but also in the Oatlands and Polmadie areas, which border the far side of Richmond Park. So many people have moved out of these areas over the last forty or forty-five years.

When we went to Richmond Park on Sunday afternoons, there would be scores of children trying to catch fish from the large pond that is in the centre of the park. The kids would take empty jam-jars along and try to scoop up the small 'tadpoles' (or 'baggy minnies') as they were called, from the pond, using some sort of small net on a stick. I did this too on occasion. Great fun it was. Sometimes at the end of the afternoon, we would walk right through to the southern end of Richmond Park and cross over Rutherglen Road to Pelosi's café at number 698. Alternatively it would be Crolla's in Main Street.

Another place that I sometimes went with my parents on Sunday afternoons during the summer was Hogganfield Loch in the North-East of Glasgow and close to the relatively new (at that time) housing schemes of Ruchazie and Garthamlock. I remember that this was a vast place; we would sometimes walk around the entire area, stopping at times to watch the boats in the loch and for an ice-cream from one of the kiosks at the loch. It was always a lovely day out. We would usually walk or get the tram down to Bridgeton Cross, then board either the number 7 tram at the bottom of James Street, or the 106 trolley bus, any of which would take us up to the loch. On the way back, I think that we would sometimes get the tram down to Dennistoun at Duke Street then get the number 46 or number 22 corporation bus to take us home.

The above pastimes seem to have stood the test of time. A few years ago, ironically, on a Sunday afternoon, I walked through Richmond Park and it was quite busy with kids still doing much the same things as their predecessors did all those years ago, though not in such large numbers.

I mentioned the swing-park in Glasgow Green. There were many of these in the area at that time. There was one in Baltic Street just along from where Springfield Primary School was at that time, situated. I think I used to go in here just about every day when I was a boy. There were a few swings and roundabouts and also a few chutes, on which you would slide down from the top to the ground, then rush up the stairs and do the whole thing again, and again... You could have spent all day just doing this. I always remember this man called Danny who was the attendant at this swing–park. He had a small hut at the back of the swing-park where he took his meals etc, as he had to be there all day. Many a time when I was in the swing-park, I would see and hear Danny shouting and bawling at the kids. He would shout at them if they misbehaved in the slightest, or so it seemed. The kids were always baiting him or as we would say nowadays, 'winding him up', but it was all harmless fun really. Poor old Danny would be trying to catch the kids and threatening to eject them from the swings. I can still picture Danny to this day; he always wore a bonnet, and always seemed to have a coat on, no matter what the weather was like. I spoke to him once or twice; he was a kindly soul, in spite of first impressions when you saw him running all over the place. One of the 'characters' of the area without a doubt. That particular swing-park survived, if in a somewhat reduced form, until the very recent past. The hut where Danny was based went a long time ago and some of the swings went too, but kids still played on the swings that remained. The last time I passed by here though, it was just a vacant piece of ground, so typical of many of the other places in the area that I remember from my childhood.

There was another swing-park in the area that I remember going to. This one stood at the corner of Dalmarnock Road and Dunn Street. I recall one day that I was on the 'roundabout' as it was called, along with a few other children and this bigger boy came along and started turning the roundabout round and round at high speed. All of us started to shout to get off it, as it was going so fast we were all scared. My mother was there at the time and when she saw what was happening, she told this other boy off in no uncertain manner. My mother was a quiet person, who would never give anyone any trouble, but she had a strong sense of 'fair play' and this to her, and to the rest of us there come to think of it, most certainly was not 'fair play'.

There were also swing-parks in Fielden Street just off London Road and at the London Road end of Kinnear Road. I would sometimes go to the one in Fielden Street that was just around the corner, when I was up at my grandmother's house. I would go here and play sometimes, during the summer holidays from school during the day when my mother was working. The one in Kinnear Road I have only a vague memory of, though I remember that this swing park had a very long 'chute' and I recall the thrill of having one slide after the other on it, I think this swing park was known as the 'American Swings' I would probably go to this one when I was visiting my Aunt Chrissie with my mother, my aunt lived in nearby Buddon Street.

As I grew older and went to secondary school, another place I used to go to regularly was Tollcross Park in Tollcross Road. I would go up here with one or two of my school pals and sometimes some of my younger cousins who lived near Parkhead Cross. Often we would spend the whole or most of the afternoon playing football on the pitches there. If we got fed up with football, we would wander further down the park to the pitch-and-putt green. This was a sort of mini version of a game of golf. As I recall, there were nine holes on the course and you could get a game of pitch-and-putt for about a shilling. It was a game that seemed to be popular all over Glasgow at that time. I certainly enjoyed it, as it required more skill than an ordinary game of putting. You had to tee the ball up to drive off and sometimes you would land in one of the 'bunkers.' I could often play two or three games one after the other, during an afternoon. When you were hitting that ball from the tee, you felt like you were a real golfer.

As I recall in the late 1950s, there was also a bowling green at Tollcross Park and occasionally in the summer my father and I would go up here and sit for a couple of hours, as a change from going to the bowling green at Glasgow Green. I remember that the bowling green at Tollcross was always crowded on the occasions that we were there. It seemed to be more crowded than the one at Glasgow Green.

There was also at that time, a place called Westhorn Park. This was quite near Tollcross Park - in fact if you walked down Maukinfauld Road southward into London Road, you would be close to Westhorn. It was situated right next to the old Belvedere hospital, and just along from Celtic's training ground. I used to go to Westhorn Park almost every day in the summer after school and during the summer holidays. By this time of course, I was at Riverside Secondary in nearby Springfield Road. I would go to Westhorn with one of my friends and the two of us would play football together for a few hours. Sometimes some of the other boys we knew from 'Rivi' would come along and join us, and we could get a game of three or four-a-side going. When there was just the two of us we would play "shooty in" where one person would go in goal and the other would take shots at him. I used to enjoy both shooting in, and saving.

I was 'one footed' in footballing terms but I had a power of shot with my right foot that Jorg Albertz would have been proud of. At just about everything else connected with the game, I was not much good, but as I recall, I used to love diving and jumping about in goal thinking I was the

'Frank Haffey' of Westhorn Park. Frank who? As I recollect, there were no goalposts in Westhorn.

For goal areas you made do with whatever was available at the time. This was usually jackets but sometimes large stones, and, if you were really desperate, bits of paper. But if it was a windy day, well, you had big problems with that!

I think there was also a putting green at Westhorn - there certainly was a bowling green, and it was on this green that I had my first and only game of bowls. This would be about 1960 or 1961 and it was when I was up at Westhorn, attending the school sports.

I recall a rather amusing incident near here a few years later. I was watching the Celtic players train at their training ground 'next door' to Westhorn and I remember seeing the players on this particular morning going through their shooting practice routine. Celtic at that particular time had a Scandinavian goalkeeper whom they had signed from the Danish club Aarhus. This morning, a shot had gone wide of the goalpost and was coming towards where I, with a few younger boys, was watching. One of the boys rushed to retrieve the ball; this keeper gestured to the boy that he could get it himself. A few minutes later, the same thing occurs and a shot goes towards these boys. Quite naturally, given what had happened the first time, the boys did not bother to go for the ball. However, this time, the goalie was virtually screaming for the ball to be returned to him. For the boys, it was a case of "you just cannot win." I remember that this goalkeeper seemed to me watching that incident, a rather arrogant-looking individual. He wasn't much of a goalie either as it turned out.

9

Playtime.

As a boy growing up in that era, I had plenty of friends from the immediate area and further afield. We would spend hours kicking a ball about after school, in the backcourts or in the quiet side streets off Dalmarnock Road. It is often said these days that the boys of the present age do not play football to the same extent that previous generations did. I don't accept this at all. I believe that kids still do spend a lot of time playing football; it is just perhaps that they do so in different places.

Football was of course our main pastime. I say football but there were quite a few variations on this. Let me explain. Sometimes we would play 'shooty-in,' - this was where two of us would mark out goal areas and we would simply belt the ball at each other's 'goal.' The one, who managed to beat his opponent the most, was the winner. Quite a good game and one in which you could develop 'skills' both as a goalie and as a 'shooter.' I used to enjoy this game. Usually these games would end up with crazy scores of about fifty each or something like that.

At other times, if there were a sufficient number of us around, we would get a full-scale game of football going. Often these games could involve 'teams' of anything up to seven a side. Quite often boys from Nuneaton Street and Mordaunt Street were coming round to our backcourt for a game. Sometimes boys would come from further afield; it was a case of the more the merrier as it were, as usually the more boys there were, the better the game was. As when we played in the parks, we would use anything that was available for the 'goals' - jackets, bricks, stones, the back or sides of the washhouses in the backcourts, or even the side of the rubbish area - or as we called it, the 'midden' or the 'midgie bins.' They would all serve the purpose at one time or another.

We would often use the same ball for weeks, perhaps even months on end. We would use it until it was completely 'done' as it were. We often played with a burst ball, as long as there was something to kick around. Finally, when the ball, if it could still be called that in its final stages, ceased to be functional, it was discarded and we would all put our coppers together. Our pooled resources from our weekly pocket money were usually being sufficient for the purchase of a new ball. This was always an occasion of great joy it seemed. Yes, the simple pleasures of childhood.

I recall that a rather flimsy and not very high railing originally separated our own backcourt at number 337. Obviously its original purpose was to divide the backcourt of number 337 from the one at number 343, which was the last one before you came to Mordaunt Street. To me though, it did not seem to serve its purpose. I remember that it collapsed completely in the early part of the 1960s. This meant that my pals and I now had what to us was a 'full length' football pitch. It also meant that we now had more solid goal areas for our games. We could now use the end wall of the backcourt at number 343 which separated the backcourt from Mordaunt Street at that end and the other one, Nuneaton Street end, which was the adjoining one to ours at that side.

Sometimes the ball would go over the wall at the Nuneaton Street end. You had to hope that there would be people playing football at the same time who would throw or kick the ball back over to you. If there weren't, you had to trek through the close out into Dalmarnock Road into this other close, retrieve the ball and then all the way back again. The wall at the Mordaunt Street was a lot higher than the one at the other side. This meant that you did not have the same problem of having to skip round into Mordaunt Street every time for the ball every time that it was kicked high into the air. One solution, of course to the problem at the Nuneaton Street end of our backcourt, was to simply climb over the old washhouses or the roof of the rubbish area. I rarely, if ever, felt energetic enough for this. Also, I had seen too many of my pals ending up with their trousers ripped apart after climbing over these roofs, to be keen to 'go over the top' as it were, even if it was your 'play trousers.' They still needed replacing when they were ruined. Most of the time when the ball went over the wall, we used to take turns to retrieve it; a sort of basic rota system in effect.

Another game we would play, and yet another variation of the generic term football, was what we called 'headers.' This involved heading the ball into your opponent's goal area where your opponent had to try to save it. If he didn't, then it was a 'goal' for you. I can recall that this was the pastime that I enjoyed best and I would spend hour after hour playing at 'headers,' usually as I

Outfitters Shop, 313 Dalmarnock Road, August 1932

recall with Jim Connor, whom I mentioned in an earlier chapter.

The sides of the old washhouses provided more than suitable goal areas for this game. As I recall, the side of the washhouse in our backcourt was about the same length as the one in the adjoining backcourt at number 343. They both faced each other, about ten yards apart, so it was ideal for a game of 'headers.' We even had 'crossbars' in the goal areas. At the top of each washhouse wall, there was a sort of ridge and this served as the 'crossbar.' Right alongside the area where we played this game of 'headers', was the side red brick wall of the 'Plaza' picture hall. When you headed the ball, you would sometimes try to confuse your opponent by heading the ball off this wall, rather than heading it straight to his goal area. So quite a lot of the goals that were scored in the course of these games, were 'in/off' affairs.

Sometimes we would play football up at the top end of Mordaunt Street, which unlike Nuneaton Street, was sealed off from London Road by the railway embankment. It was a near perfect spot for a good old fashioned kick about, with plenty of space and you would get boys from all around the area Baltic Street etc, coming over to join in the fun.

Another game that I remember playing in the backcourts, was hide and seek. But when we all got a bit older, I can remember that my pals and I got more daring as it were, and we would get involved in 'chasing,' as you might call it. This involved 'meeting up' shall we say, with packs of kids from the tenements in Mordaunt Street and especially from Nuneaton Street. We would chase them back to their "territory" and in turn they would chase us back to ours. Sometimes, we would throw stones at each other. Looking back at this all these years later, it seems a bit reckless, but I suppose compared with some of the stories you hear about what children get up to these days, it all seems fairly tame.

One thing that I particularly remember about these chases, was that when we were being chased from the backcourts in Nuneaton Street back round to the backcourts in Dalmarnock Road, we would run down the short lane that led off Nuneaton Street near the 'Plaza' picture hall. If you went to the left at the end of this, it would lead you into the backcourt of the tenements at number 327 Dalmarnock Road where the entrance to these tenements was, unlike the rest of them, ours included, at the front. If you went to the right, it would take you into another short lane and into Dalmarnock Road. If we had enough of a head start on our pursuers, we would dash into the first lane and then into the closemouth in the backcourt. Some seconds later, our pursuers from Nuneaton Street would arrive. Thinking that we had all run into the second lane and into Dalmarnock Road and to our own 'patch,' they would follow us, only to end up scratching their heads wondering how we could apparently have disappeared into thin air. All the time we would be hiding in the closemouth of number 327.

It used to give us great satisfaction that we had put one over on them in this way. The walls where the lanes were are still there to this day, but the lanes themselves long ago closed off, and small industrial units now occupy part of the space where the backcourts were.

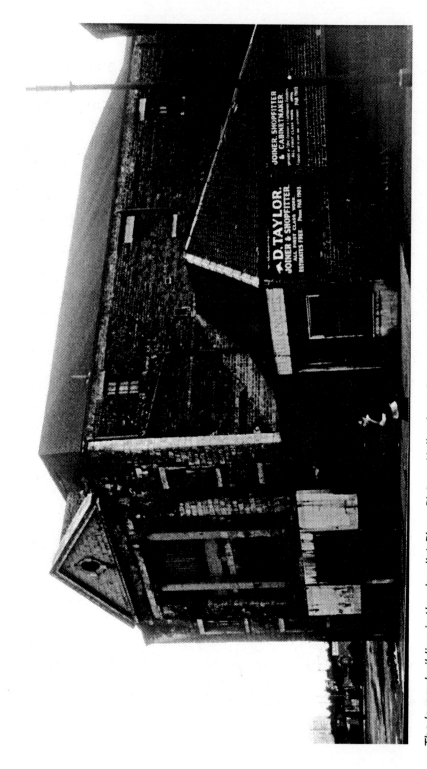

The larger building is the derelict Plaza Picture Hall, where I was a regular from about 1956 until it closed in 1962. The shop next door is Milne's Fishmongers. This photograph probably dates from the 1970s.

D. TAYLOR.
JOINER & SHOPFITTER
ALL FIRST CLASS WORK
ESTIMATES FREE   Phone: PAR 2901

JOINER, SHOPFITTER
& CABINETMAKER

Yet another pastime that I remember playing round the backcourts, was the game of marbles, or 'jorries.' This involved rolling, or sometimes throwing, these round, glass, ball-like things. Strangely enough, I cannot remember the exact object of the game. I think though, that there was this larger glass ball and you had to try and get your marbles as close to it as possible. I think that the winner was the player whose marbles were closest to the larger marble.

Something else that I recall from these 'playtime' adventures, was that some of the kids would deliberately bait Mr. Lind who lived below us, by making a lot of noise and shouting up at his back window which looked out on to the backcourts. He would go into an absolute rage and shout and sometimes swear down at them. Such was the force and intensity of his rage that they would all scamper, till the next time that is. At that time of course, it was the done thing to shout up from the backcourts. You would shout up for your mother to throw you down a 'piece' or a penny and other such everyday things. Yes, the simple pleasures of childhood right enough.

When I got older and was at Riverside I would sometimes play football after school, round the backcourt where my school friend Thomas Angell lived. This was at 722 Springfield Road and above the public-house known as the Springfield Vaults which was at that time I think called Flynn's. The pub is still there but the tenements have long since been demolished, disappearing I think about 1972. The entrance to 722 was next to the pub but as I remember it the block where Thomas lived could also be entered through the closemouth of 1297 London Road, just around the corner. As with number 722 there is also no remaining trace of this close but to the side of the Chinese Takeaway, right next to where number 722 once was there is the remains of what once was the backcourt to these tenements and where I spent many late afternoons enjoying our kickabout with Thomas and sometimes one or two others boys from the block or nearby. One of these was I think a Johnny Flannagan, who later played senior football in England.

One rather strange boyhood memory I have, is of playing in a backcourt one day, in Dalmarnock Road, just past Nuneaton Street and seeing these four or five men with what I think, were bags in their hands, running through the backcourts, heading towards Baltic Street. At that time, probably sometime in the mid 1950s, the backcourts stretched all the way down to Dunn Street and all the way up to Baltic Street. It was just like one large area with railings here and there, but no walls separating the backcourts. I wonder if I was the unwitting witness to a getaway following a robbery. I have never forgotten that incident.

10

'Springi' Primary.

I commenced my schooldays in the August of 1952. I cannot remember what day of the week it was though it was probably a Monday.

Apart from that brief but significant recall of being in the school playground on that morning, I have no memory of my first day at school.

My schooling was to commence at Springfield Primary School. This name is a bit misleading because very little, if any at all of the school, actually bordered on the main road itself. As I remember it, there were two playgrounds for us boys. The smaller of the two was the one where we had all assembled on that first morning. This playground was on the corner of Baltic Street and Connal Street. The larger one was in the middle of Connal Street, a very short street. Connal Street leads from its junction with Baltic Street, straight in to Lily Street and it was here that the girl's playground was situated. This was a smaller, much narrower playground.

I cannot say for sure why there were two playgrounds for us boys. Perhaps it was because there were many more boys than girls at the school during that period, although I don't think that was the case. Perhaps the younger boys say from about five years old up to the ages of eight or nine were put into the smaller playground first. Then as they got older, perhaps they would 'graduate' to the larger one where they would remain until leaving for secondary school, at the age of twelve. Certainly, when I think back, I have very little recall of being in the small playground at all, during my seven years at the school. On the other hand, I do have quite a lot of memories, if somewhat blurred, of being in the larger one. This would certainly be consistent with me having a clearer recall of my later years at the school.

The school had been established in 1883 and remained on the same site until 1969 when premises in nearby Allan Street became Springfield Primary. The school remains here in the present day. After 1969, the school in Lily and Connal Streets became Our Lady of Fatima School, before the Lily Street buildings were destroyed by fire towards the end of August 1973. The school never reopened. Where the two boys' playgrounds were is now partly a swingpark. There is also space for playing football at the Connal Street end, while the Lily Street part is now occupied by a community centre.

If I were honest, though, I would have to admit that my memories of these seven years in relation to the school are not very good. Certainly not as clear as my memories of my secondary schooling.

During all of my time at 'Springi,' I was in a 'mixed' class, i.e. both boys and girls. Certainly this was the case for most of the time at least. We received quite a wide spread of lessons; the usual three R's and also things like Music, some Physical Training (PT) and the occasional picture show in a darkened classroom.

I particularly remember when we got a period of PT. Unlike the later structured regime, which I was to experience at secondary school - when classes followed a time-table of lessons, I think primary teaching was very much on an *ad hoc* basis. I can still remember clearly how we would be sitting in a classroom early on in the day and Mr. Galloway, the PT instructor, would make an appearance. A cheer would echo from most of the class, as it would mean a break from whatever we were doing at the time - sums or whatever. So Mr. Galloway was always a welcome visitor when he made his appearance in the mornings, usually between nine and ten o'clock, if my memory serves me correctly.

I hasten to add that I was not among those who welcomed the sight of the said Mr. Galloway. I did not like PT one bit; I would far rather have remained in the classroom and done my sums, even if I wasn't much good at them either. I think that sometimes the teacher who was taking our class was not really altogether pleased to have his or her pupils removed from the classroom to the gymnasium. Most of the time though, I think Galloway 'won the day' and off we would march to the gymnasium – yours truly, more often than not on these occasions, with a distinct frown on his face.

As I say, these PT sessions were never my cup of tea at all. I think in the gymnasium we had to put on some sort of gym wear or something similar. Certainly I remember that in the gymnasium, there were no changing rooms as such, and you had to change right out in the open; the girls to one side of the gym, boys to the other. Even at that age, we boys were blushing, giving quick glances over to the other side of the hall in case any of the girls were looking over, trying to make the change over as quickly as possible, to avoid embarrassment. If that was not enough, the

Springfield Road Primary School in 1965. This is the Connal Street part of the school, with the two boys' playgrounds between the classroom blocks.

'gymnasium' was actually just a hall, quite a broad one though, very spacious. I think that it was just used as a make shift gym. Certainly I remember there were classrooms on either side of it and you would get children coming out of the rooms while were doing our exercises, or worse still, when we were in the act of stripping or changing.

I have little recollection of what we actually did during these 'lessons.' I think that each session would probably last for about an hour or perhaps a little shorter. Most probably, what we did was wave our hands above our head while looking rather stupid. Mr. Galloway always had his hands up in the air, so we were probably encouraged to do 'stretching exercises' or whatever. I seem to remember, if very vaguely, that at times we also practiced some sort of dancing. I wouldn't have liked that either, not at that stage in my life anyway.

I can still picture Mr. Galloway to this day. He was a small man of rather slight build, always quite cheery; but he seemed to wear 'boring' colours. He seemed always to have on this grey sweater. He had a slightly receding hairline and I think the children usually referred to him as "wee Ben". Certainly that was his nickname when our paths crossed again at secondary school. I cannot remember his real Christian name. I don't think he was based at any school in particular. I think he must have worked the schools throughout the area, on a sort of roving commission if you like. Not one of my favourite people, was Mr. G. – not I hasten to add because of any of his personal characteristics, but simply because I hated his vocation.

That hall which doubled as a gym was, if not the bane of my young life, then certainly not

This Class photograph, from 4 April, 1957, was taken in the Girls' Playground, facing Lily Street. I am in the front row, second from left, between classmates Jackie Stevenson and Drew Russell. The teacher is Mr. McPhail.

one of my favourite places during my time at 'Springi.' It was just along from here, near the exit into Connal and Baltic Streets, that we were to go when the school doctor called. There was this little room at the bottom of the hall where we would have to go in and get our 'jags' for such thing as diphtheria and polio. I think we would get one for measles too and perhaps chickenpox as well. It was also here where we periodically 'got our heads inspected' – externally only, I hasten to add. We would be inspected at an early age for lice and similar things, the doctor running his or her fingers through our hair.

That was bad enough, but the 'jags' were something else again. I can still picture to this day, in my mind's eye, that little room where we got them. It is strange how the less pleasant happenings always seem to be the ones that stick with you the longest, the things that you can recall easily, while other, perhaps more pleasant, things may be "lost" with the passage of time. Anyway, I can still picture myself in this room, almost half a century on. We would line up in a queue and, as you got nearer the doctor and of course the dreaded needle; you would start to get really frightened. You would somehow envy your pals passing you on their way out, at least the worst moment was now past for them, while all the while you would be getting nearer and nearer to the needle. When I think back, the 'pain,' if there was any, was not all that bad really. I think it was more the perception than anything else. There would be a slight soreness when the needle went through your skin but that was all. You would be relieved once your turn was past, till the next time that is. At that time, diseases like diphtheria and polio were much more common than what they are now, so although we were too young to realise it, the immunisations, to give the 'jags' their proper their proper name, were of course for our own good.

Certainly for the most part they served me well, though I did suffer from chickenpox when I was about seven. I also remember, we would get periodic general medical inspections too, and after this was finished everyone would say that they had 'passed the doctor' (it seems a little silly all these years later, not to mention ambiguous as well) - that was the 'in phrase' on these occasions.

We used to get 'films,' if that is the correct word, every so often. I cannot remember what type of films these were or anything like that at all; most probably they were *Pathé News* type films. Unlike the dreaded appearance of Mr. Galloway, this was something I *did* look forward to. I think we all did really. It was a welcome break from everyday lessons. We would all troop up to the room upstairs - it was just above the gym hal. The curtains would all be drawn, then with the room suitably dark, the good old projector would do its stuff and for about the next hour, we would all be engrossed, our eyes firmly fixed on the screen, which was draped over the blackboard, if I remember correctly. I think the room was usually one of the larger rooms and there may have been other classes in there with us.

Another event, which is quite clear in my memory, is the Coronation of Queen Elizabeth II, in June 1953. Our class was taken on a visit down to the Bridgeton Public Halls in Summer Street, near Bridgeton Cross, to see this momentous occasion. I think this would be a few days or so after the actual event and that we were seeing a recording of it. I can remember quite clearly, us marching in file, straight down Baltic Street into Heron Street, across the busy London Road into Summer Street and our destination.

Then there were the visits at the end of each term, to Dalmarnock Parish Church at 103 Springfield Road. This was just around the corner from Lily Street. I can still picture, if somewhat vaguely, the inside of this small church all these years later. I always enjoyed going there. Sadly, this lovely little church is no more, it having been demolished sometime in the late 1970s or during the 1980s.

I even tried 'Sunday School' around this time, being persuaded by a school classmate to go along one Sunday afternoon to the Baltic Hall at 518 Baltic Street, where the classes were held. For some long forgotten reason or reasons, I didn't go back a second time.

I always looked forward to 'playtime' when I was at 'Springi.' I remember that the boys from our class and myself used to play football during the breaks from classes. All my recall of these games is when I was in the big playground. I cannot remember ever having played football in the small playground that I mentioned earlier. Usually, we played over at the far corner where the 'shed' was. This was a covered area where there was a long seat and where some of the boys would go to eat their 'piece' if it was raining. If the 'footballers' got there first though, we 'commandeered' the whole area and the 'diners' would sit there at their peril, at any moment

Dalmarnock Parish Church, in Springfield Road. This lovely little church was demolished in the late 1970s or early 1980s, a few years after this photo was taken in 1975.

likely to be hit by the ball. This small area was bordered at one end by the boy's toilet and the other by the railing of the adjoining girls' playground that stretched towards Lily Street. It was these two spots that were used for the 'goals' - the entrance to the toilet and the railings of the girls' playground. Rather makeshift to say the least. Anyone coming out of the toilet was liable to be hit full blast by the ball from a kick of Jorg Albertz proportions, while at the other 'goal,' the ball often went over the low railings and into the girls' playground.

We did play in the main playground itself when the weather was better. We probably only used the smaller area when the weather was not so good and because there was more cover there. I have one rather glorious memory of playing football in the big playground that looked out into Connal Street. It was lunchtime and it was a 'big game,' that is there were about six or seven of us in either side. On this particular occasion, I was out on the 'right wing,' away over at the far end of the playground near to where the entrance to the classrooms were. I hadn't had as much as a touch of the ball since the game had started, when suddenly the ball comes to me and I blast it with all the power in my right foot. It goes screaming into the goal and I am an instant hero in the eyes of my teammates. I felt that I had scored the winning goal in the Cup Final. Actually the 'goals' we used in the playground itself were somewhat better than the very makeshift ones in the smaller, covered area. In the playground, one of the goals was the side of the toilet. The toilet was a long stretch, from the covered area described, right down to another smaller covered area at the other end of the playground. So the sidewall of this toilet, provided ample space for one of the goals. The other goal was simply the railings of the playground, in Connal Street. This was where my 'Cup Final' goal was scored.

As I got older, I used to have my lunch in the school, my mother having taken great care to ensure that I was always provided with sufficient sandwiches or whatever, to see me through the day, till I got home in the late afternoon. I then looked forward to a big 'supper.' We always referred to it as such in the McKenna household. Come to think of it, I cannot recall the term 'lunch" ever being used in our house at all. I think 'lunch' is more commonly used in middle class homes than it is in working class homes such as I grew up in, to refer to the meal in the middle part of the day. To us, breakfast was what you had first thing in the morning. Then, about midday, it was 'dinner time' - the fact that the meal at this time of the day consisted often of simply a snack, was neither here nor there. Then in the early evening, it was supper. On Sundays though, we would have our supper in the middle or late part of the afternoon. This was most probably due to the fact that on Sunday mornings, we had the traditional 'long lie.' This meant that, as we got up later, there was no midday meal and we were all hungry by suppertime.

I do remember though, that when I went to school at first and for some time afterwards, my mother would come up to the school playground every day at 'lunch' time and we would walk home together for lunch, a journey that took less than ten minutes.

There was one occasion – I think it must have been near the beginning of my schooldays – my mother had not appeared at the school playground at lunchtime. As a wee boy I was worried, but I remember walking down Baltic Street, then into Mordaunt St in the direction of our home. I had just about reached the end of this street, when I saw my mother coming round the corner from Dalmarnock Road towards me. She was worried about me and relieved to see that I knew my way home. I think the tram bringing her from work in the city-centre had been late or something like that and most unusually she had not been on time to collect me from school. I made out that "Everything was ok," and that I wasn't worried, – talk about putting on a brave face! I think that after that I did come home on my own, all the time.

Another clear memory I have from around this time is of one afternoon when there was this violent thunderstorm raging. I remember being with my school pals, all of us going along Baltic Street with our mothers alongside us and great flashes of forked and sheet lightning flashing all around us. I have never been too keen on lightning to put it mildly, and I remember that day, that I was really scared - the lightning seemed to be about to strike us at any time. I think we were *all* scared that day. Of course you don't think of it that way, you are only really aware of your own feelings when something like that is scary to you.

Strangely, I can only recall the names of one or two of my teachers during my time at 'Springi,' apart from Mr. Galloway that is. I remember that late on a Monday afternoon, we got a Miss Dodds.

A view of Baltic Street, c. 1902, looking east. The buildings of Springfield Road Primary School can be seen in the distance on the right. In the far distance the tenements of Springfield Road are visible. All these buildings survived until the mid 1970s. I remember playing, in the 1950s, in nearby back courts.

I think this was a kind of music lesson and we used to sing from sheets. Although I had nothing against music as such, suffice to say that Miss Dodds was not one of my favourite teachers.

The only other teacher I can remember with any degree of certainty, is a Mr. Peacock, a tall man with greying hair and who always seemed to wear a grey suit. I don't recall what he taught us, but I remember him as a pleasant sort of person. Then there was Mr. McPhail, whom I remember as a cheery, jovial sort of person, but that's about all.

Although I am at a loss to remember the names of other teachers, I do remember being in many different classrooms throughout the school. I remember that after the midday break, we would all line up on front of the main building in the Connal Street playground. Then we would march into the building itself and up the stairs or wherever, to our classrooms. This would all be done against the background of 'marching' music, or sometimes I think Scottish dance music. I think one of the teachers played the piano in a corner near to the exit into the girl's playground in Lily Street. It sounds a bit daft when you think of it all these years later but that was the way that it was.

In contrast to my failing in remembering the names of most of my teachers, I can remember nearly all of my classmates. I have two class photographs from my time at Primary School. One is of us in the smaller of the two playgrounds - the one I assembled at on my very first day at the school. I am not entirely certain in what year this one was taken, but it would perhaps be about 1953 or 1954. The other one has the year inscribed on the cover. It was taken in the girls' playground facing Lily Street, in 1957. I can recall the full names of all but one or two of the children in both of these photographs, so perhaps my memory is not so bad after all.

I left 'Springi' in June of 1959. Unlike my recollections of leaving secondary school, I have absolutely no recollection of my final day. I cannot recall whether or not I was looking forward to advancing to secondary school. It was about to happen though, whether I liked it or not and in August of that year, I would commence my secondary education at Riverside Senior Secondary in Springfield Road, a few hundred yards to the north.

11

'The Pictures.'

During the time I lived in the Dalmarnock/ Bridgeton area of the East End, there was a plethora of cinemas in the immediate and adjoining areas. In all, I reckon there were about seventeen of them. Even as a young boy I was a fan of the cinema. I simply loved 'the pictures' as we referred to the cinema. Looking back, I think that my favourites at that time were probably westerns and war pictures. I remember I always used to like Cowboy-and-Indian films, and for some reason, I particularly liked Jeff Chandler pictures. He, with the distinctive and premature grey hair. When I was a boy, it always seemed to be him who was fighting the 'bad' Indians. In those days of course, there was a much greater distinction between the 'good' guys and the 'bad' guys. In the modern cinema, it is a much more subjective concept; I am talking here about an era over thirty years before modern westerns such as *Dances With Wolves* put a whole new slant on the cowboy and Indian thing.

As I say, war pictures also took my fancy, although in this case I cannot remember any particular actor that stood out. When you watch a lot of the old war films on the telly though, decades later, you tend to recognise films and famous stars that you saw as a boy and names 'come back to you'.

The nearest cinema to our tenement home was just around the corner in Nuneaton Street, a walk of less than five minutes. It had been established in the early 1920s and had been previously called the Dalmarnock Picture House. It was however, by the time I was growing up, known as the 'Plaza'. The last pictures were shown there in 1962, but the derelict building remained standing for another fifteen years or so, before finally being demolished. It was a small cinema; the red brick wall of the side of the building stretched into the backcourts that my pals and I played in. We would climb on to the tops of the washhouses or the 'dykes' as we called them and we would be able to hear the sound of the picture through the air vents. It was this cinema that, as a boy, I visited the most – usually every Saturday evening, with my mother.

While I slept in the smaller of our two rooms – the one looking out into the backcourt – as the curtains were drawn first thing every morning the first thing you saw was the imposing side wall of the Plaza. In the winter I always got off to a good start in the mornings if I saw snow on the Plaza roof.

The other cinemas in the area were: the 'Olympia,' down at Bridgeton Cross, the 'Arcadia' at the Calton end of London Road, the 'Royal' in Main Street, the 'Kings' in James Street, and The 'Strathclyde' or the 'Strathy' in Summerfield Street, just off Dalmarnock Road, shortly before you cross the bridge into Rutherglen. If I remember correctly, the 'Arcadia' seldom seemed to be busy; there were often many empty seats. My abiding memory of this hall is of for the first and only time in my life walking by mistake into the female toilet. I remember the shock of two young girls about my own age on seeing me enter, and I got out of there soon as possible. I think that the embarrassment is so much greater

Summerfield Street, from Dalmarnock Road. The Strathclyde
Picture Hall, on the left, had been converted into a Bingo Hall,
at the time of this photograph, taken at the end of the 1970s
or early 1980s.

at an age when you growing up than in later life. In Rutherglen itself, were the 'Odeon' and the 'Rio.' (Or as a workmate used to call it the 'R ten.') I usually went to these halls during the week, mainly the 'Rio' as I got older

As well as these, but slightly further afield, was the 'Granada' in Duke Street, just down from Parkhead Cross. Further afield still, there was the 'State' and 'Odeon,' both in Shettleston. Then, coming a bit closer to home again, there was the 'Premiere' in Kirkpatrick Street, just off London Road and close to where my paternal grandmother lived, on London Road itself. This cinema was known locally as the 'Geggy' – why, I never did find out. There were also another two small cinemas near Parkhead Cross. One of these was in Springfield Road and was called the 'Black Cat'. The other, "the 'Parkhead Picture Palace' ('The Three P's',) was in Tollcross Road. I have a vague recollection of going on occasion, on Sunday afternoons, with my parents, to these two halls, though it was by no means a weekly thing.

I cannot recall ever having been in the 'Royal' or in the 'Geggy,' but I was at one time or another, in the remainder of all these halls. None of them is still in existence today, as a cinema. With the decline in the popularity of the cinema as a place of entertainment in the late 1960s and early 1970s, they were either used as bingo halls for a time, or demolished.

Further afield still was the 'Scotia' in Millerston Street, Dennistoun. I was never there on a regular basis; in fact I only recall one visit for sure. That was one Tuesday afternoon about 1959 or 1960, when my parents took me there and we saw a

Norman Wisdom picture, *Follow a Star*.

My favourite cinema during my childhood years, the 'Plaza', is long gone, as are The 'Strathclyde', and the 'Odeon' and the 'Rio' in Rutherglen. Likewise, the 'State' in Shettleston and the 'Arcadia' in the Calton have also gone. Most of the others are lying empty and derelict, with the subsequent decline of the popularity of bingo, although the 'Odeon' in Rutherglen is still in use as a bingo hall in the present day. The 'Premiere' in Kirkpatrick Street is the most extreme example of an old cinema lying empty and derelict. When the cinema closed, sometime in the 1960s I think, the building was never used again, apart from a brief period as a meat warehouse. In a small street, itself in a generally poor state, it has remained to the present day, in a state of dereliction and disrepair, surrounded by all kinds of rubbish.

The revival of an interest in the cinema and a resultant increase in attendances from the late 1980s has of course not resulted in the reopening of the old local cinemas or 'flea pits', as they were affectionately referred to by locals. Instead, the whole of the East End of Glasgow is now served by the 'Forge' - a multi-screened cinema, at Parkhead. This is part of the 'Forge' shopping centre on the site of the old Parkhead Forge engineering works. On the eastern outskirts of the city, there is the 'Showcase' multi-screen cinema.

12

Saturday Night at the Movies.

I have been a fan of the cinema for almost as long as I can remember. I think it would be in 1956 or 1957 – I would be between nine and ten years of age – when I saw my first film in a picture hall, though I cannot remember what film I saw. Almost certainly though, it would have been in the 'Plaza'. I remember seeing *Rock Around the Clock* about that time so perhaps it was that one, or maybe *Brigadoon* or *Seven Brides for Seven Brothers,* both of which I have fond, if very distant memories of, as well. I can remember *Rock Around the Clock* a little more clearly. It seemed everyone was 'rocking in the aisles' that night, to the sound of Bill Haley and the Comets, all the rage at that time of course with that new craze, Rock and Roll. As a small boy I was fascinated.

I went with my mother to the 'pictures' every Saturday evening from about 1956 till about 1959. Usually we would go to the 'Plaza', although occasionally we would venture up to 'The 'Strathclyde' in Summerfield Street, or the 'Strathy' as we sometimes referred to it.

The 'Plaza' cinema was situated just around the corner from our home at the beginning of Nuneaton Street and next to a small shop, Milne's, that sold fish. I can somewhat vaguely remember the entrance to the hall. The stall where you paid your admission money was right in front of you. On either side of this there was an entrance to the stalls and another door to the small balcony. The hall itself was not very long but there was a wide spread of each row of seats. As I remember it, the seats in the stalls were the basic fare as it were. If you wanted a little bit of 'comfort,' then you paid the extra old sixpence and went up to the balcony. I do not have any clear memory of ever being in the balcony on those Saturday evening trips to the 'Plaza' with my mother, though we may have been once or twice. We usually went to the stalls, hard seats and all.

In those days, the old projector would frequently break down and the screen would go blank in the middle of the picture, sometimes for as long as ten minutes. In some ways it was almost "expected" that this would happen. When it did, you would hear the boos and shouts of disapproval from the audience, but there was rarely, if ever, any trouble because of this. In fact, in a perverse sort of way, it was a bit of fun and part of the evening out really. Having said that though, I cannot imagine it being regarded as such with modern cinema audiences somehow.

In those days, the single feature was the exception rather than the rule, unlike the cinema fare of the present day, which is exclusively single feature. In those days you would get the 'big' picture and a shorter film, often referred to as a 'B movie.' There was also, of course, the *Pathé News* features, with that distinctive rousing music at the beginning. Then there were the cartoons which, even as a small boy, I somehow never liked.

Sometimes you would get a single feature with one "big" and definitely long picture, being shown. Films such as *Ben Hur* and *Spartacus* from the late 1950s and early 1960s immediately come to mind in this respect, but there were others. When there was a long single feature on, there would be an interval or intermission about half way through the picture. This intermission usually lasted about ten or fifteen minutes. It was advantageous in the sense that if you needed the toilet, you had the opportunity to do so. Usually half the audience seemed to have the same idea and you would often have to queue at the toilet. Then you would go for an ice cream or ice-lolly from the girl going round the hall with the tray of 'goodies.' My favourites were always an Orange Maid ice-lolly, or any kind of Chocolate Ice. There was usually a queue here too and you often would find that, by the time the lights went off and the picture came back on, you would still be standing in a queue. As a small boy, I recall that when the hall darkened again, it was sometimes difficult to find where you had been sitting. I had a fear of getting 'lost' and a few times I recall my mother shouting down to me that I was going into the wrong row of seats, often one or two rows down from where I had been sitting originally.

The disadvantage of the intermission was that it would come on at a bit of the film you were really enjoying or just when the film was beginning to get really interesting. The lights would come on, sometimes quite unexpectedly, and the curtains would be drawn. You would hear the comments from the audience like "some picture eh?" Another thing was that if the intermission was about fifteen minutes, you could quite easily forget where the film had stopped and it would sometimes take a few minutes before you could pick up the story again. Modern cinema of course, has omitted the intermission completely; something that I have mixed views on.

In those days, the local cinema features were widely advertised in the main streets of the area, on billboards. I can recall very clearly, that when I was out on those Saturday morning shopping trips with my mother, I used to look forward to seeing what was to be on the 'Plaza' and the 'Strathclyde' in the coming week. At that time you would get a couple of pictures on from Monday till Wednesday, then on the Thursday every week, the programme would change again. Sometimes you would get the one film or films on for an entire week - Monday to Saturday, but this was the exception rather than the rule. Nowadays you seldom see cinema features advertised on billboards in the streets. The exterior wall of the 'Plaza' used to have its programmes advertised on a billboard and in Dalmarnock Road itself; there were quite a few billboards. One in particular, I remember being just past Ruby Street in Dalmarnock Road. It was this one that I used to look at every Saturday morning when I was out with my mother at the shops.

The advertisement boards, following a long absence after the demise of the local cinemas, have recently been making something of a comeback, advertising films showing in city-centre cinemas, themselves becoming increasingly fewer in number as I write.

In those days, it was very unusual for a cinema to be open on Sunday. My own recollection is that it was only from about the mid or perhaps the early 1960s, that cinemas began to open their doors on Sundays on a regular basis. Certainly

121

the local cinemas, if they were open at all on a Sunday before that period, would only open about once every month or six weeks. It seemed to be that Sunday was given over to double bills of *X* certificate films. There were four classification codes for films. A *U* certificate meant that the film was suitable for all age groups. An *A* meant that it was suitable for most age groups, except for young children. An *AA* was similar to the modern 15-classification, meaning that it was a film, which contained scenes deemed to be more suitable for adults. An *X* was a strictly adult only film.

I remember that as I got a bit older and started going to see films with some my pals, we would be curious as to what these *X* certificate pictures were. You would see the 'trailers' for the forthcoming attractions and they would show a 'toned down' highlight of these X movies. I clearly recall seeing the trailer to that very good James Dean film *East of Eden,* and also *Blackboard Jungle*, which starred Glenn Ford. Both of these in the 'Plaza'.

Considering some of the films shown on screen in the present day, these movies seem very, very tame in comparison, but they still held a curious fascination for us school kids, even if it was only the 'trailers' we were allowed to see.

In those days of course, it was common practice to enter the cinema in the middle of a film. Then when the bit that was on when you came in 'came round again,' you would leave and go home, or, if it was a really good film, stay on until the end again. You weren't really supposed to do this and looking back now it all seems a little bit silly. Part of the fun really was the 'dare' and the risk of getting 'caught'.

One truly strong and enduring memory I have of the 'Plaza' is being there with my mother one Saturday evening and seeing this black and white picture *The Big Knife.* The film starred Jack Palance, Ida Lupino, and Wendell Corey. What I particularly remember though, from that evening, is being totally transfixed by this other actor on the big screen in front of us. This person was a short, stocky guy who was bawling and shouting at Jack Palance in a tirade that lasted about five minutes. The sheer intensity of this person was to me, a small boy, unlike any thing I had ever seen. I think this would be about 1957. I can even remember the name of the character - Stanley; he was played by an actor, who was to become, and remains to this day my favourite movie star of all time. His name? Rod Steiger. I have seen that film many times since; even when I saw it for the first time on television all those years after seeing it at the 'Plaza', I remembered that Steiger tirade; something which seems to have become his 'trademark' throughout his career. I could almost remember what he was going to say next, so strongly was that memory embedded within me.

Another occasion I remember well was being at the 'Plaza' on a Wednesday evening one time with both my parents. My father would come with us on some occasions, as, like my mother and me, he was a big film fan all his life. We were in the 'Plaza' that evening and we saw *Each Dawn I Die* that starred Jimmy Cagney and George Raft. This was a film which had been originally released away back in 1939 and had been re-released. In the 1950s, the cinemas used to bring out the old movies and show them in double bills. Seldom, if ever, do you get that nowadays. A pity really. I remember coming out of the 'Plaza' that evening, raving about the film, as I reckoned it was the best film I had seen at that time. It remains one of my favourites to this day and, like *The Big Knife,* I have it among my large collection of films at home.

When I was still at primary school, one winter's morning in January of 1957, I was sitting up in bed waiting on my mother bringing me a breakfast snack before I went to school and she to work. It was still dark outside and the whiteness of the roof of the 'Plaza' picture house building opposite, told me that there had been an overnight fall of snow. My mother turned on the wireless as usual and we heard that the Hollywood actor Humphrey Bogart had died. At that time I was fast becoming a big movie fan and Humphrey Bogart was a name that I associated with visits to the pictures. It's one of those things that stick in your mind all your life, for seemingly no particular reason. A bit like people remembering where they were when it was announced that President Kennedy had been shot in 1963.

One of the things for the better in the cinema of the modern day, is that cinema audiences are now a lot quieter than what they were in the 'old days.' I remember that, in the 'Plaza', you would sometimes hear quite a bit of noise. This was mostly from children, and most of it would occur when the screen went blank due to a breakdown. When this happened, you would see a very fleeting flash of light on the screen, a few numbers perhaps and then the screen was completely blank.

You would see the occasional drunk being evicted from the 'Plaza'; it always seemed to be some old man. You would get someone who had fallen asleep – usually someone on their own; you would hear loud snores coming from that direction. When this happened, after a few moments, you would hear cries of "oh shut up" or something like that, then the usherette with the torch would come along, waken the 'offender' and everyone could start to concentrate on the picture again.

When completing a research paper on Glasgow gangs of the 1930s I encountered a few local newspaper reports of trouble in Bridgeton cinemas involving local gangs. I never experienced anything even remotely akin to gang fights in my visits to the 'Plaza' attending as I was twenty years after the 'heyday' of the gangs and in a decade (the 1950s) that was not renowned for such incidents.

In those days too, it used to be quite common for the audience to cheer the 'good guys' against the 'baddies.' This most often happened during westerns, The Indians being the 'baddies' of course. Again this is something that would be almost unimaginable in the cinema of the present day.

13

'Rivi.'

I have no clear memory of the actual day I left Springfield Primary at the end of June 1959, so I cannot really remember if I was looking forward to going to secondary school or not. Probably, I was not. I rather liked 'Springi Primary' and it was probably a wrench to leave it, as it had held many happy childhood memories for me. Never again would I play football in the playground on Connal Street. Never again step inside that lovely little church in Springfield Road for the end of term services two or three times a year. On the plus side of things, never again would I have to endure a PT session taken by Mr. Galloway (or so I thought).

For the next three years – three years and four months as it turned out in my case – my place of learning was to be Riverside Senior Secondary School. This was situated about a third of the way up Springfield Road, (number 454) which stretches from its junction with Dalmarnock Road at its southern end, all the way up to Parkhead Cross.

For the most part, I would walk up to the school. This would be one of two routes. I could walk up Dalmarnock Road to its junction with Springfield Road and then walk straight up Springfield Road. Most of the time I would go the 'roundabout' way. This would be to go into Mordaunt Street from my home, into a short stretch of Baltic Street, before turning into Kinnear Road, then finally along any one of the side streets in the top half of Kinnear Road, usually Bogside Street. From Bogside

Riverside Senior Secondary School in Springfield Road. The photograph probably dates to the 1970s.

Street, I would turn into Gretna Street, briefly into part of Gailes Street, then into Springfield Road and cross the road to the school.

There was this large, very loud, and aggressive dog, which always sat outside a small workshop just as you turned into Kinnear Road. Hearing its barking used to lead me to pick up speed in my tracks. Not that I was in a hurry to get to school, no, it was simply to get out the way of this beast as fast as possible.

I would usually return from school this way too, but sometimes, if I was with one of my more daring school friends, we would have our very own shortcut - over the railway lines. At this time, the railway line, which stretched all the way along the embankments off Mordaunt Street and Kinnear Road up to Celtic Park and far beyond, was still very much in operation. In the present day where the tracks were, is, like a lot of other places I remember from that period, lying derelict.

There were about three of us on this particular day as we climbed the embankment in the middle of Kinnear Road and on to the shortcut, which would bring us out at Mordaunt Street. I think that this was my first railway track 'adventure' and I was a bit wary of the whole thing, only being coaxed into by my more adventurous companions. You can imagine then how I felt, when about a minute into our journey, this wee uniformed guy appears from seemingly nowhere, screaming at us and chasing us, warning of the dire consequences if he ever met us again. I think that was my first and last experience of that particular shortcut. There were safer ones.

When it was raining though, I would usually

board the number 58 bus at its terminus at Baltic Street, just off Springfield Road. It would take less than five minutes for the bus to race up Springfield Road, before depositing its school passengers at a stop opposite the main gates of 'Rivi.' I don't recall ever getting the tram to school. I think that the number 30 tram, which had formerly left from Baltic Street and journeyed all the way out to Blairdardie near Knightswood, must have been one of the services that was withdrawn before all the trams were withdrawn from the streets of Glasgow in September 1962.

The railway line that I mentioned was a thorn in my side in other ways too. Living so near the line, my parents and I would often be awoken in the middle of the night by the sound of trains on their way to some far-flung destination, like Aberdeen perhaps. The old style trains, of course, were particularly noisy.

Riverside or 'Rivi' as most of us youngsters called it had been opened in January 1933. It had been given Senior Secondary status from the beginning of session 1939-1940. The school served the East End of Glasgow and the intake of pupils was mainly from Dalmarnock, Bridgeton and Parkhead areas. Most of the pupils would have previously attended Springfield Primary, Strathclyde Primary, Newlands Primary and also Barrowfield and Dalmarnock primaries. The very first entry in the school log book read "Riverside Advanced Central School was opened today with the following staff." The names of the staff were then listed; it was reported that a total of eight hundred and fifty seven pupils had been enrolled at the school for the first term.

Strathclyde Primary School, c. 1964

My introduction to 'Rivi' occurred one bright, late August morning in 1959. I recall lining up that morning outside the school gymnasium with the other 'new starts', many of whom had been by classmates during my primary school days. There were also a few who I remembered from 'Springi Primary' the previous term. They were telling us what to expect at 'Rivi.' A lot of others though, I did not recognise at all. Although we were assembled outside the gym, it was not the case that our first taste of Riverside was to include a PT session - things weren't *that* ominous. Rather, it was where it seemed, the new intake of pupils traditionally assembled on their first day at the school.

I remember a rather amusing thing happening when we were waiting for our names to be called out. One of the boys, who had been telling us about life at 'Rivi', mentioned to us that the very first thing we would get on entering one of the classrooms, was a timetable. I, for one, had never heard of this term before and in my mind I envisaged some sort of clock or something, being presented to us. Not bad for the first day I thought. Of course a timetable was nothing of the kind. It was a list of the various subjects each class would receive teaching in from Monday to Friday. The room numbers where we would have to go for these lessons would be indicated alongside the subject. The timetable was chalked up on the blackboard in the classroom and we would all have to jot it down accurately on a piece of paper and carry it around with us at all times. We would either have it pasted on to one of our school jotters, or perhaps attached to our school bag.

Looking back on the way things were done at the school as regards assembling for classes, a lot of it to me seems rather pointless. First thing in the morning we had to assemble in the playground opposite the classrooms on the ground level and across from the gym. This was repeated in the afternoon after the lunch break. As I remember it, our names would be called when we assembled in the playground for the register to be called, then when we went into the classroom; the register was called once again. This to me seems a rather unnecessary duplication. Perhaps the teachers were expecting some of us to 'escape' between our standing in rows in the playground and our short journey to our class. Mind you, with the lack of attendance of some of my class members, maybe it wasn't such a bad idea after all.

In those days, the classes for boys and girls were mostly separate. We boys were instructed in technical subjects like Metal work, Woodwork and Technical Drawing. The girls were introduced to things like Domestic Science and Needlework etc. For both the boys and the girls these 'specialist' classes were supplemented by the more basic subjects such as Mathematics, English, History and Geography. Both boys and girls classes had 'periods' devoted to Physical Training, while the same applied in the case of subjects such as Science and Art.

A 'period' by the way, was the duration of a lesson on any of the subjects, which were taught at the school. Lessons began of course, at 9am and finished at 4pm. There were eight 'periods' to each school day and each lasted about forty minutes. So actual learning would take up about six hours, with an hour for lunch. We had a ten-minute break in both the morning and the afternoon of each day.

My secondary schooling lasted until December 1962; I wasn't allowed to leave in June of that year, as I did not reach the age of fifteen until September. You can imagine how I felt when June 1962 came around and with about 90% of my classmates leaving the school for the very last time, yours truly was merely having a summer holiday, as I had to return when the school reopened in August. I wasn't the only one, but of the one or two others whom I had known since 1959 or before, at primary school, and who had to return with me, I didn't see much again.

We were all split up and put into different classes and it was a case, once more, of having to get acquainted with a new group of pupils, most of whom I had never met before. I think I must have resented having to "serve" that extra term. During the three previous years, I had almost perfect attendance, only being absent on one occasion that I can remember and indeed winning some sort of minor 'prize' for this. However, in those last few months at 'Rivi', I was absent on at least ten different occasions, and I wasn't always unwell either!

I recall from that final term what came to be called the 'Cuban Missile Crisis.' This was a stand off between the two superpowers, the United States and The Soviet Union, over missiles that were being transported by the Soviets to Cuba. Our class was in the gym that morning, just before lunchtime, when the small tannoy in the corner began to crackle. Now this indeed was unprecedented. In the three years and more that I had been at the school, I had never heard a bleep out of the thing. Troubled times indeed. A sombre voice informed the silent listeners, that ships of the Soviet Navy were, despite the warnings of the then American president, John F Kennedy and without regard to the consequences, continuing their journey to Cuba. The situation, we were informed, was indeed very serious. It seemed that the world was closer to all-out war than at any time since 1945, and as it turned out, we have never been so near to the brink (and possible apocalypse), again since. Certainly not nearly as close as we were on that autumnal morning thirty-nine years ago.

It all ended peacefully of course. The ships eventually turned around. The world was saved from nuclear extinction and I was condemned to spend another nine weeks in a place that I had long since grown tired of. I wanted to leave it permanently, at the first available opportunity.

Looking back, although all of us in the class that Wednesday morning were only weeks away from leaving school and as it were, going out into the big wide world, we had probably at best, only a limited understanding of what was going on all those thousands of miles away. We perhaps didn't fully appreciate the seriousness of the situation, even if we did understand it. To us, it was probably all more of an adventure than anything else. I remember that on leaving the school that day to go home for lunch, the talk between a few other boys and myself was of air raid sirens and shelters. We wondered "would the *One O'Clock Gang* still be on television during all of this crisis?"

A lot of people were genuinely worried during that period. I remember my mother and the neighbours at 'number 337,' being engaged in conversation about it and about what might happen - their fears etc. Also I remember there was a 'special paper' out almost everyday during the high-point of the crisis. The term 'special paper' was what I remember my mother used to call the edition of the 'Evening Times' or the 'Evening Citizen' which used to come out every time something really sensational or dramatic, like a local murder or something like that, had occurred. We would hear the sound of the paper seller from our home, as he made his way along Dalmarnock Road or the nearby side streets. It always seemed to be around lunchtime that such a thing occurred. You would hear the cry of " Special, Special, read all about it ..." or something similar. People would rush to their windows or on to the street to see what it was all about; the 'buzz' would spread round the neighbourhood that such-and-such a thing had happened. Nowadays, that is long since an outdated practice. Society it seems is no longer shocked at anything, and events like murder, which is now such a common-place occurrence, no longer shocks people as it once would have done.

I don't remember much about my early days at 'Rivi'. I suppose I must have settled in reasonably well. The trouble throughout my time there was that there were more subjects that I didn't like, (some in fact that I actually dreaded with a vengeance) than those I actually *did* like. I was not 'into' things like Art and Science. I positively loathed the Technical subjects, and also Geometry and Algebra, while Arithmetic was a sort of 'in between' subject with me. The ones that I did like were English, History and to a lesser extent, Geography. Not surprisingly, this state of affairs was reflected in my end of term Report Card - that small booklet you had to take home to your parents every so often. It was reflected in the sense that, if I didn't like something, I just never took any interest in it at all, a lifelong trait of mine with regard to life in general terms. I subsequently did not do well in these subjects when it came to exam time. It was the same with PT; I liked the football sessions but positively dreaded both the gym and the swimming sessions.

As I say each 'period' lasted about forty minutes. It was bad enough having to sit through some subject you didn't like for that length of time but, if you got a double period, i.e. the same subject for two consecutive periods, it was absolute agony. Science and the technical subjects were the worst in my case when it came to this. Sometimes you would get a double period first thing in the morning and this always seemed to be especially hard to take. I can remember that most of the class used to look forward to the end of term and a change of timetable, when there would be a good chance that a particular teacher you didn't like, would not be teaching you in the new term. It could work the other way of course; perhaps someone you particularly liked would no longer be teaching you in the new term. The subjects though, stayed the same for the most part and I cannot remember any significant changes at all during my time at 'Rivi.' You would get some subjects at different times from the previous term, sometimes with a different teacher, but the general pattern remained largely the same.

One thing I certainly looked forward to changing were the PT sessions. Apart from the football periods, I did not like PT at all. The sessions in the gymnasium were periods that I did not look forward to. For these you had to put on special gym clothes for climbing the rope ladders and vaulting the 'horse' and all sorts of other mind-boggling movements. I think I was half way up a rope ladder when it came over the tannoy about the problems in Cuba that Wednesday morning.

For our PT instruction, we had two instructors - a Mr. MacLeod and Mr. Galloway – yes, the same Mr. Galloway from my days as a primary school pupil. And here was me thinking I had got rid of the bane of my Tuesday mornings from a few years back. These two PT instructors were like chalk and cheese. Mr. Galloway wasn't such a bad guy really. In fact he was ok – it was just that I detested what he taught. I remember him as someone who was good at his job and who just got on with it, no thrills, no fuss as it were. MacLeod, on the other hand, was always fooling around. He could be ok at times but he had this terribly devilish streak in him and used to take a delight in singling out most of the class for ridicule on an individual basis. If you had the 'wrong' colour of hair or something like that, then you were a particular target for him. I was very thin and that was his cue to single me out. There was another boy who was quite fat, so he was a favourite target too, not surprisingly. It was ok of course when it was the turn of someone else for this kind of attention, but when the 'focus' was on you personally, it didn't seem quite so funny somehow. There were one or two of the boys in the class that MacLeod never bothered in this way or at least didn't appear to, but most of us suffered at one time or another. I have to say that although he was not my favourite teacher by any means during my time at 'Rivi,' he could be quite funny at times.

What was most certainly not funny to me was when, in the few weeks leading up to the end of term in the summer, we would use the PT sessions to practice outdoors for the forthcoming school sports. If the weather was fine, MacLeod would have us all stripped to the waist and doing our paces round the track. Talk about sheer agony. The sweat would be dripping from us; it's a wonder, looking back on it, that we were fit for our afternoon classes. The 'track' was usually the small piece of ground adjoining the football pitch where the school football team played their games. It was on this smaller pitch that the girls' classes held their hockey sessions. On occasion though, he would take us over to the Strathclyde Juniors football ground and we would work out there. Looking back, I wonder if he asked their permission first.

We used to get our football sessions in a double period last thing on a Friday afternoon. This was good, as it meant that once our Geography period just after lunchtime was out of the way, we would be 'liberated' from the class desk until Monday morning. For the next hour and a half or so, we would enjoy ourselves on the football ground, fantasising that we were the top stars of the day. Sometimes when we were having a full-scale game during one of these periods, passers by in Springfield Road would stop for a while and watch us playing. This made us even keener, having a 'crowd' watching us and all that.

Most of us always dreaded when it rained; our football would be cancelled. We would sometimes be kept in the gym and perhaps given some exercises. In the middle of winter the frost and the snow would make outdoor football impossible. I think that when this happened, we would have five-a-side games in the gym.

I seem to recall though, that most of the time when the football was 'called off,' we just used to sit about the small dressing room alongside the gym and if the rain didn't go off, we would sometimes just get sent home when three o'clock came along. So, sometimes it didn't work out so bad after all and, as they say, every cloud has a silver lining of some sort anyway.

If anything, I think I hated the swimming sessions even more than the sessions in the gym. I never learned to swim when I was at school. I was always that bit too wary of the water. As I remember, for most if not all of my time at the school, the swimming sessions were held last thing on Monday afternoons, a double period. We had these sessions up at the old Whitevale public baths in Whitevale Street, just off the Gallowgate in the Camlachie district of the East End. I can still recall all these years later, the weekly routine when we were going to the baths. We would all assemble in the small dressing room alongside the gym. The instructor, usually Mr. Galloway, would then count us all to see how many of us were present. We would then make our way out of the main gate of the school and cross Springfield Road into Gailes Street. From here we would pass into the top half of Kinnear Road just opposite Celtic Park and where, at that time, there was a railway bridge. We would cross the main London Road and proceed through the Barrowfield district, along Barrowfield Street till we came to Fielden Street. This took us up to the Gallowgate and from there it was just a short walk to the baths at the start of Whitevale Street.

The swimming session itself would probably last for an hour or perhaps a bit longer. The time we took to walk to the baths was part of the 'period' and if I remember correctly, we used to finish a little before the 'official' time of four o'clock.

At the pool itself, there was the deep end, which I think was just over six feet deep and the 'shallow' end where most of us who were still learning to swim, went. Most of the time we were left to do our own thing. The boys who had learned to swim just larked about and carried on, pushing some poor unfortunate into the deep end of the pool from time to time. As for myself, I had a constant fear of this. How I managed to avoid it, I will never know. I remember that Mr. Galloway would give the rest of us some instruction down at the shallow end. I can still picture this to this day, my groping attempts at becoming a swimmer. In the end it was all lost on me.

Once the swimming session was over, we were free to go home - we didn't have to return to the school. Sometimes I went home, but on other occasions I would go to my grandmother's home, which was in London Road. That would only take about ten minutes by walking straight down Fielden Street and into London Road. The tenement building where my grandmother lived was about halfway between Dunn Street, which began on the other side of London Road, across from where Fielden Street stopped, and Marquis Street. This street has disappeared in the midst of the clusters of new homes built in the area over the last twenty-five years.

14

'Rivi' revisited.

When I belatedly left school for the very last time just before Christmas in 1962, I was glad to leave. I don't remember much about my final day at school. What I do remember though, is walking through the school gates out into the busy Springfield Road. Then crossing the road, glancing over at the red brick building that had been my place of learning for the last few years and feeling so glad, so truly elated that I did not have to go back there ever again.

Sometimes though when you look back as it were, on earlier parts of your life with the benefit of a few decades of hindsight, you begin to see things differently and schooldays are no exception.

In retrospect I do have some good childhood memories of my time at 454 Springfield Road, Glasgow SE. To name a few: playing football in the playground at break time. Then rushing home at lunch time for a quick snack prepared by my mother and watching the *One O'Clock Gang* on TV before dashing up Dalmarnock Road and up into Springfield Road to return to school for the afternoon lessons.

Other things I quite looked forward to were the end of term events like the school sports, which were held every year during the final week in June, always on a Tuesday afternoon, at Westhorn Park, which was only a few hundred yards from the school in London Road. The 'short-cut' to the park was along the north bank

R and J Templeton Grocers, at 41 Springfield Road, February, 1937

of the River Clyde from the back of the school. I used to like Westhorn. I was never much good at the actual sports events and rarely, if ever, took part in any of the deciding events where the prizes were won. But It was always a good 'day out,' a break from the drudgery of lessons and a sort of preliminary if you like, for the big event to come, i.e. the long eight week break from school. We always got a good day weather-wise for the sports. Perhaps the summers really *were* somehow better in those days.

Nowadays, Westhorn, which arguably was my favourite haunt during my school years, is lying derelict and in complete disrepair. It ceased to be a park sometime in the 1980s and is now just a wide-open space where nothing happens. The bowling and the putting greens and everything else that once made the park what it was have long since disappeared. The grass has grown unchecked for years now. The place is frankly a mess, an eyesore, and a real shame when it is remembered how it once was. I remember, sometimes when I was going along to the park to play football with my pals after school was over or during the summer holidays, we would take the 'short–cut' along the banks of the river. Then when we got there, we would climb over the fence, up the steep brae and into the park rather than walk further along the bank to where there was a gate into the park. Nowadays all the fencing has gone and you can simply walk into what was Westhorn at any point along the way.

At the end of term, twice a year, we always had a church service. I always quite liked this too, although it may have been more for its 'symbolic' significance than anything else may. It indicated to us all more than anything else, that it *was* the end of term and school was well and truly out, or at least it would be as soon as we got this boring old service out of the way.

I have quite a clear recall of these occasions. The services were held at the Calton Old Parish Church in Helenvale Street just off London Road, past its junction with Springfield Road. The church still stands today. It is nice to see this reminder of the past as it were, in the midst of all the changes that have taken place in the area over the last forty years, with hardly anything left as it was and quite a lot of places, 'Rivi' included, having disappeared altogether.

The services were always held in the afternoon. We would all make our way, the entire school, in an orderly procession, out of the side entrance to the boys' playground and into Kempock Street. Kempock Street ran off Springfield Road, on the same side of it as the school. From Kempock Street you could see, at ground level, the classrooms, which you could look right into from the street, where the technical subjects were taught, and the Science labs directly above. I think there were four of each of these. From there, we would pass through the narrow lane, which stretches alongside the now vacant ground, which at that time was the home of Strathclyde Juniors football club. This club is now no longer in existence. We would emerge in London Road and cross over to the church, the accompanying teachers keeping us in check all the way.

I can still picture the inside of that church clearly and us all standing up to sing the hymns and psalms from our books. I think in fact, we used to 'practice' the singing during our Music periods in the weeks leading up to the church service. Actually, for the most part, I enjoyed singing in church, particularly if it was one of my favourites like *O! Come, All Ye Faithful!* and other similar well-known hymns. I always enjoyed the ones that made you feel good when you were singing them, ones that made you want to sing them with *gusto*.

You had of course to be in your 'Sunday best' for these occasions, tie and all (how I hated *that.*) Aside from these special occasions, I cannot recall any rigid adherence to school dress during my time at the school. So long as you looked tidy enough, kept your hair short and well groomed, that was acceptable. Certainly there is no mention of any dress code within the regulations of the school. It would seem to be the case that the stricter rules with regard to dress and school uniform, so prevalent in the earlier part of the twentieth century, had for the most part, fallen into disuse by the time I was at the school.

Once the service was over, we would be free to go, as the service was always held on the last day of term. The actual service, I think, lasted over an hour, perhaps as much as an hour and a half. As soon as it was over, it was a quick dash home and an even quicker change into the clothes you normally wore when you were out playing football etc. If it were summer, the first place my pals and I would head for, was Westhorn, or sometimes Tollcross for a game of 'footy'. The start (in summer) of eight weeks of blissful freedom from the schoolroom desk.

While Westhorn and Tollcross were our main haunts during the summer holidays, there was also the opportunity to play football down at Riverside's own football pitch alongside. This was also where we had our football sessions during term, as part of our PT instruction. Every weekday afternoon during the holidays, the ground would be open for anyone to go in and play football. I remember going along and joining in a game of football quite often during the early 1960s. Sometimes you could have near enough a full eleven-a-side game, while at other times you were lucky to get enough for five a side. It all depended on who turned up. Anyone could join in; you didn't have to be a pupil at the school to take part. I remember that quite often the ball would end up out on the busy Springfield Road and you had to rely on some passer-by to retrieve it. Also, at that time, there were tenements across the road from the pitch and if the ball had been kicked really hard, it would sometimes land across there, never to be seen again, as some lucky kid thought Christmas had arrived early. In truth though, I only recall this happening once and we got a replacement ball from somewhere, though from where I can't remember.

I used to love the summer holidays. They were always eagerly anticipated, sometimes as much as a few weeks before the end of term. The school sports at Westhorn were always a sort of 'landmark' in that respect. When the day of the sports dawned, you knew that the holidays were not far off, just around the corner as it were. If we were not playing football, my pals and I would sometimes go 'into town' to the city-centre. This was though, the exception rather than the rule, as we usually just tramped around the East End. If it were raining, we would sometimes go to the pictures.

One day though when one of my pals and I were walking through Glasgow Green. For a change, we decided that we would visit the People's Palace Museum. We made our way up to the top floor, where a lot of portraits were on display. We had only been in this room less than five minutes, when my friend made a remark about one of the portraits upon which we both burst into loud laughter in an otherwise large, silent room. All of a sudden, this small uniformed man appears at our back and 'invites' us to vacate the premises. It was a straight 'red card' for both of us that day. I'm pleased to report that my visits to the People's Palace these days are more frequent and certainly last a lot longer than that one of just over four decades past.

The school, of course, had a football team, which was part of the Glasgow Schools' football league of the time. Riverside was, in fact, the first school in the city to install floodlights. Most of the football matches were played on Saturday mornings of course, but with the advent of the lights, there were also games on midweek evenings during the winter. I think the floodlights were installed sometime during my final year at the school in 1962. What I do remember for certain is that after I had left the school, I would sometimes go along and watch a game in the evenings. The lights really brightened up the area as you walked along Springfield Road towards the ground. The brilliance of the light beaming right on to the main road really hit you.

The floodlights at 'Rivi' were actually at least the equal of the lights at the grounds of a few of the senior football clubs at that time.

The football pitch is no longer there. Like a lot of other places from that era, it now lies derelict, with rubbish strewn all over it. There is little indication now that it ever was a football pitch, although part of one of the goalposts is still visible at one end of the pitch, or what used to be the pitch.

It's a shame really the way these places have been allowed to deteriorate. Even though the school is no longer in existence, I think the pitch could have been put to some use, perhaps as some sort of recreation area for youngsters. Or something built there. Across the road from the pitch, there is another vacant piece of ground, once Springfield Park. This was another of my boyhood haunts. At that time the park stretched from Kinnear Road to Springfield Road, bordering on Bogside Street and Irvine Street. There was a bowling green, on the Kinnear Road side; plenty of benches where people could sit on a pleasant summer's day, watching the world go by and getting a sun tan. Yes, the summers *definitely were* better in those days. It was always a busy park, and a very pleasant one. Now it is no more, until very recently it was just a grassy spot off Springfield Road, alongside which, when there was a big match at nearby Celtic Park, scores of supporters buses would park. Now rows of new flats have been built on one of my favourite childhood spots. You can still envisage where the park began and where it stopped.

There were also a few 'special occasions' during term time, some of which I looked forward to and others I didn't. I say ' special occasions' but they weren't really that at all and were in fact, part of the term timetable. They were 'special' though in that they involved the class leaving the actual school, and it was a sort of 'half day out' if you like. In session 1961-62 we commenced sessions at Stow College annexes in painting and decorating, and bricklaying and plumbing. The plumbing sessions we had were down at an annexe of the college, which at that time was just off George Street, near George Square. We went there every Monday morning, I think that the painting and decorating sessions were held there too.

We had the bricklaying sessions up at a place in Whitevale Street, up at the north end of the street, just off Duke Street, every Tuesday morning. The actual building still stands there in the present day. I absolutely loathed the bricklaying sessions, simply because although all of these sessions were designed to prepare us boys for the big wide world of work, I had absolutely no desire to become a 'brickie.' So, true to form, I was never any good at this type of class.

The painting and decorating sessions were my favourite. Even as a boy I always used to like assisting my parents with the painting of our home – though I left the papering side of things to the grown ups, as I was never much good at that sort of thing. (I did, in fact, want to become a painter when I left school but the school doctor advised me against it at the time. This was on account of my frequently catching heavy colds and this type of employment would obviously have involved being exposed to all sorts of weather. So, painting was out. Instead I became a warehouse boy.)

150

To get to these two places, I always got on the number 58 bus, down at the terminus in Baltic Street. This would travel up Springfield Road, past the end part of the Gallowgate at Parkhead Cross, and along in to Duke Street. Most of my classmates usually got on the bus at the stop at the top of Parkhead Cross. For these journeys, we would all be issued with travel tokens. These were small round yellow things, which came in various values i.e. a penny, sixpence etc. You would give the bus conductor, or conductress, tokens to the value of the fare and get your ticket. I think the school had introduced tokens to stop some of the boys walking from their homes to these places and keeping the money they got for the bus fares from the school, for sweets or the snooker hall at Parkhead Cross.

Then there were the visits to Woodburn House on Wednesday mornings - another 'half day out.' This would be during session 1960-61. Woodburn House is situated in Burnside, just before you come to the East Kilbride road on the left-hand side. From the outside, it looks very much the same as it did forty years ago. We used to go here to get instruction in gardening technique, exactly why I do not know. It was not exactly something I looked forward to every week, but on the other hand, it was not something I dreaded either. By no stretch of the imagination could these sessions be called the most exciting activity of the week. I didn't even find them particularly interesting but they *were* an 'escape', if only for a few hours. We were issued with tokens for our visits there too. The tramcars were still running at that time and I think it would be the number 26 tram that

I boarded at the stop just past Nuneaton Street. This would transport me to Burnside. Usually a few of my classmates would get on the same tram and we would all come back in the opposite direction about three hours later.

When I look back on the trips to Stow College, especially to the place near George Square, I am amazed how, when you are much younger, everything outwith your immediate area seems so far away. When you get older though, you make the same journey and you see it's not nearly so far away at all, practically just along the road.

On the minus side of my memories of Riverside is, since at the time I was a Celtic fan, I was not very popular with classmates etc. A Celtic fan in a Protestant school never really is popular – unfortunate but true. I was of mixed parentage and religion was simply never an issue with me or my parents. That was not the case at school though.

I remember going to a Wednesday evening Celtic v Dundee League Cup game in August 1962; the next day a new classmate came up to me and said that I had been spotted with a friend in Springfield Road and Janefield Street on my way to the match. The look upon his face was one of disgust; it was as if I had committed some ghastly crime. Perhaps in his view I had. The friend I was with that evening was actually another Celtic fan from my class; there were few of us, so we tended to stick together.

When I look back on that incident over forty-three years later I am of the opinion that although some progress may have been made in the near half century that has passed, bigotry is still a big problem in West-Central Scotland in the present day.

I wonder if perhaps a Roman Catholic supporting Rangers would have an even worse time of it than I had. Perhaps not but I firmly believe that separate schools should be a thing of the past and that there should be no separation. I firmly believe that it would be one huge step on the road to combating the menace of sectarianism.

15

Teacher, teacher.

I have already mentioned a few of my teachers (or instructors as you might refer to Mr. Galloway and Mr. MacLeod in the field of PT), but there are many others of whom I have fond (for the most part anyway) memories, during my time spent at 'Rivi'.

Our English teacher for nearly all of my time at the school was Mr. Boyd; a very pleasant man whom I remember had to take a lot of abuse at times from the one or two more unruly members of our class. I met Mr. Boyd in 1994 by arrangement when I was compiling a short article on the school, and he was able to recall some of the teachers whom I had forgotten. On the other hand, there were one or two that he had forgotten about, that I mentioned. Mr. Boyd told me that when the school closed in 1984, it was because of the rising level of the nearby River Clyde. Until then, I assumed that the school had closed simply because of the decreasing numbers of people living in the areas from where it had formerly drawn its intake.

I was always very good at English and I always enjoyed the lessons, particularly as Mr. Boyd was such a good teacher. It helped to bring some sort of balance to my schooling and those other subjects, which I didn't do so well in, like Science for instance.

For our science lessons during most of my time at the school, we were taught by a Mr. Dixon, whom I remember as a cheery sort of man, but another one of those with a devilish streak in him. Unlike Mr. MacLeod, he wouldn't single you out in front of the class or anything like that. No, his 'line' was more of playing practical jokes and tricks on you. He once sent another boy, who had just started at the school, having come up to Scotland from Wales, from the class, for a 'long stand.' He told the poor boy that this was needed for one of the class experiments and that he had to go down to collect it from this other science lab at the other end of the school. He was still posted missing at the time of the mid-morning break. I'm glad to say I was never taken in by any of Dixon's tricks.

I had no time for science at all. I just never got much interested in Bunsen burners, test tubes and all that sort of stuff. There was this other science teacher there at the time, a small balding man who always looked stern. His room was right next to Mr. Dixon's. I cannot recall us ever having a science lesson with Mr. Dunlop. His nickname though was 'gather', which always sounded to me like 'garra'. Apparently he got this name as, at the end of every science lesson, he would say to the class "gather in the books, boys."

For Mathematics, in the early part of my time at the school, we had a Mr. Mackintosh. He was a tall, well-built man who wore glasses all the time. He taught the three subjects, which at that time, came under the heading of Mathematics. These were Algebra, Geometry and Arithmetic. Of the three, I was best (if far from brilliant), at the last of these. The other two I had no interest in whatsoever. I remember one day when we were having some sort of class examination – I can't remember which of the three it was on – and

Mr. Mackintosh was walking around the room as the invigilator. Here was me, sitting with a puzzled expression on my face, staring at the paper on the desk, no doubt 'stumped' by one of the questions in front of me. It must have showed, because Mr. Mackintosh bent his head over the desk, spotted what was puzzling me, and to my astonishment, wrote in the answer. A kind, if very unusual gesture, I have always thought, because it certainly was not every day that you got help like that, in a class test, from one of the teachers.

I think Mr. Mackintosh left the school about 1960 or thereabouts and he was replaced by a Mr. MaCall, a rather small man whom I remember, seemed to have a permanent expression of determination on his face. I don't remember much else about him, except that I think he was rather strict. He was nicknamed 'Cash MaCall' after the character of the film of the same name starring James Garner, which was doing the rounds at that time.

Although English was probably the subject, at which I was consistently 'best' during my time at 'Rivi', my favourite subject, the one I looked forward to most, was History. For this we had a Mr. Whiteford as our teacher. I remember him as a young, slim, pleasant person, with dark hair, who did his job well. He was one of those teachers who just got on with the job without the gimmicks, unlike of some of the other teachers at the school. The way it should be done really. I always found History very interesting, and this is something that has stayed with me all of my life. Even after graduating from university in History, I continue to read books on the subject regularly.

Our Geography teacher was a Miss Dewar, a rather elderly woman (or so she seemed to us young boys). She was most definitely one of the 'old style' teachers. I cannot recall ever seeing her smiling. She stood for no nonsense, not suffering fools gladly - not suffering them at all really, if the truth be told. I also seem to remember that she was prone to using the strap quite often. All that said, I have to say also that I personally never had any bother with her at all. Looking back, she was only doing her job the way she thought it should be done, and under the circumstances, with some of the more unruly elements in our class giving her a hard time of it, she was probably correct in the line that she took. I could never see Miss Dewar though, or someone like her, fitting in to teaching as it is today, with all the changes in not only the curriculum, but also in the methods of teaching, and the more modern 'approach' of the teachers in the schools of the present day. I quite liked Geography; I developed the 'knack' of being able to relate the capital city of almost any country in the world during my time at 'Rivi.'

Art was one of the subjects that I was never particularly keen on without outrightly dreading it. I could take it or leave it, although I was never much good at it. The Art teacher, I remember, was a Mr. Parks, who, I always thought, resembled the late Roy Castle a bit. Roy Castle, at that time, had a regular show on television. The thing I remember most about this Mr. Parks was that he seemed to spend an awful lot of time talking about things which had absolutely nothing to do with his subject. Perhaps he thought it was the best way to 'win over' the class and to be popular. One year we had Mr. Parks for the final period in the morning before the break for lunch and for the first period of the afternoon too. This was quite unusual, as for the most part; a double period usually came first thing in the morning or at the end of the afternoon. One Wednesday, just before the break, having been doing his usual 'talkie' bit, he announced that in the afternoon he was going to talk about 'the facts of life.' With a laugh, he said that under the circumstances, he expected a full class attendance in the afternoon. I think that this had been at a time when there was a decline in attendance levels at classes, especially in afternoons, and he was using this gimmick to in his own way, try to improve the attendances. Just for the record, I have no recall of whether or not he ever did keep his promise or, if there was a 'full house' that afternoon. The chances are that he didn't, or I would surely have remembered it.

The logbooks for the school boast that the school had for most of the time, high or above average attendance levels. I cannot say that I saw much evidence of this during my time at the school. The afternoons seemed to be the time when pupils would fail to show up for classes. They were 'dogging it' as it was called. You often heard the expression "are you 'dogging it' this afternoon? " whispered in the middle of a lesson. There were one or two boys from our class that I remember were absent just about every Monday afternoon and quite often on some of the other afternoons as well. How they got away with it and for so long, I do not know. The main attraction seemed to be a snooker hall up at nearby Parkhead

Cross. Apparently this was where those 'dogging it' spent their afternoons. As I remember it, there seemed to be more 'dogging it' in the few weeks just before the summer holidays.

Although I was good at English and usually attained a high grade in the examinations, I was not quite so keen on the Drama classes we got once a week, as a sort of back-up to the main English classes. These I think were in my final full year at the school. For these, we were taught by a Mr. Slavin, a tall, broad-shouldered man whom I thought of at the time as quite dour, although this may have been really due to the fact that I just didn't like what he was teaching us. These classes consisted of reading out from books, which usually contained plays, and each person had to read out a line or two when their turn came round. I wasn't in to this at all, to put it mildly, and always dreaded it when it was my turn to read out my lines. I remember one day in particular; we always got these classes on Tuesday mornings just before lunch. Anyway, here we all were this Tuesday morning, reading out all this usual nonsense as I saw it; I hadn't being paying attention to the proceedings one little bit. Mr. Slavin asked me to read out this bit from the book in front of me and I must have given out one long and very audible sigh, because his next words were "And what is the matter with *you,* James? " This was accompanied by a stern expression on his face. I think I had been gazing out of the classroom window or something like that, perhaps thinking of the approaching lunch break.

Then there were the Technical subjects, which we all referred to as woodwork, metal, work and

'Techi-Drawing.' I think the last of these was the most boring of the lot. I was never much good at Woodwork and Metalwork - never much good with my hands as it were, but at least I did try. With 'Techi-Drawing' I just never tried at all, as I thought it the most boring thing I had encountered since I had come to the school. That opinion never altered during my three years and a bit at the school. 'Techi–Drawing' classes were taken by a Mr. Thomson, a thin greying man from whom I cannot say I gained much inspiration at all. For the Woodwork classes, we were taught for the most part, by Mr. Brown, a far more cheery and talkative man than I ever found Mr. Thomson to be. Then there was a Mr. Macdonald who taught the subject too. I don't really remember much about him at all, though I can still picture him vaguely to this day. There was also a Mr. Shanks for this subject, though I remember even less about him. In these classes we used to make coffee tables and the like, learning how to use the tools of joinery.

The Metalwork classes were taken by a Mr. Heilbron whom I remember as being 'o.k.' In these classes, we would stick bits of metal into vices and use files and various other sorts of tools on them. All very uninteresting stuff as far as I was concerned. The thing with the technical subjects was that the periods never came singly – it was always a double period. For 'Techi-Drawing, this was sheer agony. I think that in one of my years there, we had Mr. Thomson for the last two periods on a Thursday afternoon. The relief when the bell sounded at four o'clock was terrific. It was always good to hear the bell at the end of the school day, but if it meant instant release from one of your least favourite subjects, it was doubly satisfying.

We also had Music classes; we would sing aloud from books in front of us on the desks, while the teacher would give us some musical accompaniment on the piano. For nearly all of my time at the school, the teacher for these sessions was a Miss Croft, a small, rather elderly woman who always seemed to enjoy her work. She was never appreciated, though, by some of the less well behaved members of the class who would, when singing the songs in the classroom, add their own words to some of the them.

At that time in the school, pupils would sing stirring British songs like *Rule Britannia, A Life on the Ocean Wave* and *The British Grenadiers.* I always enjoyed these songs as they made you feel proud to be British. There were other songs of course, such as *Home on the Range.* This song was always sung with gusto. There were others too, like *The Orderly Song, which* was one of the favourite ones of those in the class who preferred to substitute their own, sometimes vulgar words, for the words, which were written in the songbooks.

When it came near the end of each term, we would be singing hymns and psalms to get some practice in as it were, for the church services held at the end of each term. I enjoyed these too. In fact, I always quite looked forward to the Music classes generally. We were not examined in any of the work we did during these sessions, so it was all rather enjoyable. Miss Croft was, like Miss Dewar, one of the 'old school' of teachers, but not the strong disciplinarian that Miss Dewar was.

One Friday morning, I think it was, in my final full year at the school, we were shocked when we went along to the room where Miss Croft taught, only to be told that she had died suddenly. I cannot remember if we had a regular teacher for our music periods after that, though I seem to recall that we had music lessons, on occasion, from the grandly named Mr. Dingle. There was also a Mr. McGill for a while too I think.

The other occasions when we got musical accompaniment during a lesson, was just before the Christmas and New Year holidays, when we would all be marched off to the gym (that dreaded place again), where we would receive dancing lessons to get us prepared for the school dance. You didn't have to go to the dance of course, but there was no escaping those lessons. I think that these may have been part of our PT instruction and that in the final few weeks of the term, the time allotted to them would be given over to this dancing practice. It would be a change from the usual routine of rope ladders and 'horses' but it was not exactly something I looked forward to. I cringe when I think back, as to how I must have looked trying to do the 'Cha-Cha' and the other ridiculous things, to the accompaniment of music. As it turned out, I never went to any of these dances. I just was not interested in them at all; perhaps those terrible practice sessions turned me off dancing, or at least that type of dancing. On the day of the dance, you would hear some of the boys talking about which girls they were going to be dancing with that evening. Then, the next day in class, you would hear these same people talking about who they walked home or went to a café with after the dance.

These are all the teachers I can remember teaching us on a regular basis, although there was a Miss Phillips who taught us English for a while. This, I think, was in my second year at the school and this person may have alternated for our classes with Mr. Boyd. Then there was a young teacher who taught Mathematics who we had, I think, in my final year. Her name was Miss MacLeod and as I remember she was very pretty, with long blonde hair. She used to get some wolf whistles and a few other 'calls' from some of the boys in my class. She did not seem to mind this at all, if I remember correctly. I cannot recall though, this particular teacher being a 'regular'. I am sure I would have remembered somehow. I don't think she was any relation to the aforementioned Mr. MacLeod.

At that time of course, the strap, or the belt, was still very much in use. Like most of the boys, I got the strap at one time or another, but I did not get it very often. There is no doubt in my mind that it was a deterrent to misbehaviour in the classroom. Nowadays, teachers are literally terrorised by wild, largely uncontrollable pupils and they have little or no recourse, in the short term, to any means of discipline. I think this is wrong. My memories of the strap are that it *was* painful, sometimes very painful indeed, especially on a cold day. After about two or three strokes of the strap, your hands were very sore. I think the maximum you could get at any one time, was six strokes. I recall boys in our class and our pals from some of the other classes, saying that so and so got 'six of it' this morning. I think the 'six of it' thing was if someone had really misbehaved, been outrightly cheeky and abusive to the teacher or something like that. As I say, that is fine by me. On the other hand though, you could also get the strap for arriving late at the class and sometimes I think, for even getting your sums wrong during a class. For this, you would probably get one or two strokes of the strap. I think in retrospect, that giving the strap for 'failing' in class lessons was wrong, as it hardly encourages a child to improve. Rather, to the less confident of pupils, it merely invokes fear.

I cannot recall ever receiving 'six of it'. Perhaps about three was the most I ever got and not very often. In practice it was a deterrent and whatever I had done wrong, I most certainly would not do again following a few hard whacks of the leather on my hands. There were those of course, who were, it seemed, getting the strap on a daily basis for whatever wrong-doing they had been found 'guilty' of. Perhaps there was a point where you just 'got used to it', but I certainly never reached that point. I recall one time, when a few of us had been 'carrying on' just before going in to a classroom one Thursday afternoon. As we approached the room we were jostling around. There were five of us; when we got right outside the room, three of our crowd suddenly rushed into the room, closing the door behind them. Within what seemed a split second, the door opened again and the teacher yelled at the two of us who were still engaged in our mock fight. Of course it was we two who got the strap, while the others got off scot-free. I think the teacher was on the point of sending us along to the headmaster, but changed her mind and gave us the belt herself in front of the whole class. I cannot recall who the teacher was, but I don't think it was on of our 'regulars'.

If you got sent to the headmaster's room, which was situated between the boys' and the girls' playgrounds; it was really 'serious' stuff. If you were the timid sort, you were really scared, I suppose. If you were one of the more wayward of the class, it was a 'mark of honour,' as it were. You would hear the buzz going round the playground at the break. "Did you hear the news? Big so-and-so got sent to the 'heedie's' (headmaster) office this morning."

Some of the time, perhaps in my final couple of years at the school, I went home for my lunch. I do remember though, that some of the time at least, I used to just hang around the school playground and join in a game of football or something like that. I cannot recall ever being in the dining room of the school. I think that it was situated at the rear of the school, towards the Clyde, though I am not sure. The dining room is rather amusingly, if unintentionally appropriately, referred to in the logbooks of the school at the time of its opening as "being for the general *food* of the school." This misprint was later corrected to *good*.

There was a lot of carrying-on during the lunch break. Most of us were content to play football, but the rougher elements, from the various classes, would roam around the playground in small packs, usually pouncing on (at first anyway) unsuspecting victims. Then they would carry them off struggling, to the back of the school near Kempock Street where the poor unfortunate would be deposited into the bushes there. These boys seemed to work a 'rota system' of sorts and would pick on different victims every day. It was my turn once or twice of course, but after a while you got wise to it or 'fly' as they say and you would learn to keep out of the way of the gangs. Once you were 'introduced' to these bushes, you did not want the experience repeated if at all possible. You came out of the bushes, sore all over with 'jaggy' nettles stinging you. I remember that when the poor unfortunate impacted with the bushes, there was always a cheer went up from those assembled as 'spectators'.

Then there was the "smokers' corner". Even in those days, schoolchildren started smoking early, although compared with some of the things pupils allegedly get up to at schools these days, it all seems rather tame if not entirely harmless. The "smokers' corner" was over at the side of the gym, beside the toilets in the boys' playground. During the short breaks from classes in the morning and the afternoon, you would see all the 'fly' smokers congregating at the entrance to the toilets, and having a quick puff. As it was a rather secluded spot away from the main part of the playground, they would probably be left alone - at least for a while. Looking back though, I find it difficult to understand how they got away with this. The teachers must have known what was going on; where they met for this 'activity' was just along from the headmaster's office. Again, I think this was something that the boys who smoked looked upon as being 'big' somehow - being grown-up and all part of the growing up process as it were, if a little too soon in some cases.

Amongst other 'extra curricular activities' that I recall, was when there was an 'event' taking place at the end of the school day. Again the participants were usually mostly the rougher elements of the school, not necessarily always the older boys either. An 'event' was when there was to be a fight at four o'clock or as soon as possible after it. It would usually involve two boys trying to knock each other senseless. Sometimes I think you would get a 'double header' - with a second fight following the 'main event' but more often than not, it would be the result of two boys coming along to a prearranged place for the fight. The place as I recall, was at the back of the school going towards the north bank of the Clyde, where there was plenty of open ground and where the participants could indulge their fancy. These things were always pre-arranged during the school day, and word would quickly go round the classes that wee so-and-so was fighting big so-and-so at four o'clock. I think sometimes there were even one or two 'events' during the lunch break and on occasion, these were 'held' in the playground. If some of the teachers saw it was getting out of hand, the braver of them would venture downstairs to the scene of the action. The boys would probably be sent to the 'heedie' for punishment.

The playground 'events' though were few and I think that, as opposed to the prearranged ones at the end of the school day, they were probably the result of some dispute that had happened on the spot as it were, at the time of the lunch break. I do not know what the motivation for the end of the day 'events' were, but I guess they were probably a lot to do with status and gaining some sort of rather misguided respect from one's peers. I think these boys were out to prove that they and they alone, were the king of the castle as it were, and that you did not mess with them lightly. There were certainly a few 'big names', that you heard every day in the school playground. By 'big names', I mean those boys who had made something of a hobby out of fighting and who were 'notorious.' We quieter ones would always steer clear of these other boys. When these 'events' were taking place, the 'spectators' were shouting loudly and cheering wildly. The two participants would each have their supporters among the crowd. The teachers must have known that these things happened, but probably because the school day was over and since the fights were taking place just outside of the school premises, they would turn a blind eye to it. Their working day was finished after all. These fights did not occur on a daily basis. You could get weeks going by without any, and then there would seem to be a spate of them.

Usually at four o'clock, I would go up to the little library which was situated just along from Mr. Boyd's room, up the stairs, almost directly above the room where we received our mathematics teaching. Even at that age I enjoyed reading. Certainly I preferred it to joining a crowd and watching two boys punching each other. I would usually spend about an hour there. I think the library was open until about five, but I cannot remember if it was open till then every day. I did this mostly in the winter months.

In the spring and summer months, I usually went to play football after school. Some of the time though, I would simply go straight home and help my mother out with some messages or things like that. As I recall, Friday was usually the day that my mother sent the washing round with me to the launderette in Nuneaton Street, at number 352 – across the road from the 'Plaza' picture hall. I remember I would go round with the washing in a bag and leave it there. You would get a ticket with a number and you would go round to the shop and collect it the next day. Like the vast majority of people living in the tenements in that era, we did not have a washing machine. The name of this launderette incidentally was the 'Snow-White Launderette.' It must have lived up to its name, as I cannot remember my mother ever complaining about the standard of its work.

When I look back all these years later at my time at the school, I have rather mixed feelings about whether I liked it or not. There is a saying of course, that one's school days are the happiest of your life. This, of course, only comes with the benefit of hindsight. There were some good times, some not-so-good times, and some downright bad times too. One of these occurred for me one Thursday morning in class, during my second year at the school. We were in the Mathematics room and we were listening to Mr. Mackintosh going on about what he was writing on the blackboard, when in walked Miss Jeffries, a woman with greying hair who was a sort of understudy to the headmaster. I think the headmaster at the time was Mr. Hill. Miss Jeffries also doubled up as the health administrator, arranging all the medicals and inspections and all that sort of thing. I remember she had a brief word with Mr. Mackintosh and then called out my name, whereupon I stood up (you always had to do that when your name was called.) I was then informed by the bold Miss Jeffries, that following my recent routine class medical, it was discovered I had some sort of throat infection, which required immediate treatment. I cannot remember at all the name of it, except that it began with an 'R', Following a visit to Dr McKechnie's surgery that night, there was nothing showing up after he examined me. My mother and I were both relieved but also very angry that a medical matter, which should of course have been private, was broadcast by a senior member of staff, in front of the entire class, without any regard for the person concerned, namely yours truly. I can imagine the uproar if a thing like that happened nowadays, with all the pupil and parent power of the modern era. Such a Miss Jeffries type of person would be hauled up in front of the 'beaks' pronto.

Time spent at school whether or not it was an enjoyable experience, is something that quite naturally remains with you for the remainder of your life. Riverside School closed in 1984 and the buildings were demolished the following year. The school remained in existence for just over half a century, not a long time as these things go. Nowadays, where 'Rivi' once stood, is in effect, one large unofficial rubbish tip, with all sorts of rubbish lying around. A huge space just being wasted. Kempock Street, which ran alongside the school at the side of the Technical classrooms and the Science labs, is no longer in existence. The old Strathclyde Juniors football ground across from the school, has remained another piece of waste ground for at least the last twenty-five years. Looking at that whole part of Springfield Road in the present day, those who do not remember the area as it once was, would find it hard to picture a large school looking out on to the main road.

Every time that I pass the area though, I try to picture in my mind's eye, the school and not the waste area which is before me, because I do have happy memories of 'Rivi.'

16

Gissa joab.

I left school in December 1962. I cannot recall much of the first few months of 1963 apart from the fact that it was one of the coldest winters on record. I remember being on a bus near to Christmas at the end of 1962. It was going up Abercromby Street, and I was making my way to Barlanark to visit my pal Jim Connor. As we got to Duke Street, the snow started to come on heavily; I remember thinking that I might be stranded in Barlanark for the night if it kept up.

As it was, that was the start of a period of at least three months when there was hardly a day went by without there being snow lying on the ground. Football matches of course were badly hit, with a long list of postponed games every week. Of more pressing concern though, were the burst pipes in the old tenement building, caused by the bad weather. I remember that we had a few of those calamities. Then the water would be turned off while repairs were going on. Sometimes this lasted for quite a while and I remember that we had to go with basins and buckets (or 'pails' as they were sometimes referred to) simply for the basics of everyday existence. I remember helping my mother with this. We got the water from the shops downstairs, that is of course if *their* water supply was unaffected by the 'panic'. When the water did come back on again, it was, more often than not, a strange colour. That of course meant that you had to wait even longer until it became clear again and thought safe to use. These were not the best of situations but we always seemed to come through them all right in the end; it wasn't every year we got a winter such as that of 1962-63. Burst pipes were common occurrences at that time and if you were not personally affected by one, you would always hear of some less fortunate neighbour who was.

I started looking for a job early on in the year but it was early in May before I eventually began to earn my living for the first time. Even then, it was only a temporary job for two weeks.

I wanted to become a painter but this had to be ruled out on the advice of doctors. I cannot remember for certain what I decided that I would do instead. Like most boys, when stepping out into the big wide world for the first time, I had a mixture of feelings. I felt relieved that my schooldays were over and the sense of being 'free' that this brought. On the other hand though, there was a feeling, if not of foreboding, then certainly of wondering what lay ahead, of what the 'journey into the unknown' would bring. At that time there were no giro-cheques or anything like that. If you were registered unemployed, you simply received your money over the counter at the office where you signed on. I think that it was twice a week I had to sign on at first. The youth employment offices as they were called at that time, were down at Megan Street off Dalmarnock Road, just before you came to Bridgeton Cross. I was in that building quite a lot at that time.

For quite a few years after leaving school, I kept in touch with some of the boys in my class –

in particular, the ones I had played football with. When we all met up, the first thing we would say to each other was "are ye working yet? " and we would relate to each other our first successful or otherwise foray into job hunting.

I had a few interviews during the first few months of 1963, but nothing came of them. I remember one in particular I was sent to by the youth employment service; I was just not interested in it, but I had to go as they had sent me for the interview. At that time, I was not really certain what type of work I wanted to go into, but I suppose I was just looking around for jobs like warehouse boys and message boys. Most youngsters from working class homes at that time went into manual occupations, unlike today where a lot more enter service and administration employment. I think what put me off at this particular interview, was the man who interviewed me. I think he was the boss himself, as is often the case in small firms such as this one was. I cannot remember the name of the company, but it was situated near the Glasgow Green and just off Kings Drive, on the road to the Gorbals area. The interviewer was rather elderly, abrupt and I thought not very pleasant – not even a trace of a smile appeared on his face. I was not performing very well with his questions, and eventually this little man blurted out "you don't want this job do you? " I mumbled something in return and the interview was over. I remember going out of the place and thinking along the lines of what a lucky 'escape' I had had there. I certainly had no wish to work in a place like that, under a boss of whom my first impressions were not very favourable. I

John Street Primary School, Hozier Street.

don't remember what he told the 'Bru' but I did at the time wonder.

At that time of course, there were plenty of jobs going. It was another five or six years before the first real signs of the downturn in the economy in the late 1960s, and only a few years after the former Prime Minister Harold Macmillan had told us all "you've never had it so good." From what I have read about the 1950s, he was most probably correct too.

In early May 1962, I eventually did get a job, as a message boy with a firm called 'The East End Dental Laboratory.' This place was situated at 3 Silvergrove Street, just past Bridgeton Cross and off London Road as you headed towards the Calton. The buildings that were there at the time have long since gone and recently a new housing estate has sprung up where my first place of work once stood.

I remember that May morning all these years ago. It was a lovely, sunny early summer morning as I made my way down Dalmarnock Road, wondering what was in store for me at this place where I was going to work. Things like "what will I be doing?" "Will I like the people that work there?" Will they like me"? And, "I wonder what the boss will be like." These were the thoughts that were racing through my mind that long ago morning. As it turned out, my first experience of working for a living was a happy one. I enjoyed the job very much. The three or four other lads who worked there were 'good sports' and I got on all right with them. I remember that one of them wore glasses and was a dead ringer for Hank Marvin of the Shadows.

As it was, I was hardly ever in the lab itself as my job was to deliver dental material to the various dentists throughout Glasgow. I remember visiting places like Shawlands, Anniesland and one or two other so-called 'better' districts of the city, places I had previously only been vaguely aware of, and names with which my only familiarity was that I had seen them on the destination boards of passing tramcars. Previous to this, the furthest west I had ever been was to the shops with my mother in Argyle Street. Now here I was visiting all these 'exciting' new places, being through at Anniesland almost every day. I remember the place I went was just along from Anniesland Cross and opposite where the Somerfield supermarket stands in the present day.

All my bus fares to these places were of course provided by my employers; what with the early summer heat wave we were experiencing at the time, it was a real joy of a time. I must have thought along the lines of "I want to do this all the time." However it was only a temporary job and I was there for only two weeks. I think that I was paid only about three pounds and ten shillings in old money but well, it was extra 'pocket money' for me and a sort of additional bonus in a job I really liked doing. I can't even remember the boss. That's the sort of boss who is a good boss - one you hardly ever see. A bit like referees in football matches. Another thing I remember from that job was that sometimes the Dental Workers would work late in the evenings, do a bit of overtime, and I had the job of going out for their suppers. This was usually to Reekie's Fish and Chip shop in James Street, close to the locally well-known 'Mermaid Bar,' which I think was still known by that name at the time. I remember the fish and suppers that I got there looked really tasty and it was difficult to resist the temptation to have a nibble. I cannot ever recall, (although I have been told otherwise) these places being called Chippies in those days. It was always 'Fish and Chip' shops as I recall.

The whole system in the place was very carefree. There was no pressure on me to be back in the lab by a certain time after the deliveries had been completed. There were no deadlines or any thing like that, so I made the most of the brilliant weather and didn't hurry too much when I was out making the deliveries and on occasion, bringing stuff back to the lab as well.

I was really disappointed that I had to leave that job after the two weeks were over, even though I was aware that it would only be a temporary job. But the two weeks came and went and it was back down to the 'Bru' in Megan Street for me again. By this time, the early summer of 1963, quite a few of my pals from my school days had found jobs. One of my closest friends when I was at 'Rivi' and whom I used to play football with up at Westhorn, had found work with a painters and decorators named Peter Dragoonis. This establishment was in Dalmarnock Road, just before you crossed the bridge into Rutherglen and across the road from where the huge Dalmarnock power station stood at that time. You can imagine how envious I was of my friend as painting and decorating was, of course, what I had in mind for myself originally as a career. However, you can't always get what you want; I was really anxious to fix up something for myself on a more permanent basis.

By the beginning of September of that year and close to my sixteenth birthday, I was still 'idle' as they say and beginning to get a bit fed-up with the whole business. Initially I wasn't bothering too much to be honest. At that age you don't really think much farther than the immediate as it were, and after all, it was summer and all this free time with no need to get up particularly early in the morning, was all right. For a while in fact, it seemed just like one extended summer holiday. As time went on though, I got really fed up and almost on a daily basis, I was hearing of my former schoolmates getting jobs - some of them with good apprenticeships too. Then I heard from my old friend Jim Connor, who I had known from my primary school days; he had kept in touch since he left the area. He told me that he had got a job, working in a furniture warehouse in Springfield Road; John Dykes it was called. It was on the right hand side as you went up Springfield Road, going towards Parkhead Cross. In fact, quite close to Riverside's football ground and on the spot where the warehouse for the chain store 'What Everyone Wants' stands in the present day.

Jim had told me to try this place as there might be other jobs going. I didn't really fancy it much but as I was anxious for a job and to earn some money, I was going to give it a try. Also my parents by this time had quite naturally become concerned that I get a job soon. They were both out working while I was lounging around and doing nothing very much at all. It was time I started to contribute to the daily life at 'number 337.'

As it turned out though, I ended up in another job. Around that time, I had seen an advert in one of the papers for a warehouse boy/message boy, with a clothing firm at Glasgow Cross. I was fortunate enough to get an interview and a few days later I got a letter through the post, asking me to start on the coming Wednesday. It was with a mixture of excitement and trepidation that I received this news. Certainly there was more of the excitement than anything else and a great sense of anticipation. There still were though, the doubts – 'what was I going into?' and all that sort of stuff. Okay, I had experienced the world of work briefly and enjoyed it, but this was different, this was a permanent thing. This was for life as it were, or so it seemed. I was a bit nervous, but still looking forward very much to presenting myself for work at number 26 Gallowgate, right at Glasgow Cross, and on the fourth floor of what was called Mercat Building. The name of the firm was Ferguson and Rippin Ltd.

This would be just after my sixteenth birthday. It was on Wednesday the eleventh of September 1963, that I made my first appearance at what was to be my place of work for the next two and a half years. I remember that on the evening prior to my starting this job, I went up to the old 'State' picture house in Shettleston just off Shettleston Road, to see a movie called *Requiem for a Heavyweight* (although it was actually billed under its alternative title *Blood Money*). This was a good boxing tale, which starred Anthony Quinn and Jackie Gleason, who at that time was one of my favourites on the TV, having seen him and Art Carney in the long running comedy series *The Honeymooners.* This was my wee 'celebration' as it were, on finding my first real and hopefully, lasting job. I remember thoroughly enjoying the movie and I made my way home that evening looking forward to the following day - my 'big day'

Looking back to the newspapers of the time for this second edition I have now discovered that there was a second film on show that evening called *Pushover,* I have no recollection at all of this film. This was during the days when there were sometimes a double–bill of films on offer, a practice which continued well into the 1970s before being abandoned completely in favour of a main feature only.

17

Warehouse boy.

On the first morning of my new job, I remember being full of anticipation. It was a nice late-summer morning. I left my home early as I wished to be at my new place of employment with plenty of time to spare. As I entered the Gallowgate from London Road, I remember looking at my watch and discovering that I was a bit *too* early.

I was not due to start till nine o'clock; it was only half past eight when I arrived. I decided therefore, to have a walk round about the busy area of Glasgow Cross to 'kill time'. There were plenty of people scurrying around, as is the usual at that time of the morning, with people going to their work.

By the time I had had a leisurely walk into High Street, down part of Bell Street, then down the Candleriggs and into Argyle Street towards Glasgow Cross again, it was approaching quarter to nine. I decided that it was time to venture forth and present myself to my new employers. I entered the building and came to a lift (or a hoist as most people referred to them in those days. A small, balding, unsmiling man approached me from the lift as he opened the doors. I asked him what floor Ferguson and Rippin was on. In a rather gruff, abrupt manner he told me where it was and immediately took me up to the fourth floor, dropping me off without as much as another word. He hadn't even said 'good morning.' My first impression of this liftman was not favourable; he didn't seem a bundle of fun

182

at all. First impressions can be wrong of course. Over the next few years Tony, as he was called, became a great friend of mine. He wasn't the sort of person I thought he was at first at all; we shared an interest in football and would often stand talking about the top players of the day for ages. Yes, a really good guy Tony turned out to be. He didn't keep all that well unfortunately and left I think, due to ill health sometime in 1965. A few years later, after I had left Ferguson and Rippin, I sadly heard from one of my former work-mates there that he had died.

Apart from my first encounter with Tony, I do not remember much about my first day in the job at all. It must have worked out ok though as I recall keenly explaining my 'big day' to Thomas Angell, who had been a schoolmate of mine at Riverside, as we walked down Poplin Street from my home that bright late summer evening, on our way to see Clyde play Forfar Athletic at Shawfield in a league match from the old Scottish Second Division. The game was to begin at seven-thirty pm. I wonder if I watched *Danger Man,* which starred Patrick McGoohan on Scottish Television that evening, starting at eleven twenty-five pm and finishing just before midnight, when of course as was the norm in those far off days, the two television channels closed down.

My job at Ferguson and Rippin involved checking incoming goods and making sure that the quantities delivered matched what was stated on the advice notes or delivery notes. Then I would transport them, either in a small barrow or simply by carrying them, to where they were kept in the warehouse.

My other main duty – the one which took up most of my time – was to make deliveries to companies with which my employers traded. Unlike my short lived first job some months earlier, there were few bus trips to distant parts of the city. Most of the places I had to visit as part of my job were in the city centre, in places like Stockwell Street, Wilson Street, Ingram Street and a place in Duke Street. There were many others of course, but these are the ones I remember most. There were occasionally some trips further afield, like to a few places in the south side and I think in the West End too, but they didn't materialise very often. Ferguson and Rippin was a clothing factory; I would be delivering clothing materials to other factories and warehouses in the area. I also had to collect various accessories, buttons for coats and all that sort of thing, from some of the other places from which we purchased goods. One of those places was a firm called William Robb and Sons which was in Stockwell Street. This was one of the places that I visited on a regular basis, in the course of my work.

One stair down in Mercat Building, we had what was called 'the factory.' This was where all the raw material was converted into the finished goods ready for despatch to the various outlets with which we traded. There would be about twenty or thirty women working here. My Aunt Betty, from my mother's side of the family, worked there for a brief time shortly towards the end of my time with the company. It was always a busy place; as soon as you entered the factory from the stairs, you could hear the machines buzzing. I had to go down here quite often every day, and would sometimes chat to some of the workers there for a few minutes or so in between transporting goods to and from the warehouse. Serious conversation though was difficult as you could hardly hear yourself speak, such was the buzz of the machines here and it was not always easy to make yourself understood to Mr. Brown, who was the foreman. It was Mr. Brown you went to see about what was ready for delivery up to the warehouse.

I remember that when I first started, things in regard to my work did not seem just as straight-forward as I thought they might be, but after a week or so, I did get the hang of things as they say. I was 'shown the ropes' by a lad called Brian who was a few years older than myself. He had, up until that time, done the job that I was coming into and now he had gotten 'promoted' to a job downstairs in the factory. He was a cheery sort of person as I remember and that helped me settle in. It is always a much smoother passage in any job if you get on well with your work-mates. I can truly say that in my time with this firm, that was certainly the case with me. That was of course after the usual 'first day nerves' are done with. You don't bother about it so much as you get older, but when you are just starting work, there is always a tendency to wonder 'what you're going into' as it were. Thankfully it all worked out all right for me.

Work began at nine o'clock in the morning in the warehouse and I think went on until about half past five, though sometimes on a Friday, the really busy day, it would be six o'clock before you were finished. This could occasionally occur during the week as well. I think the factory downstairs finished earlier though. (They started at eight in the mornings I think.) The machinists went home about half past four.

The company was run by three men, the directors of the company. There was a Mr. Reid, a Mr. Anderson and a Mr. Morrison. All of them were middle-aged but Mr. Morrison I think was a bit older than the other two. When I started work there, it was just the two of them, as Mr. Anderson had been off ill for a long time. It was Mr. Reid of whom I saw most on a daily basis though. He was very distant, an 'old style' boss without a doubt. He was tall, always wore glasses and he hardly ever smiled. He seemed to carry all the problems of the business firmly on his shoulders if his expression was anything to go by. That said though, when he did speak to you, he was usually pleasant enough.

Mr. Morrison was in overall charge of the factory down on the third floor, with Mr. Brown his second-in-command. He was a working director and unlike the other two, he wore a sort of short waistcoat-cum-overall. The only time you saw him up in the warehouse was when he was conversing with the other two directors and at staff meetings.

These were held in a small space with curtains drawn, at the top end of the warehouse. This was, you could say, a makeshift boardroom. I remember a rather amusing story connected with this place. On this day Andrew sent me out to collect some material from one of the places with which we traded. He impressed on me that this was an urgent delivery and that it should be brought back to the warehouse as quickly as possible. This was in my early days with the firm and willing to make a good impression, I hurried over to the place where I had to collect the goods and unlike most of the time, hurried back to the warehouse with them. Well, here I am thinking to myself that Andrew would be well pleased with me. I entered the warehouse and found no immediate sign of him. I asked Ina where he was and was told that he was at a meeting with the directors. I moved along to the 'boardroom' and poked my head sheepishly round the drawn curtains. Andrew was sitting nearest me with Mr. Reid, Mr. Anderson and Mr. Morrison. "Here's the cloth," I said. The reply, in a rather unconcerned, somewhat 'distant' voice came, "Oh, Oh just leave it over there, James." Andrew's priorities had changed it seemed, when he sat down with the bosses. 'Power and influence,' albeit on a small scale had gone to his head. Speaks volumes on human nature, that little incident.

Mr. Morrison could at times, be a little bit impatient, if things like targets weren't going according to plan. He could be a bit touchy. I did not have many dealings with him at all though, and any time I did have to speak to him, I always found him okay. He had this peculiar habit every evening at the end of the working day. He would come out of the lift, walk out into the Gallowgate, step back nearly to the edge of the pavement and then proceed to stare right up at the building. He would do this for a minute or two and the result of this would be that passers-by would also look up at the building to see what the object of his attraction was. I never did find out what was so interesting to him in his daily stares at the Mercat Building at Glasgow Cross. Perhaps no one else ever did either.

When Mr. Anderson finally made an appearance, I found him to be a very pleasant man. He was always buzzing around the warehouse ensuring that the orders were being assembled and that they would be despatched out to the various outlets in time. Also that the ones for the post office and the railway carriage delivery, were all ready too. Mr. Anderson spoke to the staff much more than Mr. Reid did and without being a 'working director' in the sense that Mr. Morrison was, he did a fair round of checking and hurrying along of the work. He was a small man and like Mr. Reid, always wore glasses. Unlike Mr. Reid though, he was much more 'open' and he would always come up to you and ask you how you were, while making sure of course, that if you were handling an urgent delivery, you did it as quickly as possible. A fair man though, if a touch excitable at times. I remember that when I left the firm in 1966, he wished me all the best for the future.

My immediate boss though, was Andrew. He was the warehouse manager of sorts. It was he that I had most contact with on a day to day basis and while in the first couple of days at the firm I thought he looked a bit stern – mistaken first impressions once more – he turned out all right and was always fair with me. He was the one who made sure that I was doing my work and doing it on time. He had this small space, which he used, as his 'office', right up at the very front of the warehouse, looking right out on to Glasgow Cross and Trongate. It was Andrew who assigned me my day to day tasks, and who gave me the bus fares for my journeys to the different firms I had to visit in order to deliver and if necessary, uplift goods from. So long as the job was being done, he was happy. I cannot remember any time when he put me under any great pressure to deliver something by such and such a time, or to be back in the warehouse by a certain time. If I was delivering something and I was finished more quickly than expected, I would take my time coming back and would hang about the shops in the city-centre or wherever I had been. I cannot recall when I returned to the warehouse, ever being challenged on what took me so long as it were.

Sometimes, when things were really quiet at the warehouse, Andrew would have me doing a few of his domestic errands for him. His mother lived just along London Road at the point where you enter Glasgow Green near Monteith Row in the Calton; nowadays it's just a wide-open empty space. I remember Andrew's mother as a nice friendly person who always made me feel welcome when I went up to the house with various odds and ends. At other times, he would send me along to pay his mother's rent. For this, I would go to a building right at the top of Bellgrove at the junction with Duke Street. I didn't mind these trips at all, especially if it was a nice day, as they got me out and about even more than usual, and, using a bit of psychology, I always 'spun it out' and took my time coming back. Things being quiet at the warehouse, I reckoned Andrew would not be too upset if I stayed out longer - particularly since I was doing him a favour in the first place. I sometimes wonder if the three directors knew he was sending me out on these unofficial errands.

There was one part of the working day though at Ferguson and Rippin, which was never 'quiet.' That was the last two hours or so, say from about three thirty onward. This was the time when all the parcels that had to be delivered to the various customers of the firm, would be assembled, packed and sent out in time for delivery the following day. The assembling and packing would be done by the women who worked in the warehouse. As I recall, there were five of these packers: Alice, Betty, Sadie, Ina and Ellen. So it just shows what a busy wee place it could be at times.

Some of the larger parcels would be sent by rail. I would take these down on the goods lift to the London Road entrance, which was used specifically for the delivery and despatch of goods to and from the various firms in the building at that time. After these had been taken care of, I would then await the postman arriving with his van to pick up the parcels for postal delivery. These were usually the sort of smaller or medium sized packages. On a really busy day and if the postman and the railway man arrived at the same time, you could get in a right old panic! You were up and down on the goods lift quite a few times. This was often the case on a Friday, which was the busiest day. After all this had been done, there was yet more to do. The really small parcels were simply taken along to the post office in London Road, just next to where Andrew's mother lived. It was my job to do this and it could be really hectic. Often I was even busier during this period than I had been taking the various other parcels down the lift for them to be picked up.

My job was to collect the parcels from the packers, take them over to the corner of the warehouse, which was 'my beat' as it were, and weigh them on the scale I had on the table there. By weighing the individual parcels, I would find out how much each of them cost in terms of postage, then I would pop them into the sack, which I would soon have to sling over my back en route to the post office. Sometimes I would have to make two or even three visits to the post office to get all the parcels sent out. On these occasions, it would be about six o'clock before I was finished for the day. On other occasions, there were so few parcels that you could simply carry them along without a sack. Of course when this happened, I would get finished a lot earlier. I cannot recall ever being paid any sort of 'overtime' for these busy days.

The thing was that sometimes when it seemed as if you were going to get off easily and get home a bit earlier, things would change very quickly. Last minute orders would be phoned in and they had to be assembled, packed and despatched on the day, if the material was available to do so. I can remember occasions when I thought that my work was over for the day. I would be on my way out the door, only to be called on by Mr. Anderson to wait and deliver this last parcel to the post office. It was Mr. Anderson, rather than Andrew if I remember correctly, who was so particular about everything going out to their destinations on the day. I can still picture him yet; running around in the early evening, ensuring everything was in order.

That was bad enough, but every two or three months I had to cart the machine, that issued the stamps for the parcels in the office, along to the post office to check how much had been used and for the account to be charged accordingly. How I hated this. By the time I arrived at the post office, even though it was only a couple of hundred yards from Glasgow Cross, with the thing, I was both exhausted and pretty sore, as the machine was a really heavy and uncomfortable thing to carry. On occasion, if I was lucky and the firm's salesman, big John Fitzpatrick was on the premises, I would sometimes get a lift in his car with this monstrosity of a thing. But this was the exception rather than the rule. He was a bit of a Jekyll and Hyde character was big John and sometimes I wished I had never got a lift from him, such were his scathing remarks at times. At other times he could be good company.

When I was stamping and franking the parcels for delivery, I would often be up at the warehouse office about a dozen times or more. The office was situated right at the rear of the warehouse, just past the 'boardroom.' There were three staff in the office - three females who were always very friendly. There was Rena, the boss of the three, Rose, and a young girl called Jean, who came from Easterhouse and who started with the firm shortly after I joined. The office was where all the accounts, and all other paper work, was taken care of and where all the correspondence relating to the firm was sent from and incoming mail delivered to. That was also a part of my job - to post all the letters on my last trip to the post office each evening. On a few occasions I remember being so busy with the parcels, that I would completely forget some of the mail. I would arrive home very hungry and ready for my supper and on taking my jacket off, perhaps find a bundle of letters in my inside pocket. It would of course, be too late by then for that day's post. When this happened though, I would, after my supper, always take them across to the post box on the other side of Dalmarnock Road, just past Playfair Street near our home, to make sure that they would at least catch the first delivery the following day. I never did get any 'comebacks' on this; just as well for poor old Mr. Anderson's well being that he didn't know about this 'improvisation' of mine!

At least it was a five-day week. I always looked forward to the weekends, not just for the football and all that, but also for the reason that I had two 'long lies' to look forward to - not having to get up early. I have never been a 'morning person', even in my youth. I can't remember for sure whether the factory on the third floor ever worked on a Saturday morning; they may have on occasion, but certainly not regularly. I remember one Friday though, I think it would be in January 1966 during my final few months with the firm, that I was asked to work the weekend. It was about this time that a Mr. Macdonald, who was the boss of a firm of the same name in the city-centre, joined the board of Ferguson and Rippin and became the 'top man' as it were. In the short time that I knew him, I did not like him at all. He never gave me much bother, but it was his abrupt style that I did not like. He was not like the bosses I had long been used to at the firm. This Friday afternoon, Macdonald came over to me and asked me if I wanted to work the weekend as there was some sort of promotion day or 'open day' going on. I told him no, that I never worked weekends and I was not interested. He went away without a word. A short time later Mr. Reid came over and asked me again. He said they wanted a 'sandwich board man' to advertise the 'big day' and they wanted me to do it. There was absolutely no way that I was going to parade around Glasgow Cross with a big heavy board over me, with advertisements on each side, so I told him I was not interested at all. I remember that he went away looking none too pleased. I never did find out if they ever got anyone to do it.

A few weeks later, in March of 1966, MacDonald made sweeping changes. A lot of the staff were paid off, as apparently MacDonald wanted to streamline the whole place and cut staff requirements to an absolute minimum. I was one of those deemed to be 'surplus to requirements'; after two and a half years at Glasgow Cross I was out of a job. I think that after I left, the old directors took less and less part in the everyday business of the firm. The firm itself though, continued to trade at the same premises, for many years afterwards, eventually moving to Finnieston, before going out of business sometime in the late 1980s.

Although I sometimes moaned about all the tasks I had to carry out, I think that for most of the time, I quite enjoyed my time there. I had good workmates and, for most of the time at least, good bosses too.

18

Moving on.

As well as my unpaid sidelines in going messages for Andrew, I also had another wee "job" on the lift or 'hoist' from time to time. This would occur sometimes during a busy period and especially when there were a lot of people going to and from the rent office on the second floor. It would also perhaps occur if for one reason or the other Tony or Hughie were not 'on duty' and the other had to have their lunch break. On these occasions one of them would ask me to "look after" the lift for half an hour or so. This was no problem to me and they knew that I enjoyed working on the lift. If I were not busy in the warehouse, Andrew would usually give the thumbs up for my temporary transfer to these other unofficial duties.

One day, I was working on the lift, thoroughly enjoying myself too, when, amongst the people on the ground floor waiting to board, was someone I *definitely* did not want to see at that particular time. It was Mr Reid. You should have seen the look on his face when he saw me working that lift. Perhaps he was having a bad day already and this certainly did not do him any good. He didn't say a word - he didn't have to - his expression said it all.

There was however no 'come back' on this. Perhaps he was so fed up he didn't even mention to Andrew the fact that I was working on the lift when I should, of course, have been doing my duty for Ferguson and Rippin. Whatever happened or didn't happen, I continued to enjoy my stunts as liftman from time to time, right up until the end of my stay at Mercat Buildings, Glasgow Cross,

Tony and Hughie had a small room at the basement of the building where the boiler-house was. Sometimes when I was back early from my errands and didn't want to go back up to the warehouse right away, I would go down here and talk with the two of them about football and the like. I was sometimes down in this room as often as I was upstairs. In fact Tony used to call me 'Jim doon-again' as a variation on the name Val Doonican, a prominent singer of that period.

Sometimes I would stay down there for about half an hour or more and Andrew would probably be scratching his head upstairs wondering where I had got to. This was especially the case late in the day when there would not be much work on the lift and Tony and Hughie would be having a cup of tea before going home for the day. Sometimes though, Hughie would switch off the bell mechanism of the lift altogether so he would not be disturbed. He used to go spare at times - if say Tony was on his lunch break or worse still, if he was off sick. If he was busy stoking up a fire in the boiler room and somebody would ring the bell from the first floor wanting to go down, he would blow his top, ranting and raving about lazy so and so's. You could see his point though, Hughie must have been in his early sixties at the time and I often saw him with a big shovel in his hand, dripping buckets of sweat after having been stoking up the boiler. It worked the other way too of course. If he switched the bell off, perhaps some poor sod would have to walk all the way down from the top floor, the fifth. As I remember it though, once the rush to and from the rent office had died down, the place generally was a lot quieter. Most of the workers from our firm and from Norlyn Gowns on the top floor would walk down the stairs at the end of the day on their way home.

At times Hughie could be right bad tempered and a right old 'greetin' face', but everyone liked him really - what you might call a 'loveable rogue.' Tony was always the perfect gentleman, and would sometimes visibly blush if old Hughie momentarily 'forgot himself' and cursed in front of women on the lift or on the ground floor. Tony, unlike his assistant, would never deliberately switch off the bell for the lift. He believed that you should always be there for the passenger, no matter how trying it was at times.

Mind you, I did see Tony lose the place. On one or two occasions when I would have to transport goods downstairs for either the postman or the railwayman, the goods lift would be occupied by the workers of the other companies in the building, particularly Norlyn Gowns above us. When this situation occurred, I had to use the main lift, as you couldn't keep the postman or the railwayman waiting. Tony would not be very pleased. "You can't bring that stuff in here," he would say. "This lift is for passengers only." I usually fought off his protests and just carried on. As for Hughie - when this happened he didn't say anything - the expression on his face said everything; it was not one of happiness I can tell you.

It was always Hughie who would stay till the very end of the working day. Being the boilerman, he had to be there all the time. So, once the rush for the lift was over, Tony would usually be off home. He lived out in Ruchazie so he had quite a journey home. Once I got to know Hughie a bit better, sometimes last thing in the evening, even if all my parcels had been already taken to the post office, I would ring the lift bell out of sheer devilment, knowing that Hughie would be there. I knew his work would be done in the boiler-room and occasionally I would ring the bell to go downstairs when of course I could easily have walked down. I did this simply to see the expression on his face. I didn't do it too often of course, or he might not have continued to see the funny side of it.

I remember that for two or three years after I left that job I would, when I had the time, pay a visit to my old place of employment. I rarely went up to Ferguson and Rippin itself though. Mostly I would just spend a couple of hours on the ground floor, chatting with Hughie and an elderly chap named Ben. By that time, I think Hughie was about to retire and he would often be 'posted missing.' Usually though, he could be found at the Crystal Bell public house just across the Gallowgate, a favourite haunt of his, and a pub that has happily survived till the present day.

Ben had replaced Tony before I had left and I got on well with him too. He came from Barmulloch and was always talking about football, in particular Celtic, whom he had followed all over the country in his younger days. On these occasions I would sometimes see a lot of the women from the Ferguson and Rippin factory coming down the stairs on finishing their work and they always waved to me and said hello, asking me where I was working and all that sort of thing. On one or two occasions, I bumped into Andrew and I think Mr Reid too.

By that time of course, 1966-68, I had moved to East Kilbride and worked for a number of years in a large electronics factory.

A couple of months after I left Ferguson and Rippin, I got another, temporary, job in the same area, with a firm called Copeland who traded in photographic equipment. They were based in Mart Street, which is just off the Saltmarket and close to the Bridgegate. In this job, I was based on the premises for most of the time, as opposed to having the freedom to work at my own pace as I had experienced with my previous employers. The only errands that I was allocated here were to take the mail to the post office in Clyde Street at the end of every working day. This was the only similarity with what I had been used to previously, as here my main job was to pack parcels for delivery to the various trading outlets of the firm. I was not very good at this, to be honest, though I did get used to it - just about - when my three-week temporary period of employment, covering for sick leave, was due to end. That said, I absolutely hated my time here and I had no regrets about leaving, quite the opposite in fact. I was only too glad to see the back of the place. It was a small firm with only a few workers with the boss himself in constant attendance. I got on all right with the people there, although I did not find the place nearly so friendly as Ferguson and Rippin and the East End Dental Laboratory had been. Mostly though, it was the work process itself that I did not like. It was so boring, packing bits and bobs into small boxes all day and parcelling them up. Not my idea of interesting work at all.

At that time my mother was working at a cleaning job in an office nearby in the city centre. In Mitchell Street I think it was. As she only worked the mornings, some of the time she would join me for lunch and we would go into a restaurant in the Saltmarket for fish and chips. The restaurant is still there to this day, in an area that has, in a visual sense anyway, changed very little over the thirty-five years that have passed since then.

My employment with Copeland came to an end sometime in May 1966 - I would then be unemployed and signing on until mid-August 1966, when, I started a job as a storeman with a large firm in East Kilbride.

19

Granny's hoose.

Both of my maternal grandparents had died before my birth. My paternal grandfather had died in 1946, the year before I was born. My maternal grandmother lived until 1969 - I think she would be about eighty-two when she died in March of that year. I have many happy memories of my 'Granny.'

She lived at number 850 London Road, just between Dunn Street and Marquis Street, a street that is no longer in existence, having disappeared in 1983.

At that time, just like Dalmarnock Road, the area was a hive of activity, with shops and the old tenement buildings dominating the area. My Gran's one small window looked directly on to London Road and faced another block of tenements and shops, such as Sharps the hardware store at number 847, McIver's the grocers at number 851, and Mill's newsagent at number 869, near Fielden Street. In this block of tenements and shops that stretched from Kirkpatrick Street to Fielden Street, there was, as was the case in Dalmarnock Road, plenty of activity. Nowadays there is a police station just around the corner from Kirkpatrick Street where these tenements and shops once stood. All the old tenement buildings have long since been pulled down here too, just as they had in Dalmarnock Road and the area looks very different from what it did even twenty –five years ago. A lot of new houses have been built, especially where Marquis Street once was.

London Road, with Fordneuk Street on the left. My grandmother lived in the tenement a little further up on the right.

To the back of London Road, where the old homes and corner shops were in Bernard Street, the area has changed even more. I clearly recall going round to the shops in Bernard Street, but mainly to the ones in London Road itself, to get various groceries and things like that for my grandmother. I remember also going to shops such as Britton's grocer right next door to my Gran's close, at number 852. On the other side of the close, at number 848, there was a public house, the name of which I have been unable to ascertain. Then there was Gorman's the butcher at 854, Conetta's fish and chip shop at number 862, near Dunn Street and at 872-874, just around the corner from Dunn Street, stood Leonardi's café. I have fond memories of being in this café many a time. My Gran would send me round with the empty ginger bottles, and, kind soul that she always was, allowing me to keep the pennies I would get on returning the bottles to the shop. A bit further down, just before you came to Marquis Street, was Curley's provisions shop at number 842, one of many branches Curley's had in the Bridgeton and Dalmarnock areas at that time. Often when I am in that area, I try to picture the area as it was all those years ago and where such-and-such a shop was. It is not easy at all, given the vast changes that have been made to the area.

I went up to my Gran's quite often when I was a boy. A Monday and a Wednesday were the main days that I would visit with my mother, after school was over for the day. We would always walk over, the journey taking perhaps about fifteen minutes or perhaps slightly less. We would cross into Nuneaton Street, then into

Baltic Street, past the engineering works of William Arrol - at that time a huge, very busy, works which employed hundreds of people. Then we would make our way along Dunn Street, past Dalmarnock Primary School and on into London Road. I always remember that we would pass this spare bit of open ground where Dunn Street bordered with Walkinshaw Street and there would always be men playing football there. They were probably from the many factories and plants that were situated in the area at that time.

I can still vividly picture my Gran's home. It was a 'single end' and, not surprisingly, a very small room. There was a small store type of place just as you entered. This was where the coal for the fire was kept and various other everyday things. There was no hall or 'lobby' where you would usually have expected to find the coalbunker in the old tenements of the period. The coal fire was over near the window and my grandmother would sit in her armchair here. The bed was over in the other corner of the room, just past the small store and near the front door there was a set of drawers, and I think a small cupboard too. In the late 1950s I remember that my Gran got a small rented television set that she situated just beside the set of drawers. She would sit and watch that for hours on end.

My Gran's home was on the first floor of a three-storey block of tenements. As I remember it, there were another five tenants on the landing, so it was a different set up from where I lived. I think that the single-ends were the two houses at the end of each landing - my grandmother's and the neighbour directly opposite her. The remainder would have been two-apartments. I recall the family who lived along the landing from my Gran was called Smith. There was Kate, her daughter Jessie and brother Bill. My parents knew this family well. I always knew them as Auntie Kate and Auntie Jessie, even though we were not related at all. It was more the done thing in those days that you called a close friend of the family 'aunt' or 'uncle'. I don't remember much of Bill though. I have a very vague recall of being in their home on at least one occasion and remember that there were two rooms separated by a lobby. It was around 1957 or so that Kate died very suddenly. I remember being upset, as she was a friendly person who always made you feel very welcome. I can recall the day of her funeral and my parents paying their last respects to Kate. At that time, I think it was the custom that only the men went to the actual funeral, the women remaining at the home of the deceased. I have vague recollections of this when Kate died. Jessie Smith died sometime in the late 1980s, I think.

The only other neighbour that I remember from where my Gran lived, was a man called Mr McCafferty who lived in the house you passed just as you came up the stairs, on the left-hand side. He was an elderly man who would always say hello as he passed you, the kindly sort he was.

I think the tenement block, where my Gran lived, was somewhat older than those in Dalmarnock Road. What I do remember is that the backcourt always seemed to be flooded and there was a lot of dirty water around. This is something I cannot recall experiencing in my own backcourt. The drainage system or lack of it seemed to be a problem at London Road; it always looked rather unbecoming. It was one big, sprawling open space; unlike the situation at Dalmarnock Road, there did not appear to be any barriers separating the various backcourts. When you stepped from the close at 850 London Road, you were faced by a vast space, which stretched all the way up to the tenements at Bernard Street. This faced straight ahead with the tenements on Dunn Street to your left and those on Marquis Street to your right. It was more than ideal for playing football, but the actual condition of the backcourts was somewhat off-putting. I cannot recall ever going out there to play, though I did step into them a few times and would sometimes take a shortcut to the shops in Bernard Street through them when I was out going messages for Gran. This was usually during the summer break from school and when I was still very young.

During the summer holidays, with both my parents out at work, I would be at Gran's place nearly every day and my mother would collect me from there when she finished work in the late afternoon. Most of the time I spent here gazing out of the window watching the people and the traffic, particularly the tramcars, go by, much the same really as I did at my home when I was still at school. Sometimes though, I would go out to the shops with Gran. No visits to the city centre and the 'big shops,' just a walk down London Road to Bridgeton Cross, which we both enjoyed. Invariably we would stop at a lot of the sweet shops in the area. One I remember in particular was Gordon's confectioners at 189 Fordneuk Street, just across the street from the later Bridgeton bus depot, which is now a bus museum.

At that time London Road, like Dalmarnock Road, was a hive of activity with lots of traffic, both buses and trams and the street crowded with people. My Gran always liked having me there, as I suppose she got lonely on her own in that wee 'single end' of hers and she welcomed the company.

At other times, I recall that we would walk around the fairground at Glasgow Green at the time of the carnival, during the Glasgow Fair holidays. When we went there during the day, many of the attractions were not in operation, most of them only commencing in the evening. If it were a really nice day, we would go into the adjoining bowling green in Greenhead Street and sit there for an hour or more watching the bowlers or alternatively, me running about all over the place and Gran struggling to keep a watch on me. Sometimes my mother would have arranged to meet us in the bowling-green and we would have a nice walk back to London Road and a cup of tea before my mother and I went home.

Strangely enough though, I cannot recall ever being at the pictures with Gran, though I may have just forgotten about it. What I am certain of is that it was not a regular thing. I would certainly have remembered it if that were the case. I cannot recall ever being in the picture house in Kirkpatrick Street, just across the road from Gran's home. This was the one nicknamed the 'Geggy.' The real name of the hall was the 'Premiere.'

I think it would be in the later 1950s, as I got a bit older, that my mother only worked part time. She was an office cleaner by this time, having previously worked as a bookbinder. By that time, my visits to Gran would be restricted to about two a week, usually after school on a Monday and a Wednesday. I can only recall being at Gran's in the evening on a few occasions, and then it was with both my parents. I cannot recall being there much at weekends, which were mostly the time for visiting my aunts and uncles in the various parts of Glasgow in which we lived. I do recall though, on a few occasions, as I got older, sometimes on my own, and sometimes with my older cousin, having been at a football match, paying a 'flying visit' to number 850 on my way down London Road. One of these occasions was in July 1966, just before the new football season started. Celtic had being playing Manchester United - Denis Law, Bobby Charlton and all, in a friendly. Celtic won 5-1 and I remember that when I went up to my Gran's house, my parents were there. This would be about six months after we had moved from the area.

I always looked forward to going to number 850. Apart from the fact that I obviously liked Gran, she had these little treats for me, like ginger beer. You don't see it very often now, but on the rare occasions that I do spot a bottle, I seem to be momentarily transported back to those days of my childhood and Gran's good old ginger beer. It seemed to be her favourite and she would keep it in a small cupboard or 'press.' Come to think of it, it made good sense for her to keep it 'hidden' like that, as I would finish it all off. I would always go down to Leonardi's café café near Dunn Street for more for her though, and if there were enough empties, there would be an extra bottle purchased. Another wee treat she had was potato scones. I remember I loved

At the corner of Dunn Street and Bernard Street, an old pub front, 1931

these and always used to look forward to them. The 'tattie scones' of the present day seem pale imitations by comparison.

Quite often in good weather, when I went out with my mother and Gran, we would walk away down to the Calton end of Glasgow Green. On London Road, close to the Barrows Market or 'The Barras' as it is commonly referred to in broad Glasgow dialect, there was at number 212, Rossi's café. Also, another café a bit further along the road, at numbers 320-324. We would go in to these cafés for a rest and an ice refreshment. I used to always have a Raspberry Ice or a 'MaCallum' as it was more commonly called. My mother and my Gran would have an iced drink, which was made up of ginger, melted iced cream and perhaps a drop or two of milk. I used to have one of these on occasion and it tasted good, especially on a warm day. But I still preferred my 'MaCallum.'

Another place we went to was Crolla's café. This was on Main Street at number 282, near Poplin Street and French Street, on the other side of the road. This was close to Shawfield Stadium, at that time the home of Clyde football club. Here we would have 'our usual.' I think we used to alternate our café stops between Crolla's and Rossi's. I can still picture the inside of both of these places today, all these years later. I can still recall waiting, sometimes impatiently, for the treat to be delivered to our table after it had been ordered by my mother. The anticipation was overwhelming.

These cafés are long gone, although the firm Crolla's is still very much to the fore in the present day, with its headquarters in Jessie Street near Aitkenhead Road, over on the south side of Glasgow. These visits to our favourite cafés were undoubtedly the highlight of our walks and I always looked forward to them.

During the winter months it was a case of huddling round the small, but always glowing, coal fire at my Gran's house. My mother was always a good, caring person; I remember on the occasions when Gran was unwell, she used to ensure that she was well looked after. On quite a few occasions I remember going along to the house with my mother and Gran being in bed. I think we had her spare key, so that if she was not able to get out of bed, we could simply let ourselves in. When Gran was unwell, my mother would stay by her bedside talking to her and keeping her company, while I would be sent out to get messages in for her. I would go down to the butcher's just along from the closemouth at number 850, and to the various other shops in the area, for all the little daily necessities that Gran required.

My Gran, as she got older, developed cataracts in her eyes and had to attend the Eye Infirmary in Berkeley Street near Charing Cross, on a regular basis. As I remember it, her appointments were always for Monday afternoons and my mother would always go with her. When I was on holiday from school, I would go too and I remember that we always had to wait ages before my Gran was seen to - the place was always crowded. It was though, a trip to a part of Glasgow which, as a boy, I hardly ever saw and as such, was a bit of an outing, just like the visits to the 'big shops' in the City centre were.

After we moved from the area in April 1966, I did not see Gran nearly as much as I had in the past. By that time I was a bit older of course and working, so it was kind of like the end of an era, one with very fond and happy memories. I think though, she came out to visit us once or twice in our new home.

When Gran died in March 1969, it was a sad time for us all. It was not entirely unexpected, but it happened rather more quickly than had been expected. Gran died on a Friday evening and she was buried at Dalbeth cemetery, away out at the eastern end of London Road, near the Carmyle district. Her funeral left from Taylor Brothers at the corner of London Road and Abercromby Street. I remember that on that snowy, bitterly cold Tuesday morning, as the funeral procession moved east along London Road and as we passed Gran's home, my older cousin said to me, "no more tattie scones, Jim." I'd miss the ginger beer too.

20

Visiting hours.

It seems to have been traditional, from at least the early decades of the twentieth century, for the visiting of relatives to be done at weekends. This dated from the days of what social historians and sociologists term the 'extended family' and during a time when it was common for many members of the same family to live in close proximity to one another.

Aunts, uncles and the like often lived just a few closes down the street. With the building of the new housing schemes in Glasgow from about the mid 1950s, all this began to change and during the 'overspill' as it was called, many people moved out of the city itself into areas like Castlemilk, Drumchapel, Easterhouse and Barlanark. This was something that was happening not just in Glasgow or even Scotland, but all over Britain.

From my own earliest recall, only a few of our relatives from my father's side still lived in the immediate area; most of them had moved out to the new housing schemes early on. I remember that my Uncle John and Aunt Agnes lived in London Road just around the corner from Heron Street, near Bridgeton Cross. This is only a very faint recall though, as most of my memories of going to visit them, are from when they moved to Barlanark. I can remember going here in the late 1950s so they must have moved from the Bridgeton area around 1956 or 1957.

On the other hand, all of our relatives from my

mother's side still lived nearby, being situated around the Springfield Road and Parkhead districts.

Sunday evening was the time for visiting in our family and, as a boy I would be transported to such far flung places as Barlanark, Castlemilk, Pollok and Priesthill. Perhaps strangely in a way, most of these visits seemed to occur in the dark winter evenings. I have certainly much more recall of visiting relatives in the winter months, than in the summer. Perhaps it was the attraction of the big comfortable living room in these new homes in the suburbs of Glasgow and the 'novelty' at that time, of the electric fire.

The two trips I remember most were those to Barlanark and to Pollok. When we were off to visit Uncle John and Aunt Agnes in Barlanark, we would get a bus or a tram up Springfield Road and then walk along to nearby Helenvale Street. This was where the buses for Barlanark and Easterhouse left from in those days - almost alongside the church I attended when I was at Riverside school.

When we visited my Aunt Mary and Uncle Bobby in the Househillwood part of Pollok, we would get a bus or a tram from Dalmarnock Road into the city centre at Jamaica Street. Then we would walk along to Midland Street close by where we would get a number 48 or 48a to take us to our destination. I think the number 48 still covers much the same route in the present day, quite remarkable really, after all these years.

When we were visiting Barlanark, we had to travel all the way along Shettleston Road and when we were going to Pollok and Priesthill, the journey involved travelling along Pollokshaws Road. Both roads, to a small boy, seemed very long and I remember I always used to wonder which of them was the longest. I would debate this often with my father; he always said that it was Pollokshaws Road that was the longest, while I thought it was Shettleston Road. I think that he was correct all along.

It was also much the same route we took when going to visit my Aunt Francis and Uncle Tommy, who lived in Priesthill, not far from Pollok. By this time too, my Uncle Bill and Aunt Helen who had previously lived in Elmvale Street, Springburn, where the old tram terminus was, had, by the early 1960s, moved to Castlemilk. I have a very clear memory of us going to visit them in Castlemilk for the first time, one Sunday afternoon. We knew their address was in Scarrel Drive, but although we must have, or so it seemed, walked round the whole of Castlemilk and on the way asking directions from passers-by, we just could not find them. We were just about to give up and get a number 22 or number 46 bus back to Dalmarnock, when we heard my Aunt Helen shouting on us. By that time we were of course, tired and very hungry. The meal of sausage and mash was very welcome.

I remember my parents being impressed by the new houses every time we went to any of the housing schemes. What I particularly remember was being struck, as it were, by the stairs leading up from the hall to a room or rooms upstairs, in all of these new homes. It was certainly a bit of a 'culture shock' compared with the 'single ends' or the two-room tenements we were more used to, back in Dalmarnock. We were the last of the family from my father's side to 'flit' when we left

Dalmarnock Road in April 1966. Then, of course there was the inside toilet and all the obvious advantages of that. It was, in a small way, like a whole new world.

In the new housing schemes, the street lighting was different. Here they had newer forms of lighting and the streetlights were of a yellowish colour as opposed to the white colour where we lived. Nowadays of course, the street lighting is the same everywhere. I always thought that these new lights, as they were then, made the streets look a lot brighter at night than did the more standard lighting that we were more used to.

All these visits were not particular favourites of mine but I didn't dislike them either. I liked all my aunts and uncles of course and always looked forward to meeting my cousins. Of my cousins, there was Jeanette, Nancy and Gina in Barlanark; Bill and Helen at Priesthill; Isabel. Then there was Betty, Alec and Andrew at Castlemilk and Robert, Jim and Isabel, the family of my Uncle Bobby and Aunt Mary at Pollok - all three of whom were grown up and married by that time and of course no longer living at home. The only time I ever saw any of these three was sometimes at New Year when we all got together - or occasionally at Gran's. It was the same with Helen, whose parents, my Uncle Tommy and Aunt Francis, lived in Priesthill. The cousin I saw most of was Bill, Helen's brother. We were quite close and used to go to the football together sometimes. He is about three years older than I am. On the rare occasions that I can remember us visiting on a summer's evening, I can recall playing football along with Bill on a spare piece of ground just around from Freeland Drive where they lived.

I don't have quite as clear memories of my visits to my Uncle Bobby and Aunt Mary. What I do remember, is that we used to get off the bus in Barrhead Road near Peat Road and had to walk for what seemed an eternity, before we got to their home, which was in 48 Cornalea Road, a quiet street in the Househillwood area of Pollok. Here, not having any cousins to pass the time with, I used to just sit about while the adults talked. My Uncle Bobby was a really cheery person though. He was a great Rangers fan and was always ribbing me about how badly Celtic was doing at that time. At New Year time, at the New Year party when he had a wee drink in him and Rangers had more often than not just beaten Celtic that very day, oh there was no living with him. It was all in good fun and I have very happy memories of him. I remember one particular time when the New Year Party was held in our house in Dalmarnock. Uncle Bobby came over to me in the 'big' room. He had a glass of whisky in his hand – he was slightly 'tipsy' - and he had a smile on his face - Rangers had won again I think. He was fairly rubbing it in and I remember him saying, "Join the lodge, Jim. (The Orange Lodge) "Join the lodge." I remember we both had a good laugh about that. Come to think of it, I wouldn't have had far to go to join up - there was one just around the corner from us in Mordaunt Street.

I remember that when I used to go on those Sunday evening visits with my parents, I always used to hope that whichever aunt and uncle we were going to visit would have the television on.

At that time (the late 1950s), a TV set was very much a novelty and having only recently got our own television set installed, I was hooked on the 'small screen.' I was far more amused when the TV was on, as I could focus on something while the adults sat and talked. I was particularly glad of the TV diversion when we were visiting say, my Uncle John and Aunt Agnes, as I had no male cousins to play football with there and got easily bored.

I remember though, that my cousins Jeanette and Nancy were, like myself, big Elvis Presley fans from an early age. When there was a new Elvis record on the market they would always go out quickly and buy it. I remember one time – it would be 1956 I think – they were playing the big hit *Are You Lonesome Tonight?* Having just bought it, they couldn't wait to let me hear it on their new record player. So, it was not all boredom really. As another popular music star once sang, those were the days.

On these visiting occasions, we would always have our supper shortly after we arrived. The remainder of the evening would be spent with the adults just sitting talking. Sometimes all of us would watch the television, but more than once, quite often in fact, I remember that the television would be switched off and the boring talking would begin. Occasionally though, all of us would be glued to the TV if there was a really good programme on - like a good play. They used to show a lot of them in those days, particularly the 'Armchair Theatre' series that was shown on Sunday evenings. Even at an early age, I was always keen on a good drama. I recall one occasion we were watching a play called *The*

Portrait of Dorian Gray, a sort of fantasy about a man who doesn't age at all while his portrait does. I remember being engrossed in this. It was most probably one of the 'Armchair Theatre' plays.

I think sometimes we would all play cards - games such as 'Rummy' or 'Pontoons' or whatever, though this was only on occasion. Sometimes too, our hosts would serve a few drinks, but again this was the exception rather than the rule and it was mostly at the New Year party that this happened. Neither of my parents was a regular drinker anyway.

Our relatives from my mother's side of the family lived mainly in the Parkhead area. Sometimes visits here too would be on a Sunday evening, when we used to go to visit my Aunt Helen and Uncle Bill, who lived in Malcolm Street, off Springfield Road. At other times, usually on a Thursday afternoon after school was out, I would go with my mother to visit Aunt Betty who lived in Buddon Street, just across from Celtic Park.

Some Sunday evenings we used to visit an old schoolmate of my father's - Tommy Roache. At that time, he lived at number 892 London Road, between Dunn Street and Boden Street, not all that far from where my granny lived. The Roaches later moved to Dennistoun, to a tenement building on Duke Street, near to the Parkhead Cross end. Again I have memories of visiting both of these places. When we went to London Road, we would take the same route as when my mother and I went to my granny's, except that when we reached the end of Dunn Street, we would turn to the right instead of the left and into London Road. When we visited Dennistoun it would be the tramcar up Springfield Road, past Parkhead Cross and on into Duke Street. Quite often, especially during the summer, Tommy would come along to our home. I remember that he and my father would usually open a few bottles of beer and sit talking about their schooldays - all the people they used to know and where they were now, and all that sort of thing. When we visited them, it was much the same as when we visited our relations, I think we would all sit and play cards and just simply talk.

The Roaches had a daughter and a son. I remember that when the daughter got married, she went to live just off Farme Cross in Rutherglen. I remember that my mother and father were quite friendly with Janet and her husband and we would also sometimes visit them, again on a Sunday evening. When we went here, we always watched television, so this naturally, was one of my more favoured visiting places. The television always seemed to be especially good on a Sunday evening at that time. At least that is how I remember it.

It is interesting looking back on those times some forty years ago and looking at how things have changed in relation to social habits. Visiting of course is still something that many people do. However, due to a number of factors, most notably the destruction over a twenty year period of the old tenement blocks throughout the city and many areas of the city being altered almost beyond recognition, there have been many changes to the tradition of visiting. Much of the old home entertainment patterns, of the era that I am writing about, are things of the past.

The area of Anderston to the west of the city centre is, I think, the most striking example of radical change, even more so than the Dalmarnock and Bridgeton areas. Many parts of it are almost unrecognisable from the 1960s.

In turn with the scattering of whole families all over the city and with the growth of the housing schemes, much of the old way of living has disappeared, along with the tenements. The simpler pleasures of having relatives over at the weekend for tea and chat, which I have described from my own memories as a child, have given way to different, newer forms of entertainment. Nowadays the family unit is smaller and visitors are more likely to be friends rather than relations. It would seem to be that visiting these days is for the young. When I went visiting with my parents, there was of course, no such thing as a video recorder available - television itself was only just taking off. Nowadays the television is universal. Anyone without a TV is usually in this situation through personal choice, rather than through circumstances and most people have at least one video recorder in their home. As a result of all this, the entertainment norms of a few decades ago, are no more and the sing-song around the fire, the card game and even the habit of simply sitting around talking to one another, are also no more - a shame really.

21

The Fitba'.

Like most boys, I was fond of football from an early age. What, with playing it during the breaks from the boring old lessons at school and then playing it again in the backcourts, parks and side streets when school was out, it seemed you couldn't escape it even if you wanted to – and I didn't want to at all.

My father had always been a football fan; in his younger days he had, like my Uncle John, followed Celtic regularly. As he got older, though, and at the time when I was a boy, he didn't go to many of the big games. He had by that time, taken instead to attending matches at the home of Clyde Football Club at Shawfield Park, just over the 'border' in Rutherglen, down at the end of Main Street Bridgeton and close to Richmond Park. Looking back I sometimes wonder why my father took me to see Clyde rather than Celtic. Perhaps he was in some way trying to keep me from the sectarianism so much associated with Celtic and Rangers, perhaps he had got used to watching Clyde rather than Celtic by that time. I cannot say for sure one way or the other. What I do know for sure is that when I later became a regular at Celtic games c.1966-79 it was not in any way due to any influence of my father. He never at any time said that I should follow one particular club and I have a lot of respect for his attitude on this. I can say too that I never at any time heard him utter any disparaging remarks about Rangers; sectarianism simply was not an issue in our home.

I don't even know why I chose one half of the 'old firm' to support. My paternal grandfather who had died in 1946, the year prior to my birth, had been a red hot Celtic fan; I remember my father saying to my uncle John, his brother, on one occasion (in the late 1960s or early 1970s I think) "Father would have liked Jim," referring to my, at the time, passion for Celtic Football Club. One of the reasons, perhaps somewhat ironically, that I eventually stopped going to football matches and especially those involving the 'old firm' was because of the continuing sectarianism in West-Central Scotland.

During the mid to late 1950s and even into the 1960s, Clyde, although having been relegated a few times, had some really good players. They won the Scottish Cup in 1958, beating Hibernian 1- 0 at Hampden Park and when they were in the top division, quite often finished near the top.

I think Clyde was the first football team that my father took me to see. I became of course, increasingly aware of another football team that also began with a 'C' and who played their home games about a mile or so to the north of where we lived. All of that was for later though and for the present time, I was more than happy to watch the 'Bully Wee' as they were called.

My first clear memory of being at Shawfield was one Wednesday evening in August 1957, when Clyde defeated Stranraer by 10-0 in a League Cup game. I would be just short of my tenth birthday at that time. I remember that it was a lovely late summer's evening, at the beginning of the season, and that there was quite a big crowd. It is quite possible that I had been at Shawfield in 1956 or earlier, but I cannot be certain of this. What I do remember for certain is, that the anticipation of going to a match with my father was always strong. To a small boy every game is like the cup final. We went to Shawfield on a regular basis up until the early years of the 1960s; I thoroughly enjoyed every visit.

In those days, Shawfield always got big crowds even for normal run of the mill games. At that time, Hearts was a really big force in Scottish Football and they were Scottish League champions twice within three years, at the end of the 1950s. When Hearts were at Shawfield, there was of course an even bigger crowd and I remember being at quite a few Clyde v Hearts games around this time. My father never took me, as far as I can remember, to the Clyde games involving Celtic or Rangers when I was very young. At these games, Shawfield would be packed full and I think the games would have been all-ticket and of course tickets would be hard to come by, so perhaps that influenced my father too. I also remember that around this time, on December 14 1957, early on in a league match with Celtic, there was a serious accident at Shawfield, when a wall on the terracing collapsed and spectators spilled on to the park behind the goal.

My father would always try to get us along to Shawfield in plenty time for the kick off. On the odd occasion when we were delayed though, I recall that there was always a big queue at the turnstiles and, horror of horrors, sometimes we didn't get in to the stadium until after the game had started. We were never too late though and I can still remember clearly to this day, how my father would lift me over the turnstile – as you could do in those days. I cannot recall exactly how much it was to get into a match at that time though. It was probably a couple of shillings for adults and perhaps sixpence for boys. As soon as I was feet on ground again, I would dash the few remaining yards into the packed ground, my father frantically trying to restrain me lest I got lost in the crowd. It was the roar of the crowd that excited me the most and caused me to be so impatient. Occasionally, if we were a little late in getting in and it was a really big crowd, we would have difficulty in finding a place to see the game. It was only when it came nearer half time and people started moving about, going for their half-time refreshment of a pie or perhaps a cup of Bovril, that spaces would become available to view the game properly. That said, we always saw most of the game anyway.

My father of course, knew all the Clyde players of that time off by heart. The ones I remember in particular, were big Archie Robertson, the inside left, and Tommy Ring at outside left. My father used to say that the two of them 'didn't get on.' I have no way of telling if this was true or not, but it certainly did not seem like it with Tommy Ring setting up many goals for Robertson. They formed a lethal partnership in those far off days when teams played most of the time with five attacking forwards. A time too, when wingers were the most exciting sight in football and when the players were numbered simply from number 2 at right back, to number 11 at outside left. The goalkeeper of course, made up the eleven.

George Herd was on the other wing and, like Robertson, Ring and also Harry Haddock at left back (another of my favourites from those days), had been capped for Scotland on a few occasions. This shows the wealth of football talent that the Clyde team of that time possessed. It was a lot more difficult to get capped for the Scottish national team some forty to forty-five years ago, than what it is now.

Other players that I remember from this era were Dan Currie, an under-rated player who scored a lot of goals from the old inside-right position. Next to him, a centre forward named Basil Keogh who was one of those players who could score a brilliant goal or goals in one game and do nothing in the next. Another centre forward, Johnny Coyle, who had played with Dundee United, entrenched in the old Second Division at that time, replaced him in the Clyde team round about 1958, I think. Coyle scored the only goal of the game in the Scottish Cup Final of that year.

Another 'character' in the Clyde team of that time, was big Albert Murphy at right back. He was a great servant to Clyde and I can still see him yet as it were, charging right up the right wing from the full back berth and having a shot at goal as he approached it. He was the original attacking full back in my opinion, long before the phrase was ever coined.

The half back line, as it was called in those days, was usually Joe Walters, Willie Finlay and Mike Clinton. All three of them were unsung heroes who gave their all for Clyde week in, week out. I particularly remember Willie Finlay; he was rock solid in defence and epitomised the genuine, old style centre half.

Last, but certainly not least, I have to mention the goalkeeper. When I first started watching Clyde with my father in those days, Clyde had a goalie named Mike Watson. I don't remember much about him, apart from the name sticking in my mind. Another keeper called Tommy McCulloch, who I think arrived at Shawfield from the junior club Bridgeton Waverley, replaced him in the late 1950s. What service this player gave to Clyde. I think he remained with the club well into the 1960s. I saw him making some truly fantastic saves for Clyde. When speaking of unsung heroes, Tommy McCulloch must be right up there at the very top. What a fantastic keeper he was - not all that big, but agile and with tremendous positional sense. If he had played for the likes of Rangers, Celtic or Hearts, he would most certainly have been capped by the Scottish International team, even though at that time, the national team was selected by a sort of committee, rather than the team manager.

My father and I usually stood in the same part of the ground every week. We stood to the side of the goal, which faced you as you entered the ground. Shawfield being the rather curiously shaped stadium it was, this was not ideal, but we usually got a good view of the game – which was the main thing. You would see the same die-hard supporters there week in, week out, even when the team was not doing so well, when there would be more space than usual.

Some of course, would come to air their felt grievances to all and sundry. There was one guy there who was sometimes a bit the worse for drink; he would shout and rant at the players, the referee and anyone who got on his nerves, it seemed. He would often tell the referee to 'go home to his bed' – that being some of his milder phraseology. Then there was this other guy who always seemed to have this heavy coat on, no matter what the weather. I remember that his 'speciality' was jeering some of the Clyde players when they were having a bad day and not producing the goods as it were. Yes, the place was full of 'characters.'

It was of course, a lot more trouble-free on the terraces all those years ago. In all the time I went to Shawfield and all the games that I saw, I can only remember one 'incident.' One day, we were standing nearer the centre of the terracing and almost at the back of the goal, at a game against the all-conquering Hearts. After a while, a scuffle broke out between a Hearts supporter, who was slightly the worse for drink, and some of the Clyde fans. It was all over in an instant though and was certainly nothing serious.

In those days, when you were making your way into the game, you would see vendors selling rosettes in team colours and what I think were called 'ricketies'- a thing you twirled round and round in your hand and it gave off a sound. It was an old way of cheering on your team. Both of these things, which were so popular at that time, and most especially at really big games like cup finals, are no longer part of the football scene. Nowadays, it is the team strip that is popular with supporters more than anything else and of course when a team changes their strip, as the big clubs frequently do, then the fans will beg, steal or borrow to get the latest one. Such is the state of play in the modern game and the rampant commercialisation that has overtaken it as previous generations knew it.

Music was played over the loudspeakers before the game, together with the announcement of the teams and any changes to the line-ups supplied in the match programme, and at half-time. The late 1950s witnessed the beginnings of what came to be called 'pop' (popular music), and the growth of rock and roll. I cannot recall ever hearing any 'modern' music at Shawfield, no Elvis or anything like that. It was more standard fare, Scottish dance music and the like.

When I started going to the football, you never saw anyone with a shirt in the colours of their team. It was unknown. The supporters in those days would wear scarves in their favourite team's colours, and they still do to this day. The 'tammy' hat, with the team colours, is not nearly so popular as it used to be.

One thing that has survived is the programme. When going to Shawfield, as you approached the turnstiles, you would see the programme vendors all over the place. You would, in fact, hear them before you saw them. "'Ficial Programme, get your 'Ficial Programme," would be the shout. In those days you could get a programme for about six old pence. It was of course, a very basic thing; it merely gave you the teams for the game that day - with any late changes to be announced over the loudspeaker system, the half-time scoreboard and some comment from the team manager. That said, I sometimes think the old-style programme was better value for money than its modern day counterpart costing at least £1.50 and packed with advertisements on every other page.

Then there were the other vendors who sold things like chewing gum and macaroon bars. It was the same sellers you saw there every week with their goods and the same shout would go up "spearmint chewing gum, macaroon bars." There was this small middle-aged guy who was at Shawfield every time we went there and always stood at the same spot. He traded at Clyde games for years and many years later, long after I had moved from the area, I happened to be at a Clyde v Celtic match at Shawfield and this little guy was still there. He may have looked somewhat older, but his shout had lost none of its power and apparently little of its appeal either in the intervening period. These vendors were real characters and amazingly the spearmint chewing gum shout is, I think, still part of the football crowd scene today, if in a somewhat reduced form. I suppose they still sell the macaroon bars too.

22

The Fitba'- Second Half.

As a boy, Saturday was undoubtedly my favourite day. For a start, I did not have to go to school and in the morning I would be out at the shops with my mother. Then in the evenings we would, of course, be out at the pictures. The in-between bit, the afternoons, were, for about nine months of the year, spent with my father at the football. When we went to Shawfield, it was always the same route we took. We would cross busy Dalmarnock Road from number 337 and enter the very short Playfair Street - it must be one of the shortest streets in Glasgow when I think about it now. This would lead us into Poplin Street, which stretched all the way down to the top of Main Street at the other end. We would then turn off at Dora Street, another very short street and on into French Street and walk all the way down to the end and into Main Street. As we made our way from our home, we would see trickles of supporters making their way to the game, but it was only when we got into Main Street that the atmosphere began to hit you. There would be crowds of people making their way up Main Street from Bridgeton Cross to Shawfield and there would be supporters' buses all over the place. If it were one of the big teams who were the visitors on the day, the traffic in Main Street and all the way up to Shawfield Drive would be at a virtual standstill, even in those days, when there was considerably less traffic on the roads than what there is now.

After the match was over, we would take a different route home. We would walk straight down Main Street to Bridgeton Cross arriving in time for the sports editions of the evening newspapers hitting the streets. Sometimes we had a while to wait, but it was always worth it. I was always interested to see the other scores, particularly the Celtic score. Sometimes Celtic would have been playing at home that day too and you would see all the supporters' buses at the Cross coming down from London Road. At other times we would see the Rangers supporters coming in their buses along James Street from Ibrox Park. Bridgeton Cross especially on a Saturday, at that time, was always a busy place. It still is today, but in those days it was 'absolutely heaving'.

After we got the sports papers and looked at all the results, we would make our way up Dalmarnock Road and home to mother's cooking. By that time, I would have a good idea of who had won that day and who had lost and my father would have an idea if he'd won anything on the pools that week.

In those days, for the sports papers, you had the pink 'Evening Times' which marked it out as being the sports edition of the paper as distinct from the early white edition which would come out at lunch time. Apart from the football results and news, there was very little difference in the content of the paper generally from the early edition. Over the years and indeed the next couple of decades, the 'pink' as it were, gradually became paler till it was, in effect, white. Finally, the evening edition of the paper was discontinued, the good old sports 'pink' was no more. Also at that time, there was the 'Evening Citizen' and it

A March 1932 view of the Mermaid Bar in James Street. For many decades this has been a pub popular with fans of Rangers Football Club. It is now called the Bridgeton Bar.

too had a sports edition on a Saturday evening. The 'Citizen' was a larger paper than the Times and on a windy day especially it was a bit of a struggle to open it up. The Sports edition of the Citizen was of a greenish colour – this was to distinguish it from the white edition, which was printed from Monday to Friday. 'The Evening Citizen' ceased publication many years ago. I remember the Saturday sports edition well and rather fondly too, but my favourite was always the good old pink 'Times.' Somehow it really epitomised what a Saturday was all about with its sports writers like Gair Henderson. It will have a special place in my memory forever.

Looking at Shawfield these days, it looks very much like it did some forty to forty-five years ago. Clyde left there in the mid 1980s and football is no longer played there, though the greyhound racing is still very much a feature, with weekly events. The entrances at the front have not changed at all and on the odd occasion when I pass that way on the top deck of a bus, the inside looks very much the same too, although of course, the goals are no longer there. In February 1984, I was at a Scottish Cup Tie there when Clyde were playing Aberdeen. There was only a small crowd there that sunny but rather cold day. Aberdeen won the match by 2-0. A lot of memories came flooding back to me; it was very emotional. My father had just died, and I thought of all the times we had we gone there and been entertained. I even went in the same gate we used to go in after I had got a bit older and could no longer get lifted over the other turnstile at the side.

Shawfield, in those far-off days, was always packed. Even for games against 'middle of the league' opposition, there was always a fair sized crowd. In those days too of course, there was far greater competition from outwith Celtic and Rangers, than what there is in the present day. Teams like Hibernian, Aberdeen, Kilmarnock and Dundee were always formidable opposition, as well as of course, the great Hearts teams of that time with legendary players like Willie Bauld and Jimmy Wardhaugh. Between them, those two scored a barrowload of goals. Hearts also had the Scottish internationalist Davie Mackay in their halfback line. Other sides like St Mirren for instance, were a big attraction at that time too, as well as Motherwell with players such as Ian St John, Andy Weir and Pat Quinn.

I recall that my father would point out to me the big names of the day in the visiting teams. He would say things like "see that number 7, he's some player," or, "that big centre forward, the number of goals he has scored." It was through this that I became familiar with the top players of the day and how also that I came to have my favourite players, just like any other boy my age I suppose. I also used to read the sports pages of the daily and the weekend newspapers too of course and through this I knew who was who in the various teams. Bobby Collins of Celtic was a particular favourite of mine, as well as Charlie Tully. Although I was a regular at Shawfield, I was at the time of my boyhood becoming attracted to Celtic.

That period of course, also boasted the great Rangers team who were winning just about everything the game had to offer. What a forward line they had - Scott, MacMillan, Millar, Brand and Wilson. A few years later, an even better winger, Willie Henderson, replaced Scott on the right wing. Every time I saw the Rangers team of that era on the old black and white television I was transfixed. I thought their forward line and their attacking play was easily the most exciting sight in Scottish football at the time.

In those days of course, in the 'Evening Times' on the Friday evening before the next day's games, the teams for the matches would all be listed on the back page. If there were injury doubts about one or two players it would be stated after the team name that the line up was the probable team. This was of course, in the far-off days when teams were open about how they would line up and who would be playing. It was long before that 'in' word - 'tactics' (from about the mid 1960s), dictated that openness should go out the window and that henceforth opponents would be kept guessing as to how a team would play and who would be playing. Not that there was any need for secrecy in those days of course, as most teams simply adopted the standard formation of a goalkeeper, two full backs, the half-back line of right half, centre half and left half and the five forwards.

Needless to say, the back page of the 'Evening Times' was always a favourite read of mine on a Friday evening and usually before I went out for the fish suppers for our tea, I would nip down to Mann's newsagent to get hold of the 'Times.' When I got back upstairs I would be sitting scanning the teams to see who was playing the next day. If I 'dallied' too long, my mother would give me a playful reminder that it was time to go out and get the fish suppers as "your father will soon be in from his work and he will be starving."

It would be something of a miracle if one of the big teams openly announced who would be playing for them on the Saturday before a big game these days and who produced their line-up on the back page of Friday evening's newspaper. Another tradition of the past that's long gone – but never forgotten.

Another thing I recall from that time was the half time scoreboard at the grounds. The half time results from around the country would be put up on a scoreboard at the stadium. This would be done in alphabetical order and if, say, Aberdeen were playing at home that day, then their result would come first and so on. The scoreboard at Shawfield was at the opposite end of the ground from where I usually stood with my father, right next to the electronic scoreboard that to this day is used for the greyhound racing meetings.

I remember that I always looked forward with anticipation to the half time results, particularly to see how a certain other team from the East End of Glasgow was faring. If there were a real shock result, you would hear an enormous gasp of incredulity emanating from the crowd on these occasions. It was at that time, part and parcel of the Saturday football scene, every bit as much so as the half-time pie or the spearmint chewing gum. This was in the days before the ownership of small transistor radios became almost universal. This development of course, enabled crowds at football matches to keep in touch with what was happening at other games through the medium of commentators and reporters. In spite of this though, the half-time scoreboard continued at some grounds into the 1970s, before being largely

This 1955 photograph of Shawfield Stadium shows the greyhound scoreboard, which is still in existence in the present day. There is though no sign of the football half-time scoreboard, so much the focus of my attention on those long ago but not forgotten Saturday afternoons. It should be on the left-hand side of the greyhound scoreboard. Perhaps it is hidden by the sheer size of the giant scoreboard.

replaced by the practice of an announcer reading out the scores over the loudspeaker system.

My father also sometimes took me to the reserve games when the 'big' team was playing away from home. I cannot ever recall going to see Clyde with my father outside of Glasgow. At these reserve games, or 'A' team games as they were known at that time, we would usually sit in the stand. The terraces were virtually deserted at these games, although when it was Celtic or Rangers reserves that were the visitors, there would usually be a somewhat larger attendance. I remember at the end of those games, the small crowd would huddle next to a spot where there was a loudspeaker, in anticipation of the announcement as to how Clyde's first team had fared on their travels that day. A crowd would congregate in the stand area and the rest would be gathered at another loudspeaker on the terraces near the main entrance to the ground. Sometimes it was about five o'clock at the earliest before the result came through and, depending on the outcome, the small crowd would pour onto the streets and into the gathering gloom of a winter's evening in the East end of Glasgow. They would be either elated by what they had heard, or alternatively heading for the public houses in Main Street (and there were more than a few of those to be found in those days) to drown their sorrows.

In those days too, you could get into the match about twenty minutes before the end. The clubs used to open their doors about twenty past four. There would usually be a fair sized queue and when the gates opened, there would be a mini-stampede to see what was left of the game. If it was one of the bigger games with a tightly packed crowd, it was a bit of a waste of time really, as the crowd would be so big you would not see what was happening on the field at all. I am not exactly certain when this practice ceased, but it is long gone for sure. Somehow I just cannot imagine it being part and parcel of the modern commercialised game. Like the old practice of lifting a youngster over the turnstile, it has long been abandoned. As for the lift over the turnstile, as someone said to me recently, if you tried to get lifted over nowadays, you would get lifted.

I remember getting in this way with my father on a few occasions when, for some long forgotten reason, we had not been there at the start of the game at three o'clock. But it was a rarity with us.

Another time during the afternoon when we encountered the big crowds, apart from entering the ground before the game in the first place, was at half-time when there was a huge dash to the refreshment windows at Shawfield. As I remember it, there were two of those on the terracing at Shawfield at that time. One of these was right up at the corner near where we usually stood and the other away over at the other end, on the 'long' terracing leading up to where the half-time scoreboard was situated. I cannot remember either my father or I ever being 'big' as it were on the half-time snacks, but I always liked a packet of crisps - crisps with the wee blue bag in the packet. What I remember was that when half time came, there would already be a fair sized queue at the window I usually went to. I used to think that it was smart to tell my father a few minutes before the end of the first half that

I was nipping over to the refreshment window early, so as to avoid the queue - or the worst of it. What I usually found though, was that most other people had the same idea and that there would still be plenty of people in the queue when I got there. So I had forsaken the last few minutes of the first half for nothing. Sometimes I would still be standing there when the game restarted and I had to find my way back to where I had been standing with my father. When there was a really big crowd, this was easier said than done sometimes and it was with some difficulty that I eventually found where my father was standing. Memories of trying to find your seat in the old picture halls after going for the chocolate ices, are a parallel here. This was of course, when I was getting a bit older. When I was very young of course, my father would take me up to the refreshment window himself. I cannot remember my father ever buying much in the way of refreshments at half time; he may have bought the odd pie from time to time or perhaps Bovril, but it was certainly not a weekly occurrence.

In those days, the toilet facilities at some of the grounds were nothing short of a disgrace. Even well into the sixties and perhaps part of the seventies, I recall that even at a big club like Celtic, much improvement in this respect was needed. At Celtic Park, the toilets at the back of the jungle were poor and the ones at the back of the traditional Celtic end of the stadium were little better. If anything, the toilets at Hampden for many years were even worse. This in spite of the fact that it was and still is, Scotland's national stadium.

In this respect though, Shawfield fared better than most, which may, I don't know for sure, have had something to do with the fact that greyhound racing was taking place there as well as football. One of the toilets was just up at the back of the terracing where we stood and the other one was right along at the very corner of the ground near the other exit on to Shawfield Drive. The toilets at Shawfield were well kept and they were a lot better than some of the others. When you were standing on the terraces, the smell from the toilets was one of the two which naturally 'hit' you as you stood there. The other one was of tobacco. With so many people lighting up, it was what was to be expected. Although I have never been a smoker, it was a smell that I did not mind in the least as I remember it. Like some of the other things that I have described earlier, it was all part and parcel of attending a football match on a Saturday afternoon.

In those days, they used to play Scottish dance music, or perhaps some classical music at times, over the loudspeaker system at half time. This was the time when modern popular music was beginning to take off, and, from the 1960s, this became the norm; of course you still hear popular music being played before the match and at half time too, in football grounds around the country today.

By about 1962, my visits to Shawfield with my father had largely ceased and for a couple of years after that I used to go to Shawfield along with my friend from my primary school days - Jim Connor, whom I mentioned earlier. My father still went to most of the home games and sometimes Jim and I would meet him coming out of the game on the way home. My father continued to watch the game from the same bit of the terracing where he and I had stood for at least the previous five years at Clyde games. Most of the time though, Jim and I would go and watch the game from the other end of the ground, right beside the half-time score board and close to the entrance at Shawfield Drive. I remember that we got to know the guy who put up the scores at half time and we were in the privileged position of knowing at least some of the results before most of the people in the ground knew them. It was the same guy every time we were there who took care of the half-time scores and he was a cheery sort of guy. After a while, he caught on to the fact that I was always asking the Celtic score right away and he would often tell me some horror stories of Celtic losing 4 nil, or something like that. He was, as they say nowadays, 'winding me up.' I got wise to him after a while, but looking back on the poor Celtic side of that time in the years immediately preceding the arrival of Jock Stein, perhaps he may not have been kidding some of the time.

I think I continued to go to Shawfield till about 1964; apart from a few Clyde v Celtic games in the late 1960s, I don't think I was in the stadium again until the occasion in 1984 that I mentioned earlier on. I have no definite recollection of being in the ground throughout the 1970s.

And so ended a period in my young life that I still of course, have very fond memories of to this day. It was my introduction as it were, to a game that I have always enjoyed and I shall never forget these early trips to Shawfield with my father. Every time that I pass the ground in the present day, it brings back so many happy memories of my boyhood days, and, as the ground has changed very little in appearance in forty-five years, it makes it easier to remember those far-off days of old.

23

The Fitba': Extra Time but no Penalties.

It wasn't just Shawfield that my father and I went to at that time. We used to make the 'long' trip to Cathkin Park on the south side of the river, to watch Third Lanark. The Thirds, or the 'Hi Hi' as they were more affectionately known, had a really good side at that time and sometimes finished well up in the First Division, without ever winning a major honour. They did reach the final of the Scottish League Cup in 1959, only to lose to the, at that time, mighty Hearts.

I think that we used to go to Cathkin about every month or so; in particular when we got fed up with Clyde reserves when Clyde's big team were away from home. There was always a good atmosphere at Cathkin, particularly when it was one of the 'Old Firm' that was visiting, or of course Hearts. I recall being at games at Cathkin against these teams when the place was absolutely packed and also against teams like Aberdeen and Kilmarnock.

I say 'long' trip to Cathkin; it was another one of those instances that, when you are very young, a visit to another part of the city can somehow seem like being hundreds of miles away. That said, our visits to Cathkin were always eagerly anticipated. I think too, we always picked the bright, sunny days to go there, as I cannot remember us every getting the tram over to the south side of the city. No, we always took 'Shank's

Pony.' Our route would begin very much the same as if we were heading for Shawfield and we would make our way over to Main Street. Then we would make our way through to Rutherglen Road and into Polmadie Road, just across from the far side entrance to Richmond Park. Polmadie Road is a long road and to me at that time, it seemed somehow never ending, especially in the middle where there is a sort of incline over the railway tracks. Polmadie Road leads directly on to Aitkenhead Road and Cathkin Park as it was then, was close to the main road.

It was only when you approached the end of Polmadie Road that you began to see any significant crowds going to Cathkin. You would encounter some supporters of course coming up through Richmond Park and the southern end of Glasgow Green, but until you approached Aitkenhead Road, there were no crowds to speak of. You would see a lot of supporters' buses coming into the likes of Calder Street just off Polmadie Road, and when you reached Aitkenhead Road itself, it would be really busy. The traffic would be heavy and there would be throngs of supporters on both sides of the road. A bit like it was, back at Main Street when Clyde was playing at home.

I think that my first time at Cathkin would again be round about 1957, although unlike in the case of Shawfield, I have no definite, precise recall of who the visitors were on that occasion. What I do remember though, was that this was a time when Thirds had some really good players in their side. It was just at the time when the terrific Thirds forward line of Goodfellow, Hilley, Harley, Gray and McInnes, was becoming prominent.

The replacement footbridge over the River Clyde in Glasgow Green, 1926. My father and I would cross over this bridge many times in the late 1950s and early 1960s on our way from Bridgeton through Polmadie (in the background of the photograph) to see Third Lanark F.C. play at Cathkin Park

Seldom can a team boasting such a lethal forward line have failed to win a major honour. There were other players that I remember of course; there was wee Jocky Robertson in goal - what a keeper he was. I remember that he was so agile, diving all over the place and making some fantastic saves. I remember that my father was a big fan of his. "What a goalkeeper he is, son," he used to say to me. Just like Tommy McCulloch at Clyde, wee Jocky was never capped as an international. There was also, just prior to the right wing partnership of Goodfellow and Hilley, Billy Craig on the right wing and Bobby Craig (no relation.) Those two, plus Robertson in goal, McInnes on the left wing and John Lewis at centre half, are the players that I remember most from my early visits to Cathkin.

Both of the Craigs played for Celtic briefly. Billy Craig, my father had informed me, was at Celtic Park before he joined Thirds. Bobby played for the Parkhead side after he left Cathkin. He played in fact in the Wednesday night replay of the 1963 Scottish Cup Final when, to my dismay the late great Jim Baxter once more put the hoodoo over Celtic and the Baxter inspired 'Gers trounced Celtic by three-nil, after a 1-1 draw on the Saturday. I recall that on the evening of that game, I was in the stand at Shawfield at a Clyde reserve game with my friend Jim. I was listening to the match on my recently acquired transistor radio, all the go then, and growing more distressed by the moment as Rangers piled on the agony writ large.

Wee Joe McInnes on the left wing was the type of player that my father would always refer to as 'a character.' He was one of the old style wingers, like Tommy Ring and George Herd at Clyde, and was an exciting sight to watch as he tore down the Thirds left wing, leaving defenders lying all over the place in his wake.

Unfortunately though, he seemed to get sent off by the referee regularly for getting into scraps with the opposition, or perhaps arguing with the referee. In those days, most of the time, when a player got sent off, he was sent off for what would now be termed 'violent conduct', i.e. the use of the fist or a head butt. Nowadays, a player can get sent off for two reasonably innocuous fouls. A player can even get sent off for handling the ball. The whole business is, in my opinion, a ridiculous, unsatisfactory state of affairs that has spoiled the game of football and perhaps most particularly in the Scottish game, taken a lot of the good, old fashioned passion out of playing football.

The games at Cathkin at that time were always exciting and there always seemed to be plenty of goals being scored. I can only recall being at one nothing-each draw and that was against of all teams, Hearts, who at that time scored so many goals. In fact, in one of their championship winning seasons, (1957-58) they scored an amazing 121 goals. One particular game I remember at Cathkin was against Falkirk who had a good side at that time and won the Scottish Cup in 1957, beating a very good Kilmarnock side by 2-1 after a 1-1 draw. On this particular day, there were goals galore and Falkirk eventually ran out winners by 5-3. Falkirk had, in their side then, players such as Alex Parker, a Scottish

International right back, and a good goalkeeper in Bert Slater who had a spell with Liverpool.

The one disappointing thing about Cathkin Park was that, unlike Shawfield, which was totally under cover, Cathkin was wide open to the worst of the winter elements on both the terracings behind the goals. The only shelter from the rain and the snow, apart from the stand of course, was the space opposite the stand and enclosure, to the right of where we normally stood. Most of the time we stood on the terracing nearest to Aitkenhead Road. It was here that you got the best view of the match. We never went to the stand at all at Cathkin. In those days of course, before the spread of enclosures, you could walk from one end of the ground to the other at half time. It is no longer possible to do this the way modern stadiums are built. Each section is fenced off and there are more or less separate ends for the home supporters and the visiting fans at every ground nowadays. In those days though, my father and I would sometimes walk right round to the other side of the stadium and watch the second half from the end nearest to Mount Florida.

The refreshment facilities at Cathkin were nothing like as good as those at Shawfield. The only place you could get a half time snack, as far as I recall, was right away up in the corner of the terracing on which we normally stood and close to the covered part of the ground. The refreshment stall was right in the corner of this terracing and to get to it, you had to climb a rather steep brae (perhaps this was part of the 'real' Cathkin Braes.) In the winter when it was sometimes icy, it was tricky to get up this brae and even trickier perhaps coming down as you would be slipping and sliding all over the place.

I remember one day we were standing under this covered part of the ground. It was a bitterly cold day round about New Year time and Thirds were playing Kilmarnock. How the game had even got started was miraculous in itself, as there was frost on the pitch and snow flurries threatening a heavy fall later. I remember going to the refreshment stall at half time in that game and slipping as I came back down. As I think it would be Bovril or tea that I would be bringing back to warm us up on such a cold day, my journey was most probably a wasted one. Certainly there was no way that I was going to venture back up and stand in the queue for a second time in such freezing conditions.

Third Lanark Football Club went defunct in 1967 following serious financial troubles. The actual space where the park had been is still vacant to this day and has fallen into disrepair. The goalposts are long gone of course, as is the stand and the enclosure. However the terracings, although no longer used as such, are still there. Looking all around you, you can just picture in your mind's eye, the ground as it was all those years ago. One warm summer's day in June 1997 I went with a colleague, who was working on the aforementioned *2000 Glasgow Lives* Project at the time, to what is left of Cathkin Park. We did a spot of filming with the video camera we had with us, with me relating memories of being at Cathkin as a boy. I thoroughly enjoyed the experience of recalling my days as a boy spectator on the terracing to the right of where we had the camera situated.

251

Of all the times I went with my father to the football in those days, one in particular stands out starkly clear in my mind to this day. It was one Saturday during December 1960, the 3rd to be exact. Clyde's game had been postponed as it was absolutely bucketing down with rain. I think we had gone along to Shawfield first and then found that the game had been postponed late on. My father told me that Celtic were at home to Dundee that day and he thought that it would be a good idea if we went there. This was great news for me, for some time I had wanted to go to Celtic Park to see this other team that I had heard and read so much about. This was, in spite of the fact that they were at the time going through a long, lean patch in terms of winning trophies, with Rangers and Hearts sweeping all before them.

That day I was so excited – to put it mildly – as we made our way from Bridgeton Cross towards the stadium. The rain was, if anything, getting heavier by the minute, although such was my state of excitement, it would hardly have bothered me.

We walked along London Road; just after we had passed Brook Street, my dreams were shattered, as heading in the direction of Bridgeton Cross, some mounted policemen approached. They were indicating to the fans going up to the game, that it too had been postponed due to the atrocious weather conditions. I remember being so let down, talk about disappointment. I don't remember where we ended up that afternoon. Most probably we went home to 'number 337' to listen on the radio to any match that may have survived the weather. I am sure though, that I couldn't have been very happy for the remainder of that Saturday. Perhaps though, my usual visit to the Plaza that evening cheered me up a bit. Perhaps.

For the record, I eventually did get to enter Celtic Park - about five months later towards the end of that 1959-1960 season. It was for a game against Stirling Albion; if I recall things correctly, Celtic were a bit fortunate that day to get a late equaliser, after 'playing rubbish' for most of the game. They were booed off the park at the end of the game. So my first visit to Celtic Park was not exactly a glorious one.

Then there were the junior games. My father was a keen fan of junior football and he used to take me to junior football on a regular basis. Among the teams we went to see in those days were Parkhead Juniors, who played at Helenslea Park in Methven Street, just off London Road and close to Celtic's training ground on the other side of the road. The club is no longer in existence. In another one of those instances where for some reason something remains in your mind long after, I recall that I was in Helenslea Park on that day in April 1961 that goes down as the bleakest, the most humiliating day in the history of the Scottish International Football team. They were on that very day trounced 9-3 by England at Wembley. I recall hearing the score on someone's transistor radio, near the end of the game. Not too far from here, was the previously mentioned Strathclyde Juniors ground, which spanned Kempock Street - but the main entrance was Silverdale Street just off London Road, near its junction with Springfield Road. Further along London Road and just past what, at that time, was Westhorn Park; there was Bridgeton Waverley's ground. I remember being here on a few occasions. Probably though, the Junior ground we visited most in those days, was that of Glencairn Juniors at Southcroft Park in Rutherglen and not all that far at all from Shawfield Park. The 'Glens' at that time, had a great wee team and I always looked forward to going there. Unlike the other junior clubs so far referred to, the Glens are still very much in existence in the present day and are still at Southcroft Park, which looks exactly as it did forty years ago.

When we went to these grounds, it was usually just before the senior football season started, or in the early summer when the senior season had finished. In those days, the junior season started about a week or two before the seniors got going; you would have junior football at the end of July just after the Glasgow Fair Fortnight was over. To a football-starved youngster like myself, a junior game was the first taste of football of the new season and how I relished it. There were always plenty of midweek junior games at the start of the season and with the warm summer evenings still very much part of the scene at that time of the year, it made for pleasant, comfortable outdoor entertainment - most of the time anyway.

I think that we also occasionally went to the ground of Shettleston Juniors further out in the East End and perhaps to Dennistoun Waverley's ground, Haghill - which was up near Alexandra Parade. Shettleston are, of course, another junior club still very much part of the present day junior football scene but sadly Dennistoun Waverley are no more. The club folded many years ago and modern houses now occupy part of what once was the football pitch at Haghill.

I used to go to Haghill on my own quite a lot as I got a bit older, round about the period 1963-1965. In the evenings during the summer months, there were regular games played there, involving Juvenile clubs, mainly from the Glasgow area but sometimes from other parts of the country, especially if it was a big cup –tie. These games were always lively affairs to say the least and I remember on a few occasions, they developed into all-out brawls – eleven-a-side boxing matches almost, it seemed.

I thoroughly enjoyed these. They were a diversion as it were, a good way of enjoying yourself after working all day which I had, of course, started to do by that time. They also were, of course, yet more football action for a football-daft teenager, as I was by that time. Sometimes I would walk all the way up to Haghill, especially if it was a pleasant evening. I would sometimes take the longer route of going down Dalmarnock Road to Bridgeton Cross, then straight up Abercromby Street and Bellgrove into Duke Street and along into the beginning of Cumbernauld Road, into Appin Road and to Haghill. When the game finished, it was still light, so I would follow the same route back. Occasionally I would walk down any of the side streets off Duke Street and into Gallowgate, then along say Fielden Street, down Dunn Street and into Nuneaton Street and I was virtually home. It seemed to be a short cut this. If I were feeling more lazy-like I would usually get the number 22 or 46 bus up to Duke Street and just walk along to Haghill.

I am still a football fan to this day, supporting no particular team though and rarely, if ever, going to a match. The last time I was at any game in Scotland was over ten years ago, though I have been at a few English games since then. Nowadays I do my spectating in front of the television screen and I am a big fan of the Premier League in England in particular.

I often hear it said that the youngsters of the present day do not play football to the same extent that was the case with previous generations. I don't agree with this at all. There are still plenty of young and not so young people playing football all over the place. On a good day weather-wise, you will see workers having a kick about during their break. Likewise, you will see a lot of boys playing on grassland near where they stay, just as boys have always done. Perhaps most significantly, you will see many youngsters playing football in the school playground, in what is a welcome respite from lessons, just as I myself did forty and more years ago.

Certainly, in the present day there undoubtedly are many more counter attractions. There are, for example, video games and video films nowadays to name a few. Many more than there were during the period that I am writing about, and my kick-abouts with my pals in the backcourt and round in Mordaunt Street. That said however, the playing of football as a pastime continues to flourish - and long may it do so too.

Football has changed so much and in many different ways over the past few decades. I still have these very strong and of course lasting memories though, of going to football matches all those years ago. These are memories which I cherish. I hope that the present day generation gets as much pleasure out of going to 'the fitba', and that thirty or forty years down the road of time, they too will recall the pleasures of this great sport, just as I have done here.

24

Christmas and New Year.

It's often said these days that the festival of Christmas has being spoiled and that rampant commercialisation is negating the true meaning of the occasion. To what extent this is true is most doubtful. Clearly though, there must always have been a degree of commercialisation of Christmas in times past; what we are witnessing, in the present day, is no new phenomenon but merely an acceleration of trends which have always existed to a greater or lesser degree. Where I would definitely contend that Christmas has been spoiled, is in the fact that in the present day 'Christmas' begins far too early, certainly far earlier than it did when I was a child.

What I remember from my own childhood about Christmas in the East End of Glasgow was that it was an occasion that was celebrated much more simply than it is today.

My mother would always get a small Christmas tree from Frew's shop right next to 'number 337.' I cannot recall us ever putting the tree up weeks before Christmas like a lot of people do these days. It was always just a few days before the 'big day.' I would help her to put the tree up when I came home from school. It was something I always looked forward to. We always sat the tree on a small table at the window in the 'big room', looking directly on to Dalmarnock Road. I recall how we would put the 'fairy lights', as they were called, on the tree with bits of tinsel, bells and whatever else people put on their Christmas trees. We always wanted to have it ready before my father came in from his work at just after six o'clock.

I remember too, that it was always a 'big moment' when we would put the plug into the electric socket, press the switch, and wait for the lights to come on, Sometimes they did and sometimes they didn't - it was that sort of situation. If they didn't work, then my mother would get to the root of the problem; she would not budge from the job at hand until the problem was rectified. My mother was always very good with electrical things, certainly far better than my father or myself ever were. My mother would often say to us "None of the two of you has any patience." My mother certainly had patience in abundance.

When we eventually did have the lights working, I always found it a joy to go into the dark room and just stand there beside the tree taking in the scene – the sparkling, bright lights contrasting with the darkness of the room and the streets outside. I always thought it was a beautiful scene, this little Christmas tree with its magical lights, so simple really and, so peaceful. When I was out on the other side of Dalmarnock Road at the shops, I would always look up at our window and admire our own wee tree. The best in the street I would tell myself.

Probably the other thing that I remember most about Christmas was the sense of anticipation as to what you were going to get for Christmas and when I was very young, what 'Santa' was going to bring me.

Christmas gifts were of course, much simpler in those days than what they are in the present day. I think that I would usually get a train-set or a model aeroplane kit and perhaps some sweets or fruit in my 'stocking.' Another present that I remember receiving, was the 'Sunday Post' annual. These came out every year at Christmas time in those days, with 'Oor Wullie' one year and 'The Broons' the following year. In the present day, I think they are both published at once; if the present generation of youngsters are fans of these comic strip characters, then they are getting a better deal than my generation did.

Whatever Christmas held in store for me, I certainly was never let down on the big day and my parents always made sure that I got things that would please me. Not that I was too hard to please in those days mind you. I remember though, that in 1965, our last Christmas at Dalmarnock, my parents, aware of my ever-increasing interest in pop music at that time, presented me with a record player.

I remember that I had stopped my work in the early afternoon that day for the festive period; it was a dry, bright winter's day, so I walked home through the Calton from Glasgow Cross, past Bridgeton Cross and up Dalmarnock Road to 'number 337.' It was shortly after I had entered our home that I was presented with this super record player. What a surprise! I remember being 'over the moon,'; now I could buy and play my favourite records all the time and not have to rely any more on the likes of Jimmy Saville on the wireless, to put on something that I liked. It was the best Christmas present ever from two great parents; the record player served me well for years. I bought my favourite singles and LP's on a weekly basis and formed quite a collection after a while – before the era of the record player gradually slipped into history to be replaced by the cassette-recorder and in turn the compact-disc player. I still have that old 'turntable,' as the disc jockeys of the period would refer to the old record-player. I still have it in my home to this day. It no longer works but I keep it for purely sentimental reasons and memories of a lovely Christmas all those years ago. It was probably the last 'old style' Christmas we were to have. By the time Christmas 1966 came around, we would be in our new home and away sadly, from the old tenement buildings of Dalmarnock, which in their own special way, sort of epitomised the way that Christmas was in former times.

I always wished for a white Christmas and always seemed to be disappointed somehow. I cannot ever recall us having a genuine white Christmas when we lived in Dalmarnock. There was one year, when I was very young, when it started snowing on Christmas Eve and I can remember to this day, sitting at the window looking out into Dalmarnock Road. The snowflakes seemed, to me anyway, to be getting larger by the minute and of course I anticipated a white Christmas. What a let-down come Christmas morning, as I awoke to find that the snow had turned to rain overnight and what snow had been lying on the streets the previous evening, had now turned to rain. Still, I'm sure that receiving my presents would more than make up for this.

I cannot recall any widespread celebrations in the area at Christmas. Certainly I don't recall us having any parties at Christmas and I have no recall of any of our neighbours coming into visit us or us going to their home. It seems that then, like now, Christmas was very much a family thing; only nowadays there are many more outward signs that Christmas is celebrated to a greater extent, than was the case a few decades ago. People did not mark the occasion the way that they celebrated New Year, and especially Hogmanay. I think that there is a lot of truth in the suggestion that people in Scotland now celebrate Christmas much more whole-heartedly than they did a few decades ago.

There are also many signs that the celebration of Hogmanay, while by no means dying out altogether, is not what it once was. It was very different in those days. There would be a lot going on and people would visit relatives, friends and neighbours after 'the bells' at twelve midnight, which heralded the beginning of another year.

My parents would stay up for a couple of hours, till about 2am, to see if anybody 'first-footed' us. At the stroke of midnight, my father would give my mother a big kiss and a hug and then they would have a wee drink, probably a whisky for my father with maybe a tumbler of beer too and perhaps a sherry for my mother. The traditional shortbread and fruitcake and all sorts of other things would already be laid out. I would 'celebrate' with a glass of ginger wine or blackcurrant wine.

My mother was a great traditionalist at New Year time. Throughout Hogmanay she would be working flat out to get the house in order for the big occasion. The house would be swept, washed and everything tidy and spick and span. It was a thing of great importance to my mother that this should be the case and that the New Year should begin with a 'fresh start' as it were. That meant that the house had to be in first class condition – not that it was ever anything else mind you – as my mother was a hard-working housewife and house-proud.

I don't recall us ever going into the Miller's home next door at the New Year time; they may have first–footed us on one or two occasions, but it certainly was not a regular thing. What I am certain of is that none of the other neighbours ever first-footed us. Usually, if anyone came in at all, it would be our relations from my mother's side of the family who lived in the Parkhead area - some of my aunts, uncles and cousins. There was never a crowd of them though. Usually it would just be my Uncle Bill and Aunt Helen and perhaps some years, my cousins too.

There would be no sing-song or party or anything like that; everybody would just have a few drinks and sit and talk. I think any first-foots we had would usually stay till about four in the morning, though by that time, as I was still very young, I would be fast asleep. I remember sometimes being up till about 2am. If no one had 'chapped' the door by about one–thirty, then you knew that there were not going to be any first-foots.

In those days, the Scottish Television cameras were usually down at Glasgow Cross to bring in the New Year and there would be crowds gathering there to see personalities like Larry Marshall from the One O'clock Gang and other entertainers of the day. I remember that the late actor Duncan Macrae was a regular at these New Year occasions. I remember too, that I used to watch this with my parents just after twelve o'clock, after we had toasted in the New Year.

Every year on New Year's Day, all my aunts and uncles from my father's side of the family would have a party, a get-together. There would usually be about thirty or so people at these gatherings, including all my cousins of course and perhaps some neighbours from wherever the occasion was held in any particular year. Every year the party was held at a different house. One year it would be at Pollok at the home of my Uncle Bobby and Aunt Mary. The other 'venues' were Priesthill, at my Uncle Tommy and Aunt Francis's, Barlanark where Uncle John and Aunt Agnes lived, or in Castlemilk, hosted by my Uncle Bill and Aunt Helen. And of course, in our own wee house at number 337.

So, the way it worked out, the New Year party would be held in our home every five years. I think that when it was our turn to hold the annual festivities, we always held it in the 'big room' looking on to Dalmarnock Road. In this room, there was plenty room to place a specially extended table for the dinner. After dinner, the table would be cleared away and some of my aunts would usually go into the other, smaller room to help my mother with clearing up and washing the dishes etc. My uncles and my father would be pouring their drinks and getting down to some serious talk about football, betting on the horses, or work, before my mum and the other female guests would come back into the room ready for the party to begin properly as it were. The drink would flow, tongues would wag endlessly and the songs would start once more. Later on in the evenings, there would usually be a bit of dancing as well. Certainly there was ample space for this in the big room. Looking back on this time, my mother and father probably got their 'carry out' for these occasions from Crombie's licensed grocers at 93-95 Dalmarnock Road, just past Heron Street at the bend on the road.

Once the evening progressed and the drink took affect, there would be increasingly regular visits to the toilet. The outside toilet of course, as there was no other. We used to keep our key for the toilet on these occasions, on the set of drawers near the 'lobby' so that everyone would know where to get it. Looking back all these years later, it seems like something incomprehensible, given all the modern home comforts that people take for granted these days. The present generation enjoys, almost universally, inside toilets and no need to enter into the stairway of an old tenement building on a cold winter's night, the way my generation and generations before us had to. I remember that on these New Year occasions, you could be 'needing the toilet', looking for the key and find that there were another two or three people at the same time looking for the key too. If it went temporarily missing of course, there would be 'panic'. It all seems so funny in a way with the benefit of hindsight. Mind you, it probably was funny at the time too.

I never really liked these occasions at all. New Year then and now is not a time for young children. Let's just say I 'suffered' these occasions rather than outrightly hated them. When it was our turn to host the party once again, my mother would be rushing around the house from the middle of the day getting every thing ready for the arrival of our guests. She was really great at this. Everything had to be in order - the best cups and jugs were laid out and of course, there was plenty of food and drink.

It was usually always the same format; dinner would be served, everybody would sit and chat for an hour or so, then the drinks would be brought out and everyone would do their 'party-piece,' their favourite song. My granny, who was usually at these parties, would give her usual rendition of *The Yellow Rose of Texas,* her favourite, while my uncle Bill would sing *When I Leave this World Behind*. These are the only two that I remember for sure, but everyone had to take their turn and join in the spirit of things on these annual occasions. For us children in attendance, I think it was 'optional.' (Just as well perhaps).

While all of this was going on, my younger cousins and I would be playing games like 'Postman's Knock' and helping ourselves to sweets, cakes and ginger. There was always plenty of all of these. When we got tired or fed up with that, we would go through to the main room and just sit on the floor watching the "silly grownups" making a fool of themselves and getting drunker, or 'happy', as my father used to say.

Everyone really enjoyed these occasions. It was a chance for all our relations to get together and have a really good time. All my uncles would have a fair wee drink in them by the end of the night, which was the way it was supposed to be after all. The New Year time was about the only time of the year that my father took a drink and it usually affected him after a few whiskies and a few bottles of beer. At the end of the party, he was usually 'happy' as he put it, but rarely very drunk.

The only time that I can recall him being really drunk was one year in the late 1950s, when we had been out at Priesthill for the New Year party - at uncle Tommy and aunt Francis's home. I can remember us getting into the city centre at St Enoch Square, when we found to our horror that we had missed the last tram to Dalmarnock. My father was really in a 'bad way' by this time and I recall my mother and I holding him up as we walked along Argyle Street with him singing, oblivious to our plight. I think we had to walk it all the way home that night - no late night buses - and you couldn't even think of taking a taxi. Looking back, I think that it must have been the fresh air that knocked my father for six, as certainly, if he had been in that state when leaving the party, my Uncle Bill would have given us a lift home. Uncle Bill was the only one of my relations that I can remember having a car at that time. He was not a big drinker and would only take a bottle of beer or maybe two. My father would have certainly had a 'big head' as he always referred to a hangover, the next morning.

As my parents got older, I think they went to these yearly gatherings more out of perceived 'obligation' than anything else. Perhaps it was the same with the rest of them. You never of course find out these things. I stopped going round when I was about fourteen or so, but I think the annual party continued in our family up until the late 1960s or so. As everyone got older, travelling of course became more of a burden and the occasion changed to more of a situation where you visited those relations who were nearest to you, geographically speaking.

After we left the Dalmarnock area, my parents continued to visit our relatives in Glasgow for another few years at least, but as the years went on, we saw less and less of my aunts and uncles. As far as the New Year thing was concerned, I think that it was par for the course really.

During the time that I was involved with the 2000 Glasgow Lives Project, discernible trends emerged from the interviews. One of these trends that emerged from the many interviews which I had undertaken, was that a lot of people, especially senior citizens, told me that they thought the New Year celebrations were 'not what they used to be.' Some of them, went as far as to say that the New Year was 'a thing of the past.' I wouldn't go that far, but the New Year celebrations have certainly changed from what they were in the period that I am writing about. A lot of it has to do with the break up of the old close-knit communities and the decline of the extended family. Both of these of course, were largely as result of the building of the new housing schemes and the destruction of many of the old tenement buildings over a twenty-year period. Another reason I think is that with the extension of the licensing hours through legislation in the 1970s and the 1980s, there is much more time for people to socialise in pubs and clubs than what there was for many decades prior to the 1970s.

This has resulted in a situation where you could argue that young people, especially, have the opportunity for something akin to the New Year celebrations every weekend, with places to drink being open until three and four o'clock in the morning. In the 'old days', with the pubs closing about half past nine or ten o'clock in the evening, these opportunities did, for the most part, not exist, so I think perhaps that the New Year was seen by many as something special, something different. Certainly nowadays, I think the New Year, in whatever way it still is celebrated, is far more of an occasion for young people than what used to be the case. Older people will of course, still celebrate the occasion and wait up for the bells and may still practice some of the older traditions of New Year. It is "not what it used to be" though and our wee cosy scene at 'number 337' with the shortbread, the ginger wine and all the basic trimmings at the stroke of twelve o'clock which once was the norm, is fast fading into history.

25

The Fair Holidays.

The celebration of the Glasgow Fair dates from the tenth century. The holiday making aspect of this tradition, the 'doon the watter' thing, dates from the more recent past. The late Victorian period's innovation of trips to the seaside, particularly the Clyde Coast, was largely a reflection of what was happening in the rest of Britain. By this time, the spread of seaside holidays was filtering through to the manual classes, having previously been the preserve of the more well-to-do from about the 1840's. The growth of the railway network throughout Britain in the middle of the century increasingly facilitated the growth of the seaside holiday, initially in the form of day trips and then increasingly longer holidays.

By the late 1950s, the trips to the seaside, in the form of day trips to the coast or a fortnight away during the Glasgow Fair, were still popular though soon they were to be overtaken by the advent of the package holiday to destinations abroad, most particularly Spain.

Certainly, when we went off on our holidays in the late 1950s and the early part of the 1960s, you would never have thought that the heyday of the great Glasgow Fair trek to the seaside was shortly to experience a sharp decline. What I remember from this period is that the railway stations in Glasgow were teeming with people on Fair Saturday morning, which was when we, just like thousands of others, began our annual break. This was the way it had been for decades previously; a scene from the late 1950s, in this regard, would have been one differing very little from that of twenty or thirty years previously. Many people of course, also went to destinations in England – Blackpool and Scarborough probably being the main destinations in this regard – as well as the Scottish favourites.

The time of the Glasgow Fair was always one of excitement for the three of us, perhaps most especially for me, being the age I was then. At that time, the huge majority of people took their holidays during the Glasgow Fair fortnight and whole factories would shut down over the two weeks. Over the past few decades, this has become a largely redundant practice, as nowadays most working people have a minimum entitlement of at least four weeks paid leave. This, together with the changed patterns of work over the period since the 1960s and the demise of the older, traditional industries, has led to a situation where the traditional Glasgow Fair fortnight has lost much of its significance. In past decades, everyone, or so it seemed, stopped work on Fair Friday; it was like Hogmanay in mid-summer with the pubs doing a roaring trade as the workers celebrated the fact that they were released from the drudgery of work for two whole weeks. People of course, still do go on holiday during the final two weeks in July, but it is not what it used to be and the norm nowadays is for 'staggered' or 'split' holidays being taken at different times throughout the year. Also, while people from Glasgow still do go on holiday to the Clyde Coast resorts, the continued growth and

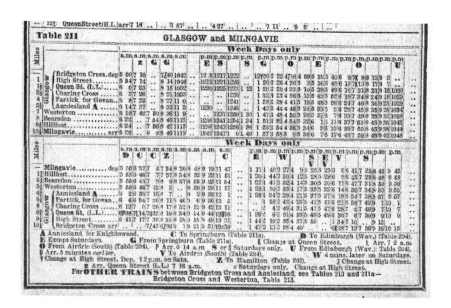

Bridgeton Cross, and the surrounding area, was well served by train services in the 1950s. Timetables from 1947, the year of my birth, show some of the services available.

GLASGOW, DUMBARTON, HELENSBURGH and BALLOCH

Week Days

Table 213

Miles		Week Days
	201 Enterarean (Wk=)204 dp	
	Bridgeton Cross ...... dep	
	High Street	
	Queen Street (Low Level)	
	Charing Cross	
	Partick, for Govan ...	
	Jordanhill	
	Scotstounhill	
	Yoker	
	Clydebank (Central) ..	
	Anniesland, for Knights	
	Westerton	
	Drumchapel	
	Singer	
	Dalmuir	
	Kilpatrick	
	Bowling	
	Dumbarton	
	Cardross	
	Craigendoran	
	Helensburgh .... arr	
	Renton	
	Alexandria, ...	
	Balloch Station ...... arr	
	Balloch Pier .... arr	

L.M.S. Workmen's Train — Third class only

NOTES

Arr. 5 minutes earlier
Calls to set down only
Except Saturdays
From Springburn — Table 215A
Arr. 1200 p.m.
From Shettleston daily and Hamilton except on Sats (Table 215)
Arr. 1.56 a.m.
Arr. 6 minutes earlier
From Springburn except on Saturdays
Arr. 4.3 p.m.
From Mount Vernon — Table 215
Arr. 7.5 minutes earlier
Saturdays only
From Airdrie (South) — Table 205
5 mins. later on Sats.
3 mins. later on Sats.
Arr. 4 minutes earlier

Week Days—continued

	201 Kennerean (Wk=)204 dp	
	Bridgeton Cross ...... dep	
	High Street	
	Queen Street (Low Level)	
	Partick, for Govan ..	
	Jordanhill	
	Scotstounhill	
	Yoker	
	Clydebank (Central) .	
	Anniesland, for Knights	
	Westerton	
	Drumchapel	
	Singer	
	Dalmuir	
	Kilpatrick	
	Bowling	
	Dumbarton	
	Cardross	
	Craigendoran	
	Helensburgh .... arr	
	Renton	
	Alexandria, ...	
	Balloch Station	
	Balloch Pier .... arr	

For **OTHER TRAINS** between Glasgow and Clydebank, see Table 215A—Bridgeton Cross and Anniesland, Table 215—Bridgeton Cross and Westerton, Table 211.

Table 316—Continued

COATBRIDGE, RUTHERGLEN, GLASGOW, MARYHILL, DUMBARTON, and BALLOCH

Week Days only—Continued

Station																													
Whifflet .... dep																													
Coatbridge																													
Langloan																													
Drumpark																													
Baillieston																													
Carmyle																													
Tollcross																													
Parkhead																													
Rutherglen																													
Dalmarnock																													
Bridgeton Cross																													
Glasgow Green																													
Glasgow Cross																													
Glasgow (Central) .... arr																													
" (Low Level) dep																													
Anderston Cross																													
Stobcross																													
Kelvin Bridge																													
Partick (Central)																													
Partick (West)																													
Crow Road																													
Jordanhill																													
Whiteinch .... dep																													
Scotstoun (West)																													
Yoker for Renfrew																													
Clydebank																													
Kilbowie																													
Dalmuir																													
Old Kilpatrick																													
Bowling																													
Dumbarton East																													
Dumbarton																													
Renton																													
Alexandria																													
Balloch Station .... arr																													
Balloch Pier .... "																													

From Newton (Table 315)

L.N.E.R. Train

L.N.E.R. Train

L.N.E.R. Train

From Bothwell (Table 315)

A Station for Celtic Park.   E Except Saturdays.   S Saturdays only.

274

Table 211a — GLASGOW CITY and DISTRICT—EAST to WEST
Week Days only

HOUR (EAST to WEST)

Springburn .... dep.
Barnhill
Alexandra Parade
Duke Street
Bellgrove
Bridgeton Cross
High Street
Queen Street (Low)
Charing Cross
Hyndland
Anniesland A
Maryhill
Jordanhill
Whiteinch (Via Park) arr.
Scotstounhill
Yoker
Clydebank (East) ...... arr.

HOUR

Clydebank (East) ...... dep.
Yoker
Scotstounhill
Whiteinch Via Park dep.
Jordanhill
Maryhill
Anniesland A
Hyndland
Partick, for Govan
Charing Cross
Queen Street (Low) { arr.
High Street
Bridgeton Cross ...... arr.
Bellgrove
Duke Street
Alexandra Parade
Barnhill
Springburn

A Station for Knightswood
B From Airdrie (South) daily and Saturdays
Bathgate (Upper) on Saturdays (Table 204)
C From Shettleston (Table 204)
D To Shettleston (Table 207)
† Departure time

E or F Except Saturdays
F From Airdrie (South) (Table 204)
G From Hamilton (Table 207)
H To and from Milngavie (Table 211)
J From Lenzietown (Table 206)
K To and from Kilsyth (Table 210)
L To Singer (Table 213)

M To Edinburgh (W.) (Table 304)
N To Balloch (Table 213)
O To Hamilton on Sats. (Table 207)
P From Shettleston (Table 207)
R Saturdays only
T To Shettleston (Hamilton on Sats) (Table 207)

U To Hamilton (Table 207)
V To and from Blackville (Table 208)
W From Balloch (Table 213)
X Third class only
Y To Airdrie (South) (Table 204)
Z Arr. 3.50 p.m.

For **OTHER TRAINS** between Bellgrove and Hyndland, see Tables 204 and 207—Bridgeton Cross and Anniesland, Tables 211 and 213—
Bridgeton Cross and Maryhill, Table 210—Bridgeton Cross and Clydebank, Table 213.

Where the MINUTES under the Hour change to a LOWER figure and DARKER type it indicates the NEXT HOUR increasing popularity of travelling to destinations abroad, has resulted in a situation where these resorts are not nearly as appealing and popular as they once were.

My parents would usually stop work about midday on Fair Friday; from then on in it was a case of looking forward to the Saturday morning when we would board the train to take us to our destination. Most years we went to Aberdeen which meant that it would be to either Queen Street Station or Buchanan Street Station we would go, as both of those stations served passengers bound for the north and the east of Scotland. Another popular haunt of ours was Saltcoats on the Ayrshire coast, and to get there it would be the old St Enoch Station we would go to, as it served the south and the west.

The main railway station in Glasgow was of course, and still is, the Central Station, which also served the south and the west and continues to do so to this day. I cannot recall though, ever being in the Central when we were going off on our holidays to Saltcoats; it was always St Enoch. I recall that, as a boy, I was always fascinated by this seemingly huge place so full of people. Perhaps I took after my father in this respect, as he was a great one for looking at where trains were going and all that sort of stuff. He always used to point out the London trains to me and I would be fascinated, as London to me, at the time, was in another world so far away – as it seemed to a boy of my age. Yes, my father and I thought alike - were we original trainspotters, I wonder?

At that time, my father worked with British Rail, so it meant that we got a set number of free

Inside St Enoch Station in August 1936. Above the newsagent the destination boards show trains to Saltcoats and Ardrossan, places I visited with my parents in the mid to late 1950s for day trips or for the Glasgow 'Fair Fortnight' Holiday. A tram from Dalmarnock Road took us to the station.

or reduced price passes to holiday destinations each year. This came in handy and meant that some years we would perhaps go away to say, Aberdeen for a week and then spend the second week of the Fair going a day 'here and there' as they used to call it. So we would have day trips to the likes of Saltcoats, Largs or Portobello on the East Coast. The trip to Portobello was one I remember fondly. We used to change at Edinburgh Waverley, and if St Enoch was to me a huge and bustling place, it was nothing to what 'Waverley' had to offer. I remember being fascinated by the size of the place.

Aberdeen was always my favourite holiday spot, though we sometimes also went to places like Arbroath and Montrose, both smaller but equally friendly and welcoming. I always did like the people of the north–eastern parts of Scotland and we always seemed to get good landladies to stay with for our holiday. I think we stayed with a Mrs Munn in Aberdeen a few times, in a street just off a main road near Pittordrie, the home of Aberdeen football club. When we went to Arbroath, it was a Mrs Cargill we boarded with. This family had a son who later played for Arbroath football club.

In those days, it took about five hours or so to get to Aberdeen from Glasgow, so, when we were bound for the Northeast, it was always an early rise. We would probably leave Glasgow about eight o'clock or so and get into Aberdeen between noon and one o'clock. My mother, being the well-organised person that she always was, would have had everything ready the previous evening so that there would be no last minute panic on the big day as it were. That said, I seem to recall that we were always in a bit of a hurry lest we miss the train. I would have usually had a sleepless night, with all the excitement of going to a 'far away' place. We would get the tram at the stop just past Playfair Street and that would take us into the city centre and to St Enoch Station. I recall once or twice though, that we got the train at Springburn, at Cowlairs where my father worked. Why this was I cannot remember for sure, but I can remember us getting off the tram at Glasgow Cross and then getting the number 37 bus up to Springburn.

On these occasions we would not have had all that much luggage to worry about on the day. In those days, it was the done thing to send on some of your luggage to your holiday destination, transporting it by train and it would be there for you when you arrived. There was this huge hamper that we used to fill with all the necessaries for the fortnight that we would be away. I remember that on the Thursday evening of the week that we were going on holiday, I would help my parents pack this hamper with clothes and other things for our holiday. Then we would cart this across the road to Dalmarnock Station at Swanston Street, for it to be transported to Aberdeen for us. It's all lightweight cases of course nowadays, but sending that hamper on in advance of us, I think would make the journey a lot easier and we would most probably have only one other case with us when we were travelling. It was there for us when we got to our destination too. I cannot ever recall it being delayed or worse still, lost in transit.

At that time the diesel trains were beginning to take over from the old steam engines which had for so long dominated the railway scene. I remember that I always looked forward to going on one of these new trains. It was a bit of a novelty really, after being used to the old trains with their smoke belching out and some rather uncomfortable aspects - like the seats in them being a bit hard. At that time, I think there were still three 'classes' of travel, first, second and third, though I cannot recall every actually seeing third class accommodation. The new diesel trains were a lot more comfortable and I thought that at times, it seemed more like being on a bus than on a train. On the old trains, when sitting at the window, I always seemed to jump when a train swooshed past in the other direction. Somehow that didn't seem so much of a problem on the new trains.

Looking back at travelling on the trains in those days, it seems incredible when you think that not all of the old trains had toilet facilities. It was only when the new diesel trains came on the scene that most trains had corridors and you could walk along to the toilet. On the old trains it was often rows of compartments. I remember that one time when we were in Aberdeen, my Uncle Bobby and Aunt Mary had come up for the second week of our holiday there. On the Saturday that we were going home, my father and my uncle had a few drinks in a pub before the train left. I remember that, when the train pulled into Forfar on the way home, my father and my uncle both had to leave the train and visit the station toilet. It turned out a bit of a panic, as I seem to recall - the two of them only made it back to the train as it was starting to take off, with the rest of us wondering if they were going to be left on the platform. I can remember this incident quite clearly, but when you consider all the things that are provided on trains in the present day, it seems almost beyond comprehension, that some trains at that time were short of the most basic conveniences.

I always dreaded the journey back from Aberdeen as it took so long. It seemed to take even longer than the journey in the opposite direction and perhaps it did. Maybe though, it was just that when I was on the way up to Aberdeen, the thought of the long travelling time was not so much of a bother as we were heading off for a week or a fortnight of fun. When we were coming back, we would leave Aberdeen in the late afternoon usually and arrive back home about nine or ten o'clock at night.

As I got a bit older, I started going my holidays with my school friend Jim Connor. We would go to places like Leven in Fife, Whitley Bay in the North–east of England and Aberdeen. The year that we went to Whitley Bay, my parents had come with us, and sometimes Jim's parents and my mother and father would all go along with us for the day, to places like Ayr and Largs.

I always enjoyed these trips to the seaside. I was never one for splashing about in the water though - I was really more a bucket and spade boy. I would happily play for ages making sandcastles and the like. There was always a carnival of some sorts too and my parents always took me round the fairground. We would usually also have a good old fish supper so in some ways, it was just like home really but a bit 'special' just the same.

The resorts were very busy in those days, the beach areas in particular being very crowded. The trains taking the holidaymakers to the seaside were always packed. It is often said, and with good reason, that good manners and concern for others have declined over at least the past few decades. I remember though, as a boy, standing on the platform at Saltcoats station with my parents, waiting to board a train to Glasgow. We had been down there for the day and there was a big crowd on the platform. I will always remember this tall man blatantly shoving both men and women out of his way so that he could be sure of getting on the train. It was supposed to be the last train for the day and everybody was in a bit of a panic. British Rail must have put some 'specials' on though, as although we didn't get on that train as I recall we did get home all right.

It is a shame really that the good old-fashioned holiday by the seaside was to be eclipsed only a few years later by the beginnings of the cheap holidays on the continent. 'Fair Friday' would never be the same again.

26

The East End: Bits and Pieces.

The area where we lived has always had a reputation for being one where there were street-corner gangs and where factions battled over territory and over religious differences. These gangs had been very much part of the scene from at least as far back as the 1920s and the Bridgeton and Dalmarnock areas were, in that respect, no different from many other areas of Glasgow. Particular gangs gradually became associated with different areas of the city, usually taking their name from a street or place in the district in which they operated.

Perhaps as a child in the 1950s, I led a relatively sheltered life, because I can honestly say that I never experienced any incident that could be realistically referred to as a full-scale gang fight. I did of course, see groups of boys fighting or two individual boys engaged in a scrap as it might be called, but at no time did I ever witness groups of people engaged in gang warfare with weapons. I have read that a lot of the gang fights in past decades took place in the wide open spaces of Glasgow Green, so perhaps this had something to do with the apparent absence of any action in the immediate area. However, I think that perhaps the era in which I grew up witnessed much less in the way of gang fights, than had perhaps been the case some twenty or twenty-five years previous to that time. So perhaps that had something to do with it as well.

All in all really, I remember the area as a fairly

quiet and peaceful place. At the weekends you would hear drunks late at night but nothing that would alarm us at all. The area was one where people lived their lives free from a lot of the troubles that plague families and individuals in all areas of the country in the present day.

Although the area has never been one of affluence, I can recall that you seldom saw anyone who was homeless. The only exception to this that I remember was one morning during my summer holidays from school. I was looking out onto Dalmarnock Road and I saw this man passing by Taylor Brother's shop on the other side of the road. He was obviously down on his luck and carried a large sack over his shoulder. My mother was at the window at the time and I remember her saying 'poor soul' on seeing the man. I remember also, that she impressed on me that you should never judge someone by his or her appearance and by the outward signs of their circumstances. That is something that I have always remembered and something that I have tried to adhere to throughout the course of my life so far.

The area, like all areas, had its share of 'characters.' I have already mentioned Danny, in the swingpark in Baltic Street. Just around the corner from here, there was this wee guy who used to hang around Kinnear Road. He was, I think, middle aged and used to come up and smile at all the children going to school and sometimes talk to them. He was harmless but in the less innocent present day he would be 'suspect' as it were.

Then there was this old guy; at least he looked old anyway. He always hung about the Gallowgate and wore an old fawn coat. When someone approached him, he would put his fists up in boxer's pose as if he wanted to fight. I think that he had been a boxer at one time and had fallen on hard times, perhaps living in one of the local 'model lodging houses.' A shame really, but as children he was a source of amusement to us when we used to sometimes see him on our way to Whitevale swimming baths on Monday afternoons. One Monday afternoon, we had just reached the top of Fielden Street and about to turn into the Gallowgate, when the old guy appeared and as usual 'squared up.' One of the boys in our class I recall took the bait and made as if to square up to the old guy, jokingly.

About five years later, having by that time started work with Ferguson and Rippin down at Glasgow Cross, I heard that the old guy had died. It's only of course, as you get older that you understand why people sometimes behave as they do and this old chap most probably had a tragic life.

One other particular thing I remember from that time was when I was still at primary school and I went round one evening to Petrie's fish and chip shop in Nuneaton Street for something for our supper, probably sixpence worth (a bag of chips). On the street I saw a tall, dark man with what looked to me like a bandage covering his head. On returning home with the 'goodies' from Petrie's, I happened to tell my mother about this and she informed me that the man was an Indian, a Sikh as I would later learn, whom she too had seen in the street a few times. It was the first time that I had seen anyone who was somehow 'different' from other people and of course I was asking my mother all sorts of questions about this man and why he had to wear that cloth thing over his head. At that time of course, it was very unusual to see anyone of foreign appearance in the area. It was only within the next decade or so that larger numbers of immigrants started to make their appearance in various areas of the city.

The area at that time was also one of great bustle and activity, as I referred to in one of the opening chapters of this book. There was always, it seemed, something going on; from the Orange Walk parades which left from the small Orange Hall in Mordaunt Street on Saturday mornings during the summer months, to the 'back court musicians.' The latter would go round the tenement blocks and play music and sing in the backcourts, hoping to get coppers thrown from the windows. I think though, by the early sixties, that these 'entertainers' were a dying breed and largely a bit of a 'leftover' from previous decades. I don't really remember many of these people coming round our backcourt, but I do remember a couple, getting on in years, who used to come around just about every week. The man was small and always wore a long coat, or so it seemed. The woman was slightly taller, and always wore the same fur coat, which by the looks of it had seen better days. They would play an accordion or mouth organ, (there were quite a few who played the mouth organ who were 'regulars'), perhaps sing a song or two, collect their coppers and then move on to the next backcourt where they would go through a repeat performance. They were well known characters in the area. All of these people appeared to live a sort of nomadic, gypsy-like existence.

As I say, the Orange Hall round in Mordaunt Street was where the local Orange members left from to go on their big parades. When these were held, you did not need a wake-up call, as on Saturday mornings, at the height of the marching season, they would be making an early start and many a time in those days I woke up to the sound of flutes and accordions. It was always an impressive sight the Orange Parade, and, as I have earlier stated, since we were a mixed family, none of us had any problems whatsoever with the parade. It was very much part of the local scene and something you grew up with.

Another thing that I recall from those days was the back–street bookie. It was September 1960 before the practice of betting on horses, greyhounds' etc. ceased to be against the law, although betting shops were not allowed to open until May 1961. A bill had been introduced into Parliament to legalise betting as early as March 1956, so it took four and a half years to become law. Prior to legalisation, the bookmakers had to operate discreetly from street corners, or more usually around the backcourts of tenement buildings. I think that by the time of the mid 1950s though, up until the practice ceased to become unlawful just a few years later, that perhaps the authorities did not use the full weight of the law against the bookies. Perhaps anyway not to the same extent that they may have done ten or twenty years earlier. Certainly, from previous research, I recall that the local newspapers of the 1920s and 1930s seemed to contain many reports of 'back streets' being caught and prosecuted.

My mother and my father always liked a 'punt' on the horses - nothing big mind you, just 'a few shillings each way.' I think that my granny liked a wee flutter on the horses too. I remember when I was very young, perhaps not even ten, going with my parents round to this back street bookie. We went up this close in Avenue Street, just around the corner from Kirkpatrick Street, and I remember my father talking to this thin little man with a bonnet over his head and handing over slips of paper and money. The area around the backcourt was, as I remember, very busy with people coming and going all the time. At that age I had, of course, little idea of what all this was about. I can still recall the name of the small man though who was the centre of attention in all of this. His name was Jimmy McKay and I can still, if somewhat vaguely, picture him to this day all these years later.

I think that I was there with my parents quite a few times and it would most probably be during visits to my granny's at weekends with both my parents, as the bookie's stance was less than five minute's walk from where my granny lived.

The tradition of the back street bookie was one of those things, which of course, is no longer part of everyday life in the present day, but is recalled as something remembered from a far-off time.

The backcourt in those days was, all things considered, a place where so much 'action' took place. As well as children playing all sorts of games in the backcourt, myself included, and the 'entertainers' and bookies, all of which I have already referred to, there were others such as the coal-merchants who would come round the backcourt and announce their arrival, hoping to all and sundry. Most memorable, in this regard, were the men who came round with a cart full of coal-brickets. These were brick shaped chunks of coal and were a popular type of fuel for many decades in the days before the introduction of electricity, when the good old coal fire was very much the norm.

As I remember it, the coal–brickets were sometimes transported in a horse–drawn cart but I think that this was the very last days of the horse and cart, as it was being replaced by motorised transport. I remember that our coal deliveries were by lorry.

When the man, sometimes with a boy helper, drew up outside the tenements, he would go round to the backcourt and the cry "coal breek- ets" would be heard all around the area.

On really cold winter days and if you were 'low' on coal etc. that cry would be the most welcome thing you could hear, sitting in a freezing cold house.

The old coal fires of course, are legendary, but it wasn't always 'plain sailing' in trying to get a fire started in the 'grate' of the fireplace. Sometimes the coal would not be of a good standard and you had to rely on adding old wood and 'sticks' and sometimes paper too, to get a decent fire going. I recall more than a few instances of this at 'number 337' on cold winter evenings.

Another thing that I remember in the area at the time was the ragstores. These were places where you would deposit all your old and unwanted clothes and you would receive a small amount of money in return. I remember that on occasion my mother would ask me to take a sackful of old clothes up to one of the rag-stores (or rag-merchants to give them their 'proper' name) in the area. As I recall, there was one of these places - Longmuir's in Mordaunt Street - at numbers 88 to 94, just past the junction with Baltic Street - on the same side of the street as the Orange Halls at number 36 and Connell's soft drinks depot at 44. This rag store is the one that I recall going to most often. There was another rag store on the other side of the road, roughly between Dale and Muslin Streets - James Collins's this was named. I think that I went down to this one on a few occasions too. I have a vague recollection of there being another one of these places just past Mordaunt Street and in Dalmarnock Road itself. It would have been near McDonald's furniture shop at number 353.

I don't remember much about the inside of these places, though I recall that the inside of one of them, the one just along from us I think, was like a long narrow passage. When you entered the rag-stores, the people there would take your bag from you and place it on a large scale. The amount in money that you would receive for the rags would be according to how much the bundle of rags weighed. The visits to the rag-stores were something that I did not mind; in fact I most probably quite looked forward to them, as it would mean a bit of extra pocket money for me at the weekend. As I recollect, it was usually always a Friday that I would take the sackful of rags down to be weighed.

Another welcome source of 'extra money' (if on a limited scale) was when the gas and electricity meters were emptied. In those days someone would be employed to collect the money from the meters and a man would come round every three months or so and empty all the shillings etc. that had been put through the slot in the machine since the last time the meter had been emptied. If you had paid in too much you got some back. Sometimes it was a huge pile of coins while at other times it would be 'a few coppers' only. It was though always a sign that I would get extra pocket money that week. The 'meter man' therefore was always a welcome sight to me.

Yet another 'haunt' of mine at that time was the Dalmarnock Tram Depot – with space for many trams inside – in Ruby Street, just off Dalmarnock Road. As a boy, I would go down here, sometimes on my own and sometimes with my pals, just to gaze at the 'spectacle' of the trams going in and out of the depot and perhaps jotting down their numbers in the passing. I remember being fascinated by the destination boards of the trams with such places as Yoker, Dalmuir West and Springburn, to name only a few, being displayed on the front of the trams. I think that if you spent too long hanging around near the entrances of the depot, someone would come out and 'ask' you to move on. This never deterred me though; it was a sort of adventure really, like many others that I remember from the time. It was also an enjoyable way of simply passing the time. I think that there were about three or four of these large doors through which the trams passed on their way in and out of the depot.

Dalmarnock Depot was damaged in a major fire in the early hours of March 22 1961. More than fifty tramcars in the depot at the time were completely destroyed in the blaze. The 'Daily Record' report of the fire, states that the blaze was at its height at 1am and that some people around Ruby Street, Dalmarnock Road and Hozier Street fled their homes in fear.

About half way between 'number 337' and the junction with Springfield Road, at 503 Dalmarnock Road, there was Pat's Pet shop. It was here that I used to go every time we added a new goldfish to our 'collection.' I think we had about a dozen or so at one time and as a boy I used to enjoy just sitting watching these little things swimming around in the bowl.

We also had a cat called 'Tiger' and we had to keep an eye on the fish every time he went near the bowl in case he fancied a quick snack. Thankfully though, I cannot remember it ever coming to that eventuality. Besides, we always provided 'Tiger' with the best of food. 'Tiger' was a handful. We didn't let him out much, only down the stairs and into the close-mouth, in case he went out on to the very busy main road and got hit by a tram or something. Of course the close was never far enough for him and many a time I had to dash out on to Dalmarnock Road to grab him, fearful for his safety. 'Tiger' lived till the year before we left the area; my father had brought him home from work one evening in 1952, when I would only be about five. I can still remember though, my father coming into the room and carrying this lovely wee kitten. He gave us many years of pleasure and we were all sad when we had him put down at the veterinary surgeons' in London Road, just past Heron Street, in 1965. Every year at the Fair Holidays he was put into a cat and dog home to be cared for until we returned from holiday. That particular year, for some reason, we could not get him put into the home we usually used; the one we eventually did use did not look after him properly. He was like a skeleton when we got him back.

Just up a bit from Pat's Pet Shop at the junction with Springfield Road, was where the early editions of the morning papers, the 'Daily Record' and the 'Daily Express', were sold. I often would go up here for the papers, as I got a bit older. At that time, I think it was still considered to be something of a novelty to get the papers the night before. I would usually go up here around ten o'clock and the papers would usually arrive by van about ten fifteen or so. Sometimes though, they would be late and by that time there would be a sizeable crowd waiting. As is usual in situations like that, the paper vendor would hardly have the time to get the papers into his grasp and to sort them out, before he was surrounded by the crowd, all of whom were wanting to be served first. There was also a paper 'stance' down at Bridgeton Cross, at the umbrella. I don't know whether or not they still sell the early papers at the Cross but the area at Dalmarnock Road/Springfield Road where I usually went is almost unrecognisable from what it was some forty years ago.

Something 'completely different' that I recall, was when the 'cossy men' were in the area. This was the name that I remember my parents giving to these workers who used to dig up the roads at night and use automatic drills on the road. I am not entirely sure how or why they got this name;

it may have been something to do with the work process they used. I remember them well, for all the wrong reasons. They would wake you up in the early hours of the morning with their working out on the main Dalmarnock Road. Did I ever get back to sleep? No chance! I think that they would be in the one place for one or two nights before moving on, either up or down the road from where, of course, you could still hear them, if somewhat less pronounced. Needless to say, their arrival was always dreaded. The 'cossy men' were the talk of the steamie (and a few other places too), for days. It is another one of those things that all these years later, you just cannot imagine having ever been, unless of course you had direct experience of it, as I and many others too had. It is something of course, that would never be allowed in the present day - keeping people off their sleep would be deemed totally unacceptable, rightly so too.

There always seemed to be something getting done to the roads in those days. If it wasn't the automatic drills, which I used to dread as they made such a noise, it was the Tar Macadam machines tarring the roads on a regular basis. You always knew it was a warm summer if you saw the tar on the roads melting in the sun. I seem to recall that it did so on a regular basis too.

In those days, as I have said, the area was heavily industrialised. This added significantly I think, to the problem of 'smog', which was a feature of Glasgow (and other big cities too) until about the later half of the 1960s. Smog was a combination of natural mist or fog and the 'output' of thousands of rooftop chimneys belching out their smoke and grime, in an era when, in most households, the old coal fire was still very much the norm. Add the smoke from the factories and you had all the ingredients for one of the famous 'pea-soupers' as they were called.

As I remember, November seemed usually to be the worst month for this phenomena and sometimes looking out into Dalmarnock Road, you could hardly see across the street. This was especially true at the time of the old fashioned streetlights, before the yellowish glow from the lights became universal as it were. It could be very bad though during the day too. I remember one time. I think it was in the very early part of the 1960s. I came out of 'number 337' and on to Dalmarnock Road when the smog was really bad. It was so dense and extensive in fact, that it was just like night time at one o'clock in the afternoon. The sky was pure black. I have never forgotten that as I had never seen it before that day and I never ever saw it again afterwards. It's all change nowadays of course. The old factories have all gone and more importantly, almost everyone today uses an electric or gas fire. The old coal fires (sadly in some ways) have long since glowed their last.

On a really foggy evening, even "Dixon's Blazes" nightly display was rendered invisible. "Dixon's Blazes" was the term that described the flashing of coloured lights in the southern night sky. The lights emanated from William Dixon's Iron Works, which were based in the old Gorbals area of the city on the South-Side. I remember as a small boy, seeing these lights for the first time in Dalmarnock Road. Perhaps somehow thinking it was some visitors from another planet, I asked my mother what these were. It was still a feature into the 1960s, perhaps even the early part of the 1970s too, until the old Gorbals was largely redeveloped and as well as the old tenements, many of the old factories etc. in the area also disappeared.

Living in the tenements in those days, another regular 'feature' of life was the appearance of the 'lamplighter', as I think he was called. This was the man who came around every evening and went into the closes to light the place up. I cannot remember when the old gas lighting in the closes and on the landings was phased out - I think that it may have been sometime in the mid 1950s but I do remember seeing this 'lamplighter' coming along on his nightly rounds. When the electric lighting was introduced, the job became a lot easier, as all the man had to do was to switch on all the lights from a box that was installed on a wall in the closemouth. In the summer evenings of course, the man would come around a lot later, say between nine and ten o'clock, while in the dead of winter, it would be around four o'clock.

Nowadays, this practice is nothing more than a distant memory to myself and the many that lived through the era when the 'lamplighter' was a familiar sight in the old tenements. In the present day, everything is done automatically, remote control as it were. That's progress for you! Or is it? I seem to recall that you could always depend on 'Wee Jimmy' or whatever his name might be, coming to light the place up in those days, whereas in the present day, I have often seen closes and landings in the modern flats in complete darkness on winter nights.

I seem to remember that in those days, there were always policemen to be seen on the streets. That era was a lot more crime-free than is the case in the present day, but at the time the 'bobby on the beat,' the old 'George Dixon' image, was still very much to the fore. I remember too, that the police used to wear the old fashioned helmet, which was by that time I think, fast becoming a relic from a bygone era. I was brought up to respect the police and I think that a lot of your opinions and attitudes to authority are formed at an early age.

27

Becoming a teenager.

It was probably in my final year at school that I started hanging around the various cafés in the area with my pals. At that time there were plenty of these in the East–End and you could spend hours just sitting with a bottle of Coca-Cola. It seemed to be the done thing at the time, or, as the younger generation might say these days, that it was 'cool.' At that time of course, the juke box in the café was the 'in' thing, as great changes were taking place in the world of popular music with the advent of rock and roll.

There was this café in Springfield Road, Pelosi's I think it was called. It was the first place that you came to when you turned the corner from Dalmarnock Road, on the left-hand side of the road. It was this particular café that I went to most often at that time. In the wintertime, when it was starting to get dark when you came out of school for the day, it was really the best place to be, as you couldn't play football at that time of year.

I remember sitting in that café and playing and listening to the big hits of the day. Records such as *Runaway* by the late Del Shannon, *Apache* by the Shadows and *The Young Ones* by that great survivor of pop music, Cliff Richard are a few from that era that spring to mind. There were many others of course. Anything at all by the late and truly great Billy Fury would be played over and over again by me, as although Elvis Presley has been my all-time favourite performer, I think that perhaps he may have taken second place then. At that time, I think Billy Fury was my number one as it were and probably the idol of my early teenage years. What a voice he had. I could have listened to him all day and it's always a treat to put on a tape of his greatest hits in the present day. I even had my hair styled in a wave after the way he had his own hair groomed. I kept it that way for a few years. This was at a time just before long hair began to become popular - from about the mid-1960s, with a lot of the new 'pop' groups of the time sporting long hair and, especially from the late 1960s beards too. The looks and the styles of the late 1950s and the early part of the 1960s soon became like much else of the period, as is the way with things, things of the past.

Looking back on that period, I would have stayed in that café all day if time had permitted. I simply loved the music of the period. Every time I hear a song or tune from the early 1960s especially, it fills me with nostalgia. Those really were the days, as they say in the passing. You could spend hours really, just sitting with a bottle of Coca-Cola or whatever and listening to the sounds of your favourites of the day.

There was this other café up at the other end of Springfield Road, on the other side of the street and just past the junction with London Road. This was another haunt of mine after school, although I was not in here nearly as often as the other one. I used to go into this other one with another school friend who lived in the first close in Springfield Road, past its junction with London Road. There was, I think, a juke box in here too and if my memory serves me correctly, we used to go into this café during the summer months, after playing football at Westhorn or at Tollcross. We would always be tired after kicking a ball and sometimes each other about for a few hours and it was nice to relax in here. As I remember, sometimes some of our classmates would come in during the evening and we would all sit round a table together, sipping our drinks and listening to the music on the jukebox. There are not nearly so many cafés in the area in the present day. I think that the sight of teenagers spending their time in cafés in the way that my generation did, is largely a thing of the past. Nowadays, more and more young people go to public houses and wine bars, than what was the case a few decades ago. When I think about it, who would want to sit in cafés and listen to what passes for pop music nowadays anyway?

By this time of course, my Saturday nights round at the Plaza with my mother had come to an end and I had started to go to the cinema with some of my friends from school at the weekends. Our favourite haunt was the 'Granada' in Duke Street, just down from Parkhead Cross. This became a regular thing with us for a couple of years or so. Also, when I was through visiting my friend Jim Connor in Barlanark, we would sometimes go to the 'State' cinema or the 'Odeon' that were within a few hundred yards of each other in nearby Shettleston. For many years then, the cinema was very much a big part of my Saturday night 'scene.' It was only really in the 1970s, when I started going out to pubs, that this pattern was broken. I did continue to go to the cinema at other times of the week though and I still do so to the present day.

In those days, I cannot remember ever going to the dancing. Although I liked so much of the music of the period, I just was not a fan of the dancing. There was the 'Palais' in Dennistoun, more commonly known as 'The Denny Pally' or of course 'The Barrowland' in the Gallowgate. But somehow dancing just never appealed to me at that time. It was only in the late 1960s and the 1970s that I started going to the dancing with friends, to the big halls in the city centre like 'The Locarno' as it was then called. Even then though, I was never what you might call a "regular" at dance halls or the later discos. I have always enjoyed listening to song and music but dancing to it was a different matter.

One particular thing that I remember from around this time (c.1964), was that I had taken a fancy to the girl who had started work in the offices at Ferguson and Rippin, where I was working at that time. She was about my age. Jean was her name; she came from Easterhouse. She was always very friendly to me in any dealings that I had with her at work. She was also pretty and always seemed to have a nice smile. I grew quite fond of her, if from a distance, but being quite shy in those days, I never had the courage to ask her for a date. Come to think of it, I never had the opportunity either, as her two office colleagues were never very far from the scene. A few weeks went by and I began to think of ways to surmount these problems and arrange a date for the pictures or something like that - or at least try to. Eventually, I had a 'plan of action' and I intended to put it into operation the following week.

The end of that week, when I had formed my 'plan' saw me out at my pal Jim Connor's home in Barlanark on the Saturday evening. I got off the bus at the end of Westmuir Street that Saturday evening, on my return from Barlanark and crossed the road, going towards Duke Street, near the 'Granada' cinema where I would get a number 58 bus down to Springfield Road and home. I was just approaching the corner with Duke Street and the crowds were coming out of the 'Granada.' Suddenly I saw a familiar face in the throng. It was the 'girl of my dreams', arm in arm with a young man, on their way to the Easterhouse bus stop in Westmuir Street. Talk about shattered dreams! On the 'bright' side, I thought at least now I don't have to worry about my plan to ask her for a date failing.

A few months later, I went into work one Monday morning, I think it was April 1965. I was taking the orders from the office staff for the tea break - the rolls with bacon etc, purchased from the dairy in nearby James Morrison Street. I did not see the office girl, Jean, and asked if she was off sick or whatever. I was told that she had left on the Friday of the previous week. I think my face must have spoken volumes on me hearing this news. Life at Ferguson and Rippin would never be the same again. Not so of course, but it did seem like that at the time.

It's funny when you look back on these years. I remember getting my first pair of 'jeans' or denims as they were sometimes called sometime in the later 1950s. It was a kind of 'big deal' at that time to get your first pair of long trousers, after years of wearing short ones. Nowadays you rarely see boys wearing short trousers at all.

Then, when I was in my later teens, the pointed shoes, or winkle-pickers as they were called, became all the rage and it seemed just about everyone was wearing them. When I got my first pair of these shoes, I thought they looked great and couldn't wait to get out and about with them on. I felt really good with them on. Nowadays when I recall them, I wonder how on earth we ever got our feet into them in the first place - so narrow did they seem.

Looking back, it seemed no time at all really, since, as a small boy, I would go out with my mother to the clothes shops and get new clothes selected for me. Then, only (what seemed) a few years later, here I was 'on my own can' and fast becoming an adult.

28

Mum and Dad.

Both my parents grew up in the East End although my father was born on the south side of Glasgow. They were also born in the same year, 1906. My mother was born in Bridgeton, at 7 John Street Lane (which in the late 1920s became part of Landressy Street), on June 12 of that year and lived in the Bridgeton area until the mid-1930s.

My father was born on September 20 at 24 South Wellington Street. This was on the south side of Glasgow, in the Gorbals area. The street was renamed Lawmoor Street in the late 1920s. I am unsure at what point he moved to Bridgeton but he attended St Anne's school in Crownpoint Road, Bridgeton. This rebuilt school in the present day, is situated in nearby David Street.

He would have originally been raised, I think, at 850 London Road, where my grandmother continued to live until her death in 1969. From 1929 to 1939 he lived at 962 London Road, at a building I am told was referred to locally as the 'hairy ham close' and which would have been between Boden Street and Nuneaton Street. There being no electoral registers during the Second World War I am unsure at what point he returned to number 850 but he is listed there in 1945 and by 1946 he is of course listed at number 337 Dalmarnock Road, having by that time married my mother.

My mother and father were married on 21 September 1945, on the day after his thirty-ninth birthday, in Saint Francis in the East Church in Queen Mary Street, just around the corner from where my father lived at the time. I arrived on the scene two years later.

My mother had been married previously; to someone she had met called David Brownlie (or Brownlee) who at the time lived at 21 Washington Street, Anderston. This was directly across the road from 584 Argyle Street, to where my mother had moved from Bridgeton some time in the late 1930s - just along from Anderston Cross. They were married at Saint Martin's Church in Anderston on 1 September 1939. This was the day that the first shots of World War 2 were fired in Europe. She went to live at 584 Argyle Street, which would be just about where, at the corner of North Street, the Marriott Hotel stands in the present day. David Brownlie was I think an industrial chemist or similar and worked somewhere on the South-Side of Glasgow. He died in February 1941 as a result of an explosion at the plant where he was based. He would have been in his early forties at the time. The explosion was not, as far as I have been able to ascertain, related to the Luftwaffe air raids of the period. Rather it was a tragic accident.

My mother continued to live in the Anderston area until 1944 or 1945. At that time, rows of tenement buildings occupied the spot and stretched all the way into the city centre. The massive redevelopment of this area in the late 1960s swept away all the old tenement buildings and the area is much changed today with motorways, bridges and all sorts of modern urban characteristics dominating the scene. So

A photograph of my mother taken in the State Studios at 581 London Road on June 5 1935 just before her twenty-ninth birthday.

much so, that the old Anderston Cross is almost entirely unrecognisable from how I remember it when I was a boy and when in the summer my mother, grandmother and myself would occasionally walk all the way up to this area for a wee change of scene. This area must have held a lot of memories for my mother.

She moved back to the East End and to number 337 Dalmarnock Road. At this time my father was still living at London Road. They met through being introduced by friends, got married and lived at 'number 337' for over twenty years.

My father had worked in labouring jobs for most of his working life. At one time he had worked with the British Oxygen Company in Polmadie Road on the South Side of Glasgow. Since as far back as I could recall, though, he had worked as a labourer with British Rail in the Cowlairs Depot at Springburn. Springburn at that time was one of the most heavily industrialised areas in the whole of Glasgow. My father took redundancy from the railways in 1963 and got a job with The Sunbeam Electric Company in Nerston Industrial Estate, in East Kilbride. In those days, if you had regular employment in the 'new towns', you had a better chance of being allocated a house there and so it proved in our case, as we left the East End in April 1966. My father worked with Sunbeam until about 1968, when he took early retirement.

My mother stopped working in her trade as a bookbinder after I was born, to care for me, while my father continued to work with British Rail. As I got older, my mother took part time cleaning jobs and it was in this line of work that she stayed, until she retired in the late 1960s.

This is a block of flats at 568-588 Argyle Street, Anderston. My mother lived at number 584, on the left of the photo, during the years of The Second World War prior to her return to Bridgeton. The photo is from 1959 about a decade before this whole area became almost unrecognisable from former times, owing to massive redevelopment. Where these buildings were, the present

For quite a few years my mother had worked with Lander Burglar Alarms, a company that was based at numbers 6-10 Playfair Street. You could see the premises from the window of our room, which looked out on to Dalmarnock Road. I have many memories of when I was very young, sitting at the window watching for my mother coming out of the front door of Lander's, which was a small firm where everybody knew each other. Next door at number 4 was Wainstain's, a shoe repairs shop or cobblers, as they were more commonly referred to in those days. Later on, my mother worked in offices in the city centre, mainly in the mornings. She worked with a company named Begg, Kennedy and Elder, who were based in Cadogan Street, and later with a firm in Mitchell Street. It was here that she was working when she retired.

We were a close family, the three of us, particularly with me being the only child. I recall things from the earlier part of my childhood such as my mother always taking care of any cuts and bruises I had from being out playing in the backcourts or in the parks. The 'magic' Elastoplast always seemed to do the trick somehow in these situations. When I had a cold, it would be a hot orange or lemon drink she would make me and perhaps as I got older, a 'hot toddy'. My mother was a very patient and naturally caring person in these situations.

My mother was always the patient one of the three of us. When something in the house broke down, the likes of a small matter like a fuse needing fixed, it was always my mother who had the patience to sit down and mend the thing. It

Bridgeton Library, in 1907, although it hasn't changed much. Reminiscence sessions, at which I collected some peoples' memories of the area were held in the hall above the Library during February and March 2000.

was the same when the old wireless went 'on the blink', or even when occasionally my cherished record player wouldn't work. My mother would always take the time to get to the root of the problem. My mother was a very practical person in every way.

My mother was a great cook. I have fond memories of Sunday dinner especially when it would be soup, (usually lovely home-made broth for the first course), followed by stew, potatoes and peas (or some variation on that). The 'sweet' or dessert would usually be tinned pears, peaches or my favourite weekend treat, mandarin oranges.

Then there was the 'clootie dumplings' one of her 'specialities' which she would make every so often as a special treat for my father and I. What I particularly remember about this was that it always seemed to take ages to make. I would see my mother putting this large bundle in a pan with a cloth over it. She would always tell me to be patient and that it took so long to cook because it had to be done properly. Wise words, but words that were always 'lost' on me, as all I was thinking about was the lovely taste of the finished product. Yes, dumpling as cooked by my mother was always one of my real favourites and what a priceless memory all these years later.

My father always gave the impression that things did not bother him to any great extent. He had a sort of 'inevitability' mentality as it were. 'Whatever will be will be'. He also believed that everything could be done an easy way. "It's as simple as that" was his favourite saying. My mother on the other hand, always showed great concern over everyday things and showed her feelings I think, more than my father did.

St Francis's In The East Parish Church, in Queen Mary Street, off London Road, where my parents were married on 21 September 1945. The photograph dates from the 1980s; the building survives today.

My mother, like most women, was very house-proud. I have already mentioned how every thing had to be 'just right' at New Year time. Well, throughout the year, it was much the same thing. My mother was always busy doing one thing or another about the house. The carpets would be hoovered on a regular basis, the windows cleaned and the furniture polished to a fine art. My mother never ever complained about housework. At times, in fact, she seemed to thrive on it. Often, when I was very young, I would hear her singing to herself in the middle of the chores. Songs like *You Are My Sunshine* spring to mind in this regard. I have to admit that I was never much help in these respects around the house when I got older.

I think that my one saving grace was that I was always keen to go the messages and to help out in that respect. My mother was always a great believer in paying bills on time. I think that in that era most people were like this. The house rent was something that was given priority. On quite a number of occasions, I went with my mother up to the house factors Danskin and Fletcher in Springfield Road, just down from Parkhead Cross, to pay the rent. We would get the old number 30 tramcar up Springfield Road and on returning, would wait at the tramcar stop just along from the factors offices, to get the tram for the return journey. The premises of Danskin and Fletcher have relatively recently been converted into a laundrette, changed times indeed. I would sometimes accompany my mother out to pay the gas bill in George Square, where the office of the Gas Board was at that time. I remember

John Street (renamed Tullis Street from 1926), from Greenhead Street in 1906. My mother was born at 7 John Street Lane (which became Landressy Street from 1928), on the far left opposite John Street School.

that this was an occasion akin to a 'day out' for a small boy. The same as going to the 'big shops' like Lewis's and Woolworth's 'in town.'

I also have a very distant memory of going with my mother to this place down off Dalmarnock Road. Part of the building was in Acorn Street and part of it in Megan Street. I remember that we waited for what seemed like ages, in this long, winding queue. I think that it must have been the old Health and Social Security building, which I think at that time, was situated next to the old labour exchange.

During the winter months when our favourite parks etc. were closed for the season, we would sit and play games like cards, 'Snakes and Ladders' or 'Ludo.' As for the cards, I think we must have, at one time or another played every game that it was possible to play with the full deck of 52 cards. The one I remember most, was Rummy, but there was also Pontoons, Snap, and Find the Lady - to name only a few. Sometimes, when some of my aunts and uncles came to visit us, my parents would move the table from its usual position against the wall in the small room at 'number 337' and place it over in the centre of the room. A few chairs would be placed around the table and a game of cards, sometimes lasting in total a few hours, would begin. I think that it was nearly always 'Rummy' they played and, to make it a bit more exciting, they would play for a few pence or shillings. I cannot remember ever playing in any of these games. I think that it was an 'adults only' affair. Most, but not all of the time as I remember, it was my Aunt Helen and Uncle Bill from my mother's side of our family who would come to play cards. At that time, they lived in Malcolm Street, off Springfield Road, before moving out with their young family to East Kilbride in the early 1960s.

Sometimes though, my aunts and uncles from my father's side of our family would come to play cards too - almost invariably on a Sunday. I think that in the present day, all these indoor games are seen as things of the past. However, at a time when television was just beginning to make an appearance in the living rooms of ordinary people, then pastimes like these were very much the staple diet of many households.

My father was always very accommodating when it came to sport and games. I have already mentioned the football and also our weekend visits to Glasgow Green. We would sometimes kick a tennis ball about in the house. When my mother was in the other room doing the ironing or whatever, I tried to persuade my father to line up the armchairs facing each other and we would sit down and kick the ball to each other. The base of the chairs would serve as the 'goal' but this action never lasted very long, as father would usually get fed up with it after a few minutes, saying he'd had enough and wanted to watch TV or something like that.

My father was usually a bit keener when we played table tennis. I remember buying a full table tennis set when I got a bit older, minus the table of course. We just made do with the kitchen table – with the cups and saucers removed first though. I used to really enjoy playing this game, perhaps for a brief half-hour or so imagining that I was Johnny Leach (a table tennis champion of the period) who was often involved in televised games around this time. Table tennis was a sport I watched on TV quite regularly. It was a big attraction for me for a while but after a year or two it, like a few other things, fell by the wayside, the novelty value eventually wearing off.

My father was also a great one for going on long walks, especially at weekends. I have very few, if any, recollections of my father and myself being on public transport when the two of us were out together. My father simply loved the fresh air and this love of the outdoors was something that remained with him right the way through to old age and only in the last few years of his life, did wear and tear force him to curtail his walks. I remember as a boy, we would walk all over the place. In the summer, when there was not as much football on down at Glasgow Green, we would sometimes walk all the way up to Cambuslang, through Rutherglen and back. I remember that on a few occasions, we would take an alternative route home and come down from Rutherglen, past Shawfield and over the bridge near Glasgow Green. There was (and still is) a pathway that led along the North bank of the Clyde and we would walk along this until we came to Cotton Street, then along Swanston Street and home. At that time, there was this old derelict mill in Cotton Street and one day we passed this and heard the sound of a piano playing. It was so eerie as there was no immediately obvious source of the sound and we seemed to be the only people in the immediate area at the time. Every time that we passed this mill after that, my father used to jokingly refer to it as the 'haunted mill.' We never did find out where the music came from, incidentally.

At other times we would play putting in one of the many putting greens, which were located in the East End at that time. My father was quite good at this game and as I became quite adept at it too, it was always a thrilling contest between us.

My father was a great fan of boxing as well as, of course football. I remember that he would watch any boxing match that was on television. Thursday evening in those days always seemed to be when the amateur boxing was on the TV and I remember that he was 'in his element', when this was on. He also of course, used to watch the World Heavyweight Championships of the period - Cassius Clay (or Muhammad Ali as he was then known), Henry Cooper, Sonny Liston and all that. He also had his very own variety of rhyming slang, always referring to a clock as 'the knock.'

Looking back, I think that, in those days life was very much more home centred than what it later became. Except when visiting relatives and going to the pictures, my mother and father did not go out together a lot, as far as I can remember. On special occasions though, like birthdays, they would always go out for a wee treat; perhaps a visit to the cinema or something like that. My father, like my mother, was always generous with money. In fact, I remember that he always believed in giving 'tips' to barbers etc. He was always supportive in every way to my mother and me.

My father was always more 'at home' quite literally, when watching television. My mother of course, was also a TV fan, but perhaps not as much as my father. She became a great bingo fan in the 1960s and was often out with her friends or my aunts at this. My mother continued to be a regular at the bingo halls almost right up to the year of her death. My father too, in his later years, got hooked on the bingo. Every Saturday night over a long period, my parents and a few of my aunts and uncles on my father's side of our family, would meet up at Sloan's lounge bar in the Argyle Arcade in the city centre. Then they would go on to a bingo hall in the Gorbals area.

My father, and my mother to a lesser extent, for as long as I can remember, always had a gamble on the football coupons at weekends. In all the years that my father especially, tried the coupon, I can never recall him winning any sizeable sum of money, though there were one or two minor windfalls. This relative lack of success though, was most certainly not for the want of trying, as, my father especially, filled in his coupon almost 'religiously.' When one of these minor windfalls did occur though, I was always guaranteed some extra pocket money. I have already mentioned the routine of going up for the early papers to Springfield Road. In those days, I think the early Monday morning papers were the first to give the payouts in the football pools dividends and as soon as I brought the paper home, my parents would be scanning the appropriate pages to see if they were 'in the money.' This situation of course, only came about when they had about twenty points or so from the weekend's coupon. I also have a very vague memory, of there being at that time, some sort of announcement on the wireless every Sunday evening, as to the payouts of the football pools. I think that it was on 'Radio Luxembourg' or something like that. What I do remember quite clearly is that the old wireless was always crackling when we tried to tune into this station and it was very unclear. My parents would be round the small wireless on the set of drawers near the door of the smaller of our two rooms at 'number 337' trying to get the wireless tuned into the station they wanted. Sometimes it worked ok but at other times you had to give it a subtle (or perhaps not so subtle) bash.

I have already mentioned my visits to the cinema with my parents, as well of course, as weekend outings to parks etc. and also going on holiday. There was one other outing that I always looked forward to, and as it only came around once every year, it was all the more eagerly anticipated when the time came near. I am referring to the carnival on Glasgow Green, which takes place every year in July during the Glasgow Fair Holidays. In those days, it was a lot bigger and much noisier than the greatly reduced version of the present day. I don't think that it even lasts as long nowadays.

We would usually always go along in the middle part of the evening. This was when the place was 'jumping' as they sometimes said in our part of the world. There would be things like the 'steamboats,' the 'dodgems' the 'waltzers' and much, much more. I was never one for going on things. I much preferred the stalls where you would throw balls at tin cans and try to knock them down for a small prize, or things like that.

My parents would sometimes go on the dodgems but in the main they preferred to play a few games of bingo, or 'lotto' as it was sometimes called. Alternatively, my mother especially, would play the fruit machines quite often and often get lucky too. About the only thing that I actually went on, apart from the dodgems on one occasion, was the 'ghost train.'

The carnival though, was one of those things that you didn't actually have to take part in to fully enjoy. Rather, it was the atmosphere of the occasion that I think was the main attraction. I remember that, on walking down Tullis Street from the main part of Bridgeton towards Greenhead Street, the atmosphere would start to hit you and you would hear the familiar sounds of the carnival-like the music and the sounds of children. Perhaps loudest of all though, were the screams and shrieks from those souls brave enough to go on the 'big wheel' which as well as turning you upside down and doing all sorts of other things to you, I suppose gave you the thrill of a lifetime. Never having been brave enough ever to venture on it, I wouldn't know for sure.

By the time we were heading up the path off Greenhead Street into the Green itself, I remember seeing the 'steamboats', which were always just to the right as you entered the Green from the path. Seeing the boats going up and down was the signal to me that this magical fairground was less than a minute away.

We would usually spend about a couple of hours in the fairground. As I say, in those days, there was a lot more to see and do, than what there is nowadays and it would take quite a while to go from one end of the Green to the other. Invariably we would stop off for a fish supper or some bags of chips on the way home. Then it would be all over for another year and the long wait for the next visit of 'the shows' as my mother and father called them, would begin.

During this period too, there was a mini-carnival up at Vinegarhill, off the Gallowgate, near Parkhead Cross. I have some, admittedly very vague memories, as it were, of supplementing my visits to the main 'shows' on Glasgow Green, with trips to Vinegarhill. Us kids of the late 1950s were spoiled for choice I think, as regards fairgrounds.

I was always closer to my mother than my father, but quite naturally I remember both of them with much love and affection. It is often said that the 'norm' in families is for the boy to be closer to his mother, with girls having a greater bonding with their father. If this were indeed the case, then I would say that my own family must have been very much the 'norm', but I am not sure if generalisations can be made on this, as like most things in life, it depends on many, both interrelated and variable factors. Being the only child, I suppose that I was 'spoiled' as they say, at least to an extent. It cannot be any other way when you have no brothers or sisters. I was brought up by both my parents to know what was right and what was wrong though; what you could do and what you could not do. It was not a rigid, strict upbringing though - rather it was one where certain values and respect came naturally to you. You learned by example. Throughout my life I have tried to hold to the values and principles that were instilled into me by my parents during my upbringing. For the most part anyway, I have been successful in this, though inevitably one or two have 'bitten the dust'.

29

Then and Now.

The area in the present day is vastly changed from the time about which I am writing. Quite apart from the disappearance of the vast majority of the old tenement buildings, there are other significant changes. Almost all of the old factories, mills etc. have gone. Those that have survived and that once echoed to the sound of machines are now business centres or the like. The streets that once were filled with hundreds of workers on their way to and from work are a lot quieter. The streets themselves, in fact, have changed greatly, with parts of the area almost unrecognisable from thirty or forty years ago.

All the old picture houses have either been totally demolished or are no longer in operation as cinemas. The only two that I can think of that are still standing, are the old 'Premiere' building (the 'Geggy') in Kirkpatrick Street and the building down at Bridgeton Cross which was once the very popular 'Olympia.'

The 'Geggy' building was for a while called 'Andy's Joint' – a meat warehouse I think – but seems now to have returned to its former empty and derelict state. Some of the halls, that during the years of slump in cinema audiences were converted to bingo halls, have in turn, ceased to function as bingo halls. The 'Olympia' itself is a case in point. The 'Strathclyde' or the 'Strathy' in Summerfield Street is another example. Used for many years as a bingo hall, the building was demolished. Houses now occupy the spot where it stood.

Likewise, almost all of the shops that I have referred to in my memories of childhood are no more. The shops in Dalmarnock Road on the right–hand side of the road as you go towards Bridgeton Cross, have totally disappeared, as have most of the ones mentioned on the other side of the road. The little shops in the side streets that I have referred to in, for example Nuneaton and Mordaunt Streets have also gone.

The area in and around Main Street – the haunt of my mother and I every Saturday morning – has completely changed. The only original shop, still in existence in the present day, is the premises that were once Timpson's shoe shop. This is now a general store. All of the other shops and buildings were demolished and there are many new shops there now. The area in London Road, though, just around from Bridgeton Cross where the State Studios and the City Bakeries once were, is almost unchanged and the premises that once housed these are still in existence.

It was in the later part of the 1970s that most of the shops started to disappear. As people moved out of the area in ever-increasing numbers, there would be less need for the shops. The old tenements were being pulled down from the early 1970s after being in existence for a hundred years and people were being rehoused in places like Easterhouse, Castlemilk, Drumchapel, Cumbernauld and East Kilbride. This was a process that had been ongoing for almost twenty years, accelerating during the 1970s with the vast redevelopment of the area.

At one time too, there was a public house at almost every corner. I have already mentioned that I recall taking empty beer bottles with my pals into the 'Station Bar' at the corner of Dalmarnock Road and Mordaunt Street, trying to get a few pennies. There were also many pubs in the side streets off Dalmarnock Road. In the immediate area, apart from the area around Bridgeton Cross that is the most unchanged part of the whole district, I can think of only one public house from that period which remains standing in the present day. That is the former 'Gushet' public house in Old Dalmarnock Road, just alongside the old Dalmarnock Gasworks. This pub is now called the 'Hayfield.'

More than ever though, every time I pass through the area, what saddens me is that almost all the old 'playgrounds' of my childhood - in the form of public parks, swing-parks and bowling greens etc – are also no longer in existence. I think that the most notable example of this is the old Westhorn Park in London Road, just across from where the old Belvedere Hospital stood for many decades, until quite recently. It was at Westhorn, as I have related in a previous chapter, that I spent many a late afternoon and evening, playing football with my school pals. In the present day, what used to be Westhorn is just a mess. There is long grass everywhere, the place having been apparently untended for years. The bowling and the putting greens have long since gone too and the whole place is barren and empty. It would be difficult to even try and play football here today such is the rundown condition of the whole area. Stillness engulfs the whole place, in contrast to the busy and bustling place it was some forty years ago.

Then there is the former Springfield Park in Springfield Road. What a lovely little park this was! Nowadays, unless you knew it as it used to be, it is almost impossible to imagine it ever being a park, as it is now just a flat space, albeit with grass. Even the old bowling green in Greenhead Street at Glasgow Green, perhaps the most fondly remembered of all the parks etc., is no longer used for bowling. Likewise with the old and once beautiful 'Daisy Park' almost next to the bowling green. The bowling green has been like this now for several years or so.

Of all my old 'haunts', only Tollcross Park resembles anything like it used to be. Even here though too, there have been sweeping changes, with the old bowling green also gone, along with the old pitch-and-putt green.

Until a few years ago, the old swing-park in Baltic Street still existed – the one where I got dizzy if I stayed on a swing for too long and where the caretaker Danny was endlessly telling children off for misbehaving – if in a somewhat reduced form. Now it too has gone completely. I think that it was the sole survivor of the many swing-parks I have mentioned earlier on in the book.

Especially with the parks and bowling greens, I feel a bit sad that these spaces have been permitted to deteriorate in the manner they have. Even given the reduced population of the East End over the years, from the time that I am writing about, until the present day, surely these places could have been retained in some form, rather than being turned into vacant spaces of ground where nothing ever happens. To some extent, the demise of these places is related to

Museum, Tollcross Park, Glasgow.

Originally a private house designed by David Bryce in 1843, this is the Museum in Tollcross Park, in 1924. I remember playing football and pitch-and-putt in the Park.

the changing social habits over time, with many more youngsters being attracted to indoor games involving computers etc. rather than going out to play football. I am not convinced though by the argument that playing football in parks etc. is becoming a thing of the past.

Also, in the so-called 'better' areas of the city, many of the old bowling greens continue to flourish; yet in the East End they seem to have all gone. I mean, it's not as if the game of bowls has suddenly become unpopular. Its continuance in these other areas of the city is testament to that. This is in fact, true of the parks and their amenities in a more general sense in the 'better' areas. They have remained, while in the less prosperous East End they have all but disappeared from the scene.

Some parts of the district have changed more than others. Walking down Baltic Street from its junction with Springfield Road, it is still fairly recognisable from what it was forty or fifty years ago, until you pass the junctions with Mordaunt and Nuneaton Streets. After that, it is completely changed. All of the old corner shops have long gone here too, as well as the pubs. The mills, which once were such a feature of the area as you neared Heron Street and Bridgeton Cross, are no more than a distant memory now. For the most part, it is modern homes which the spaces where the shops and the mills etc. once were, but there are many empty spaces, including where the vast works of Sir William Arrol's once stood in both Baltic Street itself and in Dunn Street too. Dunn Street itself has changed radically. The part nearest Dalmarnock Road has been widened and as I have said previously, the street is now part of a motorway link to the south side of the city. The part of the street that carries on into London Road, though greatly altered too, is still recognisable, even if all the old houses and shops have disappeared. Just off Dunn Street, in Albany Street, Dalmarnock Primary School still stands. In Ruby Street though, close to where the old tramcar depot once stood, there is this very small stone building with a row or two of bricks on top of it that has survived all the changes in the area over the years. I am not sure what it is or what it once was. I can only assume that it was part of the old tram depot, although I may be wrong. Whatever it is I certainly cannot see what purpose it serves in the present day.

The area where my grandmother lived is another part of the district that has been radically altered over the past few decades. As I have suggested earlier, perhaps even more so than the part of Bridgeton where I lived. This is particularly true of the part around Bernard Street, where again there once were many shops and works. In the present day the part of Bernard Street, which stretches right down to Heron Street from its junction with Dunn Street, is totally unrecognisable from when I knew it as a child. Again, it is new houses that dominate the present day scene, although the eastern end of the street still looks a bit like it once did.

London Road itself has completely changed too, or at least the part of it that stretches between Bridgeton Cross and Springfield Road. All of the old tenements have gone, as again have the shops and yet again, the main feature

Dalmarnock Primary School in Albany Street, around 1964.

of this part of the district is the modern homes, which predominate. Even the old railway bridge at Celtic Park is no longer there. It wouldn't be much use even if it were still there, as the railway line ceased to be used over twenty-five years ago. Strangely enough though, the bridge in Dalmarnock Road – on the same long disused railway line – is still in existence in the present day, though I can't think what function it serves, apart from of course, as a relic of a past era.

Further up Main Street, it is sometimes a bit difficult to picture the area as it once was all those years ago. Here though, one or two of the old shops are still in existence, in the area between Franklin Street and Rumford Street. I don't mean that they are still the same types of shops as they once were; it's the actual building I am referring to. When I lived in the area, there was a passageway under a sort of arch that led off Savoy Street near Dale Street, which led into Main Street. Likewise another "shortcut" was to enter Megan Street and Acorn Street off Dalmarnock Road; if you went through one of the backcourts and into the close-mouth, it would bring you out in Main Street. These two fondly remembered 'alternative routes' are long gone. When coming down Main Street recently, I found it quite difficult at first to picture where the shortcut from Savoy Street actually was. Such have been the vast changes within the area as a whole. The streets leading off Main Street, such as Franklin Street, where my mother lived as a girl in the 1920s have not greatly changed from when I knew them. Dale Street though, has changed quite a bit.

Workshops in Dale Street, in 1924. New homes have been built oi this ground.

Bernard Street School, 1964

The building that once housed the old 'Kings' picture house in James Street is still in existence. I think that it is now some sort of warehouse or something similar. The area on one side of James Street near Bridgeton Cross looks similar to what it did as I used to walk up towards Glasgow Green as a child. The other side though, which once housed shops and a pub, has completely changed. A short road from James Street into Main Street, through part of the greatly altered Mackeith Street has been built, as an alternative route for traffic, near where the shops once were. Just round from the Cross there are yet more new houses.

I pass through the area by bus, almost every day, on my way into the city centre; I often try to picture the tenement building where I lived as it used to be, sort of comforting, in the midst of so much change. I am usually successful in this, in spite of all the changes.

Vast and far-reaching as these actual physical changes to the area have been, they are secondary to the changes in the whole tone of the area. By this I mean the crowded streets, the traffic and the general hustle and bustle of what at that time, was an area which probably had changed very little in the preceding seventy or eighty years. The whole area at that time was one that was typical of any industrialised, heavily populated and largely working-class area throughout the whole of Britain. It was a typical product of especially the later part of the nineteenth century and the final stages of the Industrial Revolution in Britain, with the continued growth of the major cities and the spread of heavy industry throughout the country.

Walk down Dalmarnock Road or London Road in the present day; compared with the time that I am writing about here, it is like a ghost town. The hustle and bustle in the streets belongs to an era long since past and even during the day, the main roads, apart from the area around Bridgeton Cross, are not at all busy.

In this 'post-modern' Bridgeton then, the crowds no longer stream from the factories into Dalmarnock Road to jump on trams and buses taking them home, because there are no factories. The trams themselves are no more; the buses, perhaps fewer in number, go to places new. No longer does the back-street bookmaker precariously ply his trade while keeping an eye out for the 'polis.' There are premises for that nowadays.

The crowds no longer queue outside the local 'flea pits' like the 'Plaza' and the 'Geggy'; rather they file in leisurely manner into the multi-screen cinema up at the Forge. A wide choice of the latest offerings from Hollywood awaits them for their four or five pounds handed over at the cash desk. A big change from my day when it was six old pence or a shilling for the 'big picture.' The 'wee picture,' with perhaps a cartoon and then the Pathe News thrown in as an'extra', followed this. This was during a time when continuous performances were the norm. You could sit on and watch John Wayne fight the nasty injuns all over again or see Jimmy Cagney breaking out of jail yet again. Or at least you could *try* doing this in defiance of the usherette, because that's what it was all about more than anything, a 'dare.' Try staying in the hall nowadays and watch Bruce Willis saving the world again or Robert De Niro planning his latest heist or whatever and you are liable to be swept away by the cleaning lady tidying the hall for the next showing. Yes, times do change, places will change, but for the better? I sometimes wonder.

The 'dear green places,' the parks, which I played in all those years ago, are now empty, barren stretches of wasteland. Truly 'dear green places departed.' The corner shops and most of the 'main road' ones too, closed their doors for the last time long ago, just before the bulldozers arrived to sweep them into oblivion. Only the memories of Brigtonians like myself, perhaps a few thousand others, perhaps some photographs, serve as proof that they ever existed.

Even my schools, dear old 'Rivi' and 'Springi Primary' are no longer part of the scene. In the case of the latter not as and where I knew it anyway. In the case of the former, the scene today is an eyesore, pure and simple. I recently passed one of the places that I visited as part of my schooling, the former Stow College building in Whitevale Street off Duke Street. Stow College was where we learned the 'art' of bricklaying, or were supposed to. I never did, simply because I hated it. It looks much the same in layout as it did forty years ago. I could even pinpoint the spot where the bricklaying sessions were held on Tuesday mornings all those years ago. The building is no longer a college annexe. These days, the premises house the Dennistoun Neighbourhood Centre.

Further down Whitevale Street, at the Gallowgate end, there is the old Whitevale swimming baths building. It has been derelict for many years now and there are now notices posted on it warning that "THIS BUILDING IS DANGEROUS. KEEP OUT!" I think they should have had those posters up forty years ago when I was going there with the school, because to me it was *always* a dangerous building, with my constant fear of the deep end of the swimming pool.

My sentiments on the area of my childhood, the area of which I have everlasting memories, are not of course unique to 'my' area of the city. There have been people from such areas as Maryhill, Springburn and Govan, to name a few, who in books broadly similar to my own, look back to their own area as it was forty and more years ago. Like me, they sometimes bemoan the great changes that have taken place in their area and how "things ain't what they used to be."

In almost every area of Glasgow, since at least as far back as the 1960s, there have been changes which, in varying degrees, have made the areas concerned almost unrecognisable in some cases. For instance, the Anderston area has changed even more than Bridgeton.

Not all of the changes have been for the worse, in Bridgeton, as in other areas of the city.

That said, when I look back at the area as it was in the late 1950s and early part of the 1960s, with its hustle and bustle and the throng of people in the busy streets, the old, noisy trams hurling along the rails, the shops, the tenement buildings with people 'hanging' out of their windows and watching life go on below them, it induces strong emotions. I immediately feel a strong sentiment for a dear old place to which I will have a permanent attachment. Few people forget the area and the environment in which they were raised. I am no exception and wish that it could be like that again. It can't of course but the memories will always be there and so will Bridgeton.

30

Last Exit from Bridgeton

My final day as a resident of Glasgow S E was the 14th of April 1966, a Thursday. In the weeks leading up to the 'big flitting' out to East Kilbride, my mother had made many visits to the flat we were moving into in the Westwood district of the new town. I think quite a bit of our furniture had been moved on there in the days leading up to the Thursday. I had not been out at East Kilbride at all prior to the flitting, mainly because the move out, of what had been my home for over eighteen years at that point, did not appeal to me at all. I simply did not want to move. I cannot remember exactly why my mother had wanted to move in the first place. I suppose though, looking back, it was probably because there had been so many glowing reports on the new town of East Kilbride from people that my mother knew who had moved out there - my aunt being one.

Also, it could possibly have been due to the fact that it was becoming obvious by that time, that there would be big changes in the area shortly and that the old tenements, at that time close on a hundred years old, would not last for much longer.

Further, all of our relations from my father's side of our family had been moving out of the East End since the mid 1950s. We were the only ones from that side of the family still living in the old tenements, so it may have been a case of my mother wishing to have a 'new house' like the rest. And why not, I suppose?

Over the previous decade there had, of course, been a steady exodus of people from the old tenements all over the city, as the new housing schemes began to grow. During the course of my work on the 2000 Glasgow Lives Project, many of the respondents told me that the "happiest day of my life" was moving into a new home. These people were recalling moves to such districts as Drumchapel and Castlemilk. Almost invariably they described the first visit to their new home as being like entering a 'palace', with things that all these years later, we now take for granted - like an inside toilet and a bath. Certainly, it would be a palace compared to the old tenements. This was of course, before the later regrets expressed at the alleged loss of the old close-knit communities caused by mass flittings to the new housing schemes. There were and are, of course, the accompanying theories that it resulted in isolation and was one of the causes of the break-up of long standing friendships and even families and, in a wider context, the fracturing of the community as a whole.

I suppose that my mother's reaction to entering our new home for the first time would be little different from the opinions of the people I have mentioned above. With all the mod cons suddenly available, it is very difficult to imagine how it could have been otherwise. I refer mainly to my mother in this context; if I remember correctly, my father was not bothered one way or the other about our moving. I have to say, though, that he did express some enthusiasm about it, so at least he was more looking forward to going than I was. That would not be too difficult, mind you. My motivation level for the move to East Kilbride was a large round zero.

When we moved, I was halfway between my eighteenth and nineteenth birthdays. Bridgeton was the only place I had ever known. I had played in the streets and the parks there, gone to school there and even begun my long 'career' as a film buff there. But now I was leaving it for the last time. It was not something that I was happy about.

I really have only vague recollections of that Thursday of just over thirty-six years ago, but my one abiding memory is of taking one final look at our old tenement building as my mother and I came out the closemouth of number 337 Dalmarnock Road for the very last time. The tenement itself would survive for about another seven or eight years, before inevitably falling victim to the bulldozer.

Then we entered the van that would transport us, and the remaining pieces of furniture, to our new home about ten miles away. The van started to move away slowly along Dalmarnock Road and I remember taking one last look out the window at places I had known for literally as long as I could remember. All of that had now come to an end and I was entering a new phase of my young life. It truly was the last exit from Bridgeton.

Dalmarnock Power Station, for decades situated just before the 'border' with Rutherglen. A landmark in the area, the Power Station was a major employer in the district.

People's Memories

The contributors to the original edition of this book were from people who, at one time or another, have lived in the Bridgeton and Dalmarnock areas or close by. They were related to me during the course of my work on this book in the form of one to one conversations, group meetings and a few written reminiscences.

The same is true of the new contributors; however, the new contributions which form part of this edition were obtained from e-mail messages sent to me.

Contributors are in alphabetical order; the names of new contributors are prefaced by an asterisk, thus *James McKenna*.

Guest Spot. *Willie Miller*:

Former Aberdeen and Scotland footballer, now Director of Football with Aberdeen.

Willie grew up in Bernard and Marquis Streets. He recalls the 'Gas Lamps' of the streets. Here are some of his other memories of the area.

"Tony's Bar, for pie and chips." This was situated at the corner of Bernard Street and Queen Mary Street It was an off licence where he and his mates went for their pie and chips.

"Piece and Jam." He and his mates playing in the backyard, shouting up to his ma' for a piece and jam and the sandwich would come flying out the window for them to catch. Also, *"Jumping the Dykes."* Out in the backyard where the bins were kept there were dykes separating the bins. Willie and his mates used to jump over between the dykes to test their agility.

"Juice bottles used for hot water bottles." Another memory of that era. (Late 1950s - early 1960s) No-one could afford the real thing.

"Irn Bru Jubilee." Seemingly drinks were frozen in summer time and ate as icicles. (From shop opposite Glasgow Green).

"Picking tar off pavements" Another memory from that time.

Arrols Xmas Party: "Sir William Arrol, local employer, steel works, threw a party for the neighbourhood every year."

"ABC Odeon-Minors Club": Saturday morning outing for Willie and his mates, although not much of the matinee was seen as they all had a hoolie stamping their feet etc. in support of the hero who never got killed.

Willie Remembers the last tram make its last run to Ruby Street depot.

Willie recalls too "the 'Tongs' and the 'Spur'." Although he was too busy playing football Willie remembers these as the two rival gangs of the time.

On a lighter note Willie once found a frog in his backcourt and it became his pet. To this day he does not know where the frog came from.

Tommy Adams from East Kilbride, who was born in 1944, lived in Comely Park Street just off the Gallowgate as a boy. Like myself, he recalls shouting up to his mother from the backcourt for a 'piece.' He remembers his grandmother hanging out from her tenement window with a pillow used as a cushion for this, as was the done thing of course.

Tommy also refers to the binmen coming to empty the bins with lamps attached to their foreheads. He tells me they were called 'scaffies' which I have to admit is a term that I am not familiar with.

On more familiar territory, Tommy recalls playing games like hide and seek and 'heedies' (a form of football) in the closes.

Finally, Tommy produced a gem of a memory about coalbunkers. He tells me that if you had a coalbunker in the 'lobby', or anywhere in the house, you were considered a 'toff.' Most people he said had them on the 'landing' outside.

Margaret Douglas Aitken was born in 1943 in French Street. Later (aged five) she moved to Main Street, and now lives in Texas, America. Margaret relates this amusing little tale from long ago.

"I can remember the rag man wi' his horse and cart. One time my older brother wanted a balloon. Unbeknowst to my Ma he took my Da's Sunday coat and gave it to the ragman who was very happy to have it for a balloon. When my Ma found oot about it she went tearing doon the Main Street in hot pursuit, dragging my brother along with the balloon clutched in his wee fist. When she caught the ragman there was quite a barny, but needless to say she got the coat back. These Glesga wimen would take on anyone. This particular brother was always up to something."

Bill Auld now living in East Kilbride was born c.1920. He lived in Baltic Street, Bridgeton and mentions living near a swing-park, probably one that I referred to.

Bill has memories of playing football on Glasgow Green as a youngster and also mentions games of 'moashy' (what I have earlier referred to as marbles or 'jorries') round his backcourt.

Andy Baird was born in 1925 and grew up in Franklin Street in Bridgeton; he now lives in Muirhead. He remembers that in the 1930s his family had to survive on ten shillings week for the five of them. Food had to be obtained 'on tick' from the shop across the road. The pawnshop was a regular feature of life and Andy tells me, "you were always in debt."

Andy relates how Bridgeton Cross was "always mobbed at lunch time" with workers from the various factories, like Lyall's in Broad Street and the dyeworks in Tullis Street.

Andy played in junior football, for Parkhead Juniors amongst others. He also recalls playing football as a youth. "All we had was a ball," he says. It seems too, that my memory of the Glasgow Green always being full with people playing football on a Sunday, was one which people a generation earlier would remember too, as Andy tells me that "you couldn't get a pitch at Glasgow Green." Andy tells me though, that on a Sunday, contrary to what I had thought, there was no booking system. You simply went along early, probably about ten am, and hoped that you would get one of the fifteen or so pitches on the Green. Apparently it was the schools' teams, that played on the Green on Saturdays, who had to book the pitches in advance. On the Sunday it was 'street and corner' teams that would be playing on the Green and Andy recalls local gangs such as the 'Billy Boys' and the 'Norman Conks' being there. Here Andy is referring to the period of the late 1930s and early 1940s. Andy informs me that he would play junior football on the Saturday, perhaps a game for a team called League Hearts on the Sunday and then on the Sunday evening at the Green, he would play for the Franklin Street team. This was, of course, in the summer and Andy says that they would play football till it got dark.

Andy also recalls visits to what was apparently a well-known local billiard hall in its day, 'Collie's.'

I am informed that this establishment was in Dalmarnock Road, just past Ruby Street. It later became McKendrick's bookmakers shop and while I don't remember the billiard hall, I vaguely remember the bookmakers of that name. Andy recalls going here on finishing work for the day at Welma's bakery in Dennistoun.

On a different note, Andy remembers seeing gang-fights at Bridgeton Cross, with bottles etc. being thrown. On the other hand though, Andy recalls how, in times gone past, that "you could leave your door open." Neighbours it seems were a lot friendlier in those distant days.

Andy remembers a well-known 'character' of the area; "Wee Willie." Andy recalls that Willie was less than five feet tall, was forever whistling and used to go messages for people around the Main Street area.

*May Ballantyne, now living in Canada, was born in 1936 at 100 Bernard Street, "a wee single-end, we moved to a room and kitchen (106 Bernard Street) when I was three. My very first memory is standing in the close watching the searchlights looking for the German planes."

"I remember going to the 'Wee Geggie' picture house on a Saturday morning to see the 'follow-uppie' to Flash Gordon. The real name (of the picture house) was the Premier, in Kirkpatrick Street. It cost 3d in old money.

"I went to Queen Mary Street School and I remember going to the dinner school. My favourite dinner was mince and tatties and dumplin' and custard.

We used to play rounders roon the back. We had a great big back because all the pailins were cut down for the war and never put back. I've got lots of memories of Bernard Street."

Michael Bell was born in Main Street and lived in Bridgeton until he was forty when he moved to Canada. He still lives there.

Michael's contribution is an amusing little tale from Old Bridgeton.

It's about a character called 'Torchy.'

"The story was that he got that name because he was the first guy to shine a torchlight while he was shipwrecked at sea. His real name was Will Dunbreck. He came from Pentland Place. I came from the corner of French Street and Main Street. I knew him well. Anyway, he was barred from all the pubs on Main Street. One day he came into our local pub, the Park Bar, and the bartender at that time, big Jim Eamons, wouldn't serve him. Of course we were all giving the barman a hard time, telling him to serve him and give him a break. Well, big Jim wanted to see the color of his money, so 'Torchy' put a half quid on the bar, and asked for a half and a beer. So, when Jimmy put the half and the beer on the bar, he put his hand out to grab the half quid. But 'Torchy' put his left hand on one end of the half quid, and Jimmy had the other end, it stretched all the way over the bar, meanwhile 'Torchy' snatched the half and swallowed it, and ran for the door. Meanwhile Jimmy's squealin' like a stuffed pig and calling him for everything and we are all lying on the floor laughing. Of course big Jim saw the funny side of it."

Martha Best, now a resident of Kerrvale Nursing Home in Bridgeton, was born in 1918 and grew up in a room and kitchen in Marquis Street, just off London Road. Margaret recalls "happy times" in Bridgeton. She says that Bridgeton was a happy place and that she had "great neighbours." She adds, "We didn't have much money but we were happy."

Martha recalls, as a child, playing on the top of the 'dykes' round the backcourt and also pursuits like skipping ropes and running the stairs chapping other peoples' doors, then dashing off as fast as you could.

Martha recalls Willie Black's pawnbrokers in Marquis Street. It was always busy on a Monday as everyone was 'skint'." says Martha. Then there was Hynds, who was a 'bookie' in the Marquis Street area.

Among her memories of the Second World War, she remembers that a local mill (Wilson's) was converted into an air raid shelter. She also remembers that during the 'blackout' people had to find their way about with a torch and that everyone was issued with a gas mask.

A particularly interesting recall from Martha, is that of seeing and hearing 'jazz bands' in Marquis Street, "All the weans would sit in the street singing" she says. "People would sing on coming out of the local pubs at night time. Lovely singers they were," she says.

Martha worked as a 'bottler' in Moore's ginger works in Mordaunt Street, bottling Ginger and Guinness. She also worked in a canteen with a small firm near the old 'King's' picture hall, in James Street.

Martha frequented the 'Geggy' picture hall across London Road in Kirkpatrick Street. She remembers that the manager's name was Mr Christie.

*Alex Brown was born in the mid 1940s, and grew up at 16 Savoy Street. His father and grandparents had also lived here. Alex says "so this could be called our family home."

"I went to Hozier Street school, Mrs Stewart was the teacher ... boy, did she hit hard."

"In Savoy Street there was a Bookie's Runner called 'Chick,' he was always getting chased by the police He used to pay young lads to 'watch for the polis.'

"Stewart's Engineering works, and Alfie Elsworth's Wafer factory were in Savoy Street."

"I remember the picture houses, the 'Wee Royal' in Main Street. Used to get into the Matinee with Jam/Jeely Jars. And the Olympia at the [Bridgeton] Cross."

"I remember when Clyde beat the Celts in the Scottish Cup Final, the crowds were huge, all down the Main Street, right up to Shawfield."

"Most of my male relatives and myself, worked for Sir William Arrol's, In Dunn Street. My grandfather was a caulker; my father myself and my uncles were steel erectors. I served my time as a steel erector with Arrol's, on cranes and bridges etc."

Cathie Brydson, who now lives in East Kilbride, was born in 1924 and lived in Pentland Place,

Bridgeton near Main Street. Her first thought was of there being "a bookie at every corner."

Cathie recalled working in Lean's mill, just off Reid Street, as a loom worker. She also worked during the Second World War in the works of Sir William Arrol's, as a jig worker. Cathie well remembers Blair's the butcher in Main Street, which I refer to a few times. Cathie interestingly recalls that a pal of her sister was a domestic servant, to the very same Miss Dewar who was my Geography teacher at Riverside school. One horrific story from Cathie's schooldays was when she witnessed one of her teachers lashing out at a pupil (or pupils) with a cricket bat. Cathie also mentions the 'spray baths' at Riverside School (what we would now call showers).

Another interesting memory from Cathie was of the East End gang, the 'Norman Conks', attacking a street band that played the drums and flute. Other people used to throw pennies to them, she tells me.

*Mary Cairns was born in 1938 at 16 Sunnybank Street and grew up there. She now lives in Leven.

"We stayed in the middle landing of 16 Sunnybank Street, as we were on the gable end of the building there were no other houses on that landing. It was a three-apartment Corporation house, with a kitchenette and a bathroom. My parents shared one bedroom and the children slept in the two double beds in the other bedroom; my two brothers in one bed, and me and my two sisters in the other bed. We had a gas fire in our bedroom and one of our special treats was when one of my brothers would sneak some bread in and make toast. When any of us were ill we were isolated from the others and put in my parents bed and they slept on a bed settee in the living room."

"My mother was scrupulously clean and seemed to work from morning till night. I can never remember her going to bed, she was there in the morning no matter how early I awoke, and she was there last thing at night. No matter how hard she tried to keep dirt at bay, the house was infested with cockroaches. We had to make sure none were lurking in our cups, or hiding in our shoes before we put them on. I was terrified of them. They crawled up the water pipes from the house below, so the sanitary man said."

"Our playground was the backcourts. During the war a deserter from the army was shot by two MP's [Military Policemen] as he was trying to escape through our backcourt. I was playing there with other children and our safety was disregarded. I remember all the women shouting at the MP's and running with blankets for the unfortunate deserter, who had only wanted to see his wife who had just given birth to their first child."

"As we got older, we were allowed to wander further from the confines of the backcourt, a favourite playing area was the "brickie" park in Millerfield Road. It was a disused building site and we played there for hours using all the materials we found lying around. Further up Millerfield Road was the [The Eastern] Pie Company; you used to be able to get a penny bag of the ends that had been cut off by the "fly cemeteries" (fruit slices), what a treat if they were still hot."

Some wartime memories from Mary. "I remember my brother taking me to some place in Dalmarnock Road to get my gas mask changed, during the war. All the family had khaki gas masks and I had a "Mickey Mouse" gas mask. I remember going to school with my gas mask. All the streets, and the backcourts too, had air raid shelters. In front of the closes "baffle" walls were built to stop the blast from air raids entering the closes. When the bomb in Allan Street fell, my brothers told me that all our neighbours' windows were smashed, but ours were intact. However, when they went upstairs they found that all the cups which had been hanging from hooks in the scullery were broken.

At the corner of Sunnybank Street and Springfield Road was Cochrane's. I remember that their back shop's wall had collapsed and our street was covered in sugar and jam and all the women shaking their heads at such waste, none of it could be salvaged because of broken glass. It must have been caused by an air raid.

I remember the air raid shelters well. Our shelter was in the backcourt but there were shelters in the middle of Sunnybank Street too for the people who lived in the red sandstone houses across the road. These houses had tiled closes and were for the "toffs." We used to plague the life out of them, playing kick door run fast, tying door knobs together, playing jumps on their washhouses and raking their middens."

"I remember vividly my first day at "Springy" (Springfield Primary School), even down to the exact clothes I was wearing. I went home at playtime, I thought that was it but I soon got marched back again. The boys didn't have access to the wee shop in Lily Street at playtime and they used to pass farthings and halfpennies to the girls for us to go and get treacle scones from the shop, you got one big round one for a penny, it was marked off in quarters."

"I attended Dalmarnock Parish Church in Springfield Road and also went to the Sunday School and Girls Guildry there.

"Our greatest entertainment was going to the pictures. Our local picture house was the 'Strathies' or the 'Strathclyde,' to give it its real name. My sister and I use to go every Monday and Saturday, as the programme changed twice a week. It was fourpence to get in before four-thirty and sevenpence after that. We always had a mad rush on a Monday getting home, going to the toilet, getting your money and rushing round to the pictures. One Monday we returned crestfallen because they wouldn't let us in for fourpence, even though we got there on time. My mother went round and kicked up such a rumpus because she accused them of discrimination. It was a 'holy' day and the Catholic children were off school and they were all already in the pictures so they put the prices up early. We got in for fourpence. But I always remember how angry my mother was."

"Before I started school (Springfield Road School) I remember my mother taking me in my push-chair to the gas works down near Bridgeton Cross. She would stand in a queue for ages to but charcoal to eke out our ration of coal. The push-chair would be filled with the bags of charcoal for the return journey, so I had to walk home. I remember the Salvation Army would provide cups of tea for the women and children waiting in the queues."

"We never went hungry, my mother was a marvellous cook and baker. We never knew we were poor, because due to our good housekeeping and thriftiness we were better dressed than many of the children around us.

My father was a riveter in John Brown's in Clydebank. Both my brothers followed my father to Brown's, one serving his time as a painter, and the other was a caulker. During the war he was in the Auxiliary Fire Service and his uniform used to hang in the lobby. His gas mask was different from ours, his had a long trunk like an elephant. He also had an axe that hung at his belt. Often he would be out fighting fires at night after a long gruelling day repairing damaged warships. He was a quiet man who didn't show any affection towards his children; I was a wee bit afraid of him when I was young. He didn't drink or gamble or swear, but was a great bowler, and also liked to go away cycling. An avid reader, he was very politically aware. I think our parents influenced us very much, especially in our love of books.

"So, growing up in Dalmarnock in the forties may have been harsh compared to modern values, but we were certainly not deprived of anything, our parents fed our bodies, minds and souls."

David Cameron, at present living in Carmichael House Care Home, has spent all of his life to date in Bridgeton. He was born in 1919 in Great Eastern Road (the former name for present day Gallowgate). David later lived in Dalmarnock Road, just across from the old Dalmarnock Power Station. He also lived in Sorn Street (off Springfield Road) and close to Springfield Road Primary School, which he attended over quarter of a century before myself. He also attended Newlands School near Parkhead Cross. During his time at 'Springi Primary' he encountered the 'spray baths.' These were a modern form of the present day shower and would be, I expect, a feature of a number of schools of the period, as at the time, very few people in manual class homes would have access to a shower or bath.

David worked as a labourer with William Arrol's in Dunn Street and Baltic Street and also with an engineering firm called Duncan Stewart and Company. He later worked as a barman in 'Teacher's' public house, down at Bridgeton Cross, across from the famous Umbrella. This pub is now called the 'Drayman's Arms.' David recalled that when he worked in this pub "even the customers were not allowed to smoke," perhaps indicating that 'smoking consciousness' is not as modern a trend as we might think.

David recalls seeing the first 'talkie' film at the 'Plaza' in Nuneaton Street, which, at that time he says, was known as the Dalmarnock Picture House. He remembers on occasion, that gang fights would erupt inside the hall, spilling out on to Nuneaton Street and Dalmarnock Road.

David recalls a well known 'character' from the

area c. 1940s to 1960s who apparently would challenge passers-by to fight. He also recalls a street corner news vendor in the area who would 'announce' the death of royalty etc. in 'jest.' (Strange sense of humour some people had). Then there was the one who every two months or so, would hurl no less than a 'midden can' through the windows of Teacher's pub (1940s). These were wild times indeed. As David says, "The place was full of characters."

I am especially indebted to David for his 'solving' of the 'riddle' as to who and what were the 'Cossy Men.' This was something that until now, I had not been able to find out. I am reliably informed by David, that the 'Causey –Men' (note the changed spelling), were the workmen who repaired the old tramcar lines on the main roads. Their work was done at night time because obviously, with the trams running during daytime, it would not be practical then. Apparently the word causey comes from the process of putting the bricks between the tramlines.

David remembers 'Revellers' Dance Hall, near the old 'Olympia' cinema. David went here when he was young and remember the old time ballroom dancing (this would be during an era when nightly dancing in local halls would be commonplace, before the growth of the larger dance halls led to a decline in locally based dancing, at least in the halls.

One extremely interesting recall of David's is of during the time of the 'Depression', in the first half of the 1930s when he lived at Kinnear Road. David recalls that the drivers on the trains on the nearby railway line, would throw coal down the railway embankment to people below in Kinnear Road who could not afford to light a fire in their homes.

Finally, David mentioned that the famous Glasgow entertainer, Tommy Morgan, originally lived in Lily Street and that a famous Glasgow 'street busker' Willie Greig, also lived there.

Ronnie Campbell was born in 1935 and lived in Cambuslang; he now lives in Leeds. Ronnie's connection with Bridgeton was that his mother had moved from Nuneaton Street when she married. "I still have family in the Bridgeton area, so my connection goes back over sixty years" says Ronnie.

"I remember very well the fish and chip shop you knew as Petrie's but Petrie's did not own it then, just after the war; it was owned by an Italian family, Pelosi I think they were called. Tony, the owner, would sell you four chips for a penny because most of us kids couldn't afford anything more."

"In those days when we played football in the back courts, using jerseys for goal posts, we would play all afternoon, sometimes until the team that scored fifty goals was declared the winner. If we got hungry we shouted up at the back windows for a 'chit,' a cool name for a sandwich. These were wrapped in newspaper and thrown down to us. One game, around 1947 took place on as Sunday between some Baltic Street lads and a Nuneaton Street team. We agreed that the first team to reach thirty would be the winners. There were about seven boys in each side to start, but as the afternoon wore on the teams swelled to about fifteen a side. Nuneaton Street won thirty to twenty-two after about three hours of play.

Two of the Baltic Street boys who played that day were sent to prison a few years later for being involved in a gang fight using razors. Their gang was known as the 'Baltic Fleet.'

"My cousin has reminded me that Chant Murray, of 'rogue charities' fame was also in charge of a pitch and toss gambling school which was run at weekends in a piece of spare ground near your house in Dalmarnock Road. He kept order with threats of a razoring for anyone who stepped out of line. He was given large dropsys, tips by the winners. Apparently the top bet allowed was half a crown, although God knows who had that kind of money in those days. I believe the spare ground was the result of some tenements that were brought down by German bombs meant for the power station." Chant Murray, a bit of a singer, was one of the real characters after the war; he lived near the 'Plaza' (picture house) and was a guy then in his thirties. He once knocked on every door in Bridgeton asking for books and mags for the hospitals and various charities; he even had me and my cousins collecting them. We took them to a house in Mordaunt Street where they were supposed to be bundled and distributed. To our horror and surprise, Chant opened a stall in the Barras where he sold the books and mags and pocketed the money. He worked the scam for months until he was found out. He moved to London in the fifties and never came back as far as I am aware."

Ronnie rounds his contribution off with this little tale. "My Granda, James McAleer, came over from the troubles in Ulster around 1875 to settle in Bridgeton and raise a family. He and a lot of his friends took picks and spades and helped to level the ground for the original Celtic Park, near to the present one. He also helped to construct 'The Grant Stand' in the stadium ; it was named after a Celtic director. As a point of interest the stand was at the East End of the ground and the sporting term 'Grandstand finish' is derived from the players' efforts to impress the directors when attacking 'that' end of the ground. Indeed, the word grandstand is simply a mispronunciation of the word Grant Stand."

*Ruth Conner, now living in Australia, was born in 1951 at 518 London Road, "directly facing Abercromby Street and above the café owned by George and Lena Cappoci. This was my grandparent's home for thirty years or so."

"I lived initially with my parents at 263 Bernard Street, which was a single end on the ground floor of a handsome red sandstone building, and moved to a top floor room and kitchen at 257 Bernard Street at some stage before starting school. We had the best end of Bernard Street, we kids thought, because it was a dream to roller skate or cycle on. We were at the top end of the street, beside Sir William Arrol's huge green gates; at night I was often 'spooked' by the sound of clashing steel coming from the night shift there."

"To the right of our house was some spare ground that led to Dalmarnock; you had to pass a factory, with very noisy thrashing and clanging machinery. You could see into it through some kind of wire fencing and I hated passing there as the noise was overwhelming."

"Neighbours I recall in particular are: the gas lamplighter who lived in the bottom house at number 251, Eddie Carroll, an Englishman with a wife and son who knitted Arran jumpers, and the Martin family, mainly because one of the sons had a car, the only car in the street. He was always dressed in a suit and had shiny jet black, probably brylcreamed hair. I remember gathering around watching them cranking up the car and riding on the running board. Two of my mother's aunties lived in 257 and 263. The only way you could get a house after the war was to have someone 'speak' for you, or pay someone for the keys of a house."

"No-one was allowed to play in any of the closes. They were kept immaculate and although three families had to share an outside toilet it was spotlessly clean. I remember there used to be a little oil lamp there on the window sill. There was stained glass on the corners of the windows on each landing, and the banisters were polished weekly. We all had our own 'calling' as we came up the stair, a sort of "open, pee-en" that we did. We could tell when it was my father coming upstairs as he used to whistle "our" tune."

"Leisure and entertainment was pictures at the 'Olympia,' walks around the park, towards Tollcross, Glasgow Green by tricycle. Sunday School at the Bethany Hall, Brownies, the Barras, Saturday afternoon dancing at Barrowland, ABC Minors, Rollerina at Dennistoun Palais. Carnival at Glasgow Green, Richmond Park, fish teas in James Street, hot peas at Capocci's Café followed by ice cream and a 'MaCallum,' in a pink cone, drinking mussel-brae and eating mussels and whelks at the Barras. Playing peever, aleevio, whip and peerie, bogies, hide and seek, marbles, dolls and prams etc."

"Shops; there was Sellyn's Carson the jeweller, Jim Wilson's the newsagent, McEwan's the newsagent, the Christian Bookshop, the City Bakeries, Carr's shoe shop, Margaret Forrester's, Capocci's Café, the Fair Isle knitting shop, Silvergrove Dairy, The Book Exchange, Woolworth's, the 'Arcadia Bar,' Walker's, Galls, Easiephit, London Road Co-op, Conetta's fish and chips, Joe Doran's barber shop, Radio Rentals, Kirkcaldy Linoleum Shop."

"There was this 'character of the district. 'Orange Betty,' tram conductress who wore her Orange Sash as part of her work uniform. In think she was from Dennistoun, but worked on the Bridgeton trams" recalls Ruth.

Rick Cooper was born in 1939 and lived at 166 Dalmarnock Road. He has lived in Perth since 1986. "We stayed opposite the tram car depot and on the corner was the Imporium. Nearby there was the 'Depot Café.' We stayed in the top flat. There were four houses per landing. Some of the neighbours were the Bryants, Mrs McCreadie, and the Thomson family."

A school memory from Rick. "At the time of me being at Dalmarnock School there were (schoolteachers) by the name of Miss White and Miss McCormack, and a Miss Bell, who went to America and came back with lollypops for all the children."

"The entertainment in those days for me was 'Olympia,' 'Arcadia,' 'Plaza' and the one that my parents did not allow me to go to, but I did, the 'Royal' in Main Street [all cinemas]. I had a girl-friend. I was nine, her name was May MacFarlane. My real pal was Tommy Gilmore who lived in Dale Street. I left Bridgeton when I was eleven and went to live in Carntyne but although I did leave the area very young, the memories are still there."

Elspeth Crosbie was born in 1947 at 23 Sunnybank Street and grew up there. She now lives in Rutherglen. Elspeth attended Springfield Primary School (she was a classmate of mine) and later, Riverside Secondary.

Elspeth begins, "my most vivid memory 'out playing' is round the backcourts playing at wee shops, raking the middens for old cans, packets and bottle tops to use as 'money.' If we found a 'gold' one we thought we were rich. Using a whip and peerie and drawing circles with coloured chalk on the top and watching the colours merge as it spun. Bouncing rubber balls off while singing our favourite rhymes a wall. Running along the dykes and up onto the wash house roofs."

"[I remember] living in our single-end, three storeys up, inside toilet with a loft up above where our presents were always hidden at Xmas. Having to hyke our feet into the sink in the scullery for a wash. The bed in the recess and the heavy coats thrown on top us in the winter. Sitting at the coal fire and getting 'corn beef' legs. Our wee cat hinging oot the windae just like the neighbours. Buying post office stamps with our pocket money. Roller skating along Millerfield Road, just outside the chapel, the smoothest surface, and a factory nearby where we could get bags of broken biscuits."

"[I remember] the shops in Springfield Road: Cochrane's the grocers, Nan's the newsagents, Brownlie's Café, Watts the bakers (great chocolate snowballs), Kit Cat Café and Gus and Molly's sweet shop. Going to Sunday School in the Church in Springfield Road, I think the minister was called Mr Fyfe. In Dalmarnock Road I remember going to Adamson's the dentist, and having to eat ice cream after having a tooth extracted."

"My father worked as a bus driver with Northern Roadways in Old Dalmarnock Road, doing school runs in other areas; sometimes he would park the bus at our close for a break. What excitement for us kids. I will never forget the novelty of running up and down the stairs and pressing the bells; still have his badge to this day."

"My mother worked in Gilmour and Deans, the printers, in Fordneuk Street as a bookbinder, and Lairds in Carstairs Street. As a fourteen year old I had a Saturday job in a dry cleaners in Dalmarnock Road. Only remember it as Jeff's."

"Oh yes the 'Pictures." It was the 'Strathies' (Strathclyde) for us and remember the Saturday matinee *Flash Gordon*, and the *Bowri Boys* and for a special treat it would be the Olympia at Bridgeton Cross. My favourite memory of this cinema is being taken there after getting a jag for polio or something. I remember the film was *The Pyjama Game,* with Doris Day.

"I remember, attending Springfield Primary and marching down the stairs as the teacher played the piano. The tin of sweets at the Coronation (1953) and the street parties. Being taken to Bridgeton public halls to see a play."

("I remember) the record sessions at our pals house when we would listen to our favourite records on the Dansette and sometimes more than one would fall down at once. Playing 'Postman's Knock' in the lobby. If anything revives the memories of that time then it's the great music. Yes, it was smashing being a wee lassie in those days."

Andy Crossan is now a resident of Kerrvale Nursing Home in Bridgeton. Born in 1930 in Cambuslang, he has spent a lot of his life in the Bridgeton area.

Andy at one time worked in Martin's Leather Works in Baltic Street, as a labourer.

His favourite 'flea-pit' was the 'Arcadia' in London Road. "You could get in with a bottle. I liked it," says Andy. "If you were 'skint', you just played at 'Bedlium' (apparently this was some variation on the better known 'kick the can.')

Andy alludes to the closeness of neighbours. "If you made soup, it was for everybody." he says.

One of the 'characters' of the area recalled by Andy, someone by the name of Willie would play a mouthpiece while standing in a puddle of water in the Dalmarnock Road and Old Dalmarnock Road area c. 1950s. (I wonder if he sang 'Singing in the Rain' at the same time?). Apparently Willie came from as far away as Blantyre.

Another person from Blantyre was a boxer in the 1930s – 'Boy' Mackintosh – whom Andy informs me used to run from his home every morning to Martin's Leatherworks in Baltic Street.

A wartime memory from Andy is of Allan Street, close to Dalmarnock Power Station, being bombed. "There were air-raid shelters in every street," I am informed by Andy.

Apparently bookies were not confined to street corners and backcourts. Andy recalls someone who 'took lines' while working at the Forge Engineering Works at Parkhead.

Andy mentioned the time that he was in the 'Fireman's Club', which he thinks was in the London Road area, when it was "set on fire."

Andy "ran about" with the local Billy Boys gang and recalls a fight with the rival 'Norman Conks' in Norman Street, when he says, "I got my head split open."

Tommy Crossan was born in Lambert Street, Calton, in 1937, he now lives in the U.S.A. "I will always claim to be a true East Ender" says Tommy. "My earliest adolescent memories and experiences come from living in the Camlachie, Bridgeton, Calton and Dennistoun areas while staying with my Grannie Rennie and Dad Jimmy Crossan at 5 Glenlyon Street, between Whitevale and Millerston Streets. The period was between 1940 and 1950, the 'War' and early 'post-war' years."

"Although I have some memories of my mother's illness (TB) and death, the things that stand out are, starting school, the air-raid sirens, air-raid shelter, blackout, rationing, evacuation for some, metal for scrap, "any gum chum?" and Pathe Newsreels at the pictures."

Bob Currie is now living in South Lanarkshire. He was born in 1937 at 5 Silvergrove Street in Bridgeton and later lived at 555 London Road, close to Arcadia Street. He tells me that in Bridgeton at that time, tenements with bathrooms [hot and cold water] were few and far between. In Bob's home there was an inside toilet, within the 'lobby.' The house rent was paid at 'the factors' at 534 London Road, Messrs Spiers and Knox (this recalls my own visits to the factors' at Danskin and Fletcher's office in Springfield Road with my mother).

Bob attended John Street Elementary School and recalls that there were large photographs of the Royal family at the top of the stairway leading to the upper floor classrooms. He says that this was something that was "imprinted in his mind."

Bob recalls too, that in those days, the national anthem was played every evening in the local cinemas at the end of the final screening of the film. He says that this had to be respected by the film audience.

Bob recalled a part of Glasgow Green called the 'Daisy Park', just past the bowling green. This 'Daisy Park' is the place where, in one of the chapters, I recall seeing the old men play draughts during the summer. I had completely forgotten the particular name, but recognised it once it was mentioned. Bob relates the folklore that the famous Scots inventor James Watt often walked here, as it was a quiet, serene place where he could think over his ideas.

Bob tells me that the "keep off the grass" regulation was strictly enforced here. I seem to recall that too.

Like myself, Bob recalls playing popular backcourt games like 'Hide and Seek' and 'Rounders.' I don't remember 'A Leevie-O', (perhaps I knew it under a different name).

In a memory similar to one of my own, Bob relates how he first heard of the death of King George VI, in 1952. He was making his way home from school along Landressy Street, when he saw the death announced on a newspaper billboard. Bob recalls seeing the King's funeral on a television set in the window of Mason's electrical shop at Bridgeton Cross, next to Scobie's barber's shop and Annacker's grocery store.

Bob provided some good memories of the area during the time of the Second World War. He recalls the very strict enforcement of the 'blackout' those years. Bob recalls how, as a boy during the war, a policeman would take him and his parents from their home to the air-raid shelter just along the road at Blackfaulds Place. He even remembers the name of the policeman, big Joe Nicol.

Bob recalls how, at the end of the war, people were literally "dancing in the streets" when Dalmarnock Power Station switched the lights back on, ending the long 'blackout.' Vividly capturing the mood of the times, he says that people were pulling the wood off the bomb-shelters in the middle of the street, to use as firewood for VE and VJ Day celebrations.

Bob recalls too, that at the end of the period of imposed rationing during the years following the war, the sweet shops in the area, such as M&M's in London Road and Finlayson's near Anson Street, were quickly sold out of sweets. Bob says that the government had to reintroduce rationing.

So the great 'sweet rush' seems to have been a national thing. Other shops in the area that Bob remembers, were Cockburn's the chemist at Bridgeton Cross, Dunsdale's in Dalmarnock Road and most notably perhaps, the State Studio premises in London Road.

Another Bridgeton 'occasion' is remembered by Bob. This time it was the 4th of September 1962 when the people of the East End lined the route of the final procession of Glasgow's trams from Ruby Street Depot, as they were finally consigned to transport history (and a few other varieties as well). People were "hinging oot" their windows to watch the procession says Bob.

Bob also remembers what he refers to as the 'open–air gymnasium', close to the famous 'sawny (sandy)-pond.' I remember this gymnasium as part of the swing–park, just along from King's Drive.

An early example of rhyming slang is also provided by Bob. He tells me that the 'wee Royal' picture house in Main Street, was locally referred to as the "Dan Doyle." Nice one!

Bob recalls how, on Sunday mornings at Silvergrove Street, he and his family would awaken to the musical strains of the Salvation Army and their promises of the world hereafter. Then, on Sunday evenings they were alerted to the needs of this world by the famous Independent Labour Party politician James Maxton. He remembers that Maxton expounded his political doctrine at the corner of Silvergrove Street, close to where the offices of the I.L.P. were then situated, in London Road. Bob refers to Maxton as "undoubtedly Bridgeton's most colourful Parliamentarian of the twentieth century."

*Margaret Davies-Hale was born in 1950, at 19 Norman Street. She now lives in Warwickshire.

"I went to Sacred Heart Primary School when I lived in Norman Street, a little one room tenement, with my ma, da, me and two brothers."

"I remember playing in the backcourts of Norman Street. I remember my granny taking me down Main Street and her shoe getting stuck in the tram lines and throwing me across the road to save me because she thought the tram would run over her before she got her shoe released. Lord knows how she got free in time."

"She, Granny Donachie, always went to the pub on the opposite corner of the 'Olympia' Picture House at Bridgeton Cross after work every Friday night (now Whitelaw's) and my ma worked as a waitress in the restaurant [probably the Windsor tea rooms] next door to it." .

"Granny Brown, my da's mother, was of Irish descent, and apparently a holy terror, and when she got drunk the police had to send for the priest, because he was the only person she was afraid of, and she was all of five foot tall."

"I was about eight when I moved to London Road, I then went to Barrowfield School until I went to live in Dalserf Street when I was about ten or eleven. The bread factory in Dalserf Street is where ma went to work when we moved there. I remember when I lived in Barrowfield I had to go to the 'Steamy' (washhouse) for my ma every week. Also, when I was young my father used to sell brickets with his horse and cart and I used to go with him on a Sunday morning. It was hard cold work for a little 'un."

"When I lived in London Road I loved going to the Saturday matinee at the 'Olympia' and when I was older to the 'flea pit' the 'Scotia'(Millerston Street Dennistoun) for six pence.

Margaret relates how she got her first job. "I went to Pirn Street School at twelve. Just before I was fifteen, people from companies came round the schools to offer us jobs, and that's how I started at Templeton's carpet factory, just up from Bridgeton Cross."

"In the 1960s I used to go to the 'Palais' dance hall (Dennistoun) on a Saturday afternoon and the 'Barras' on a Sunday. My da even had a stall, selling second hand glasses.

"I then went to work at Gelfort's machining factory."

Mrs Docherty from Easterhouse formerly lived in Swanston Street. She remembers such firms nearby as Martin's Leather Works and Lairds Box Works. She also refers to the 'nine-penny grope' in connection with the old 'wee Royal' Picture House in Main Street.

Rachel Dryburgh was born in 1917 and lived in Fordneuk Street. At present she lives in Kerrvale Nursing Home in Bridgeton.

Rachel enjoyed living in the area. She liked school too, and was a pupil of Annfield Street and Bernard Street schools. She later worked as a binder in Pratts in Fielden Street, who made baskets.

During the Second World War, Rachel worked

as a munition worker in Alexandra Parade, where she "Made a lot of different things." Rachel also remembers going to the air-raid shelter in Fordneuk Street.

Another memory is of the bookie in Fordneuk Street, where people went to 'put a line on.' (This would be very close to where Jimmy McKay, from my own time, plied his trade as a bookie). Rachel fully captures the context of these times by saying, "People would run when they saw the 'polis' coming."

Rachel also recalls one of the 'characters' of the area - 'Rab', who would get a singsong going at the corner of Fordneuk Street, hoping to collect a few pennies

Rachel remembers the 'Geggy' picture hall in nearby Kirkpatrick Street. "I liked it. It was a wee place. It didn't hold a lot."

Amongst the shops in the area that Rachel recalls was Cooper's sweet shop in Fordneuk Street.

Jean Dundas was born in 1914, just before the outbreak of World War One. Apart from a brief stay in the Gorbals area, she has lived all of her life in the Bridgeton area. She is now a resident at Carmichael House Care Home in Bridgeton.

Jean was born at 68 Brown Street (now Megan Street), just along from Bridgeton Cross. She recalls her first job after leaving school, as a 'message girl' in a fruit shop at 541 London Road, where she delivered produce to Arrol's works in Dunn Street and Nuneaton Street.

Jean went to John Street and Hozier Street schools and recalls many happy days as a small girl out playing with her pals and going to such places as the 'sawny pond' (sandy pond) at Glasgow Green, and to Richmond Park. She also tells me that one day, when very small, she fell in the water at Richmond and was "greetin' all the way home." Jean has always liked the Bridgeton area. She tells me, "I was just so happy in Bridgeton."

Jean recalls being a customer at the local Eastern Co-op, the one near Bridgeton Cross, in Dalmarnock Road. She can even remember her Co-op number all these years later, 1756.

Jean has very interesting memories of one of the local cinemas, the 'wee Royal' in Main Street. It apparently was a very small hall and such was the demand to see films, that the 'chucker out' was literally pushing people out the exit so that the usherette or whoever could let people in the main entrance. (I hope they got to see the film first). Jean recalls that the 'wee Royal' "was dirty."

Jean remembers too, one of the 'characters' of the Bridgeton area from the late 1920s. This was, she tells me, 'flannel feet' - a middle-aged tramp who walked about Dalmarnock Road. Also, Jean told me, that on the very spot where Carmichael House (a care home for the elderly) now stands and where I spoke to her, there once stood working-mens dwellings, in the earlier part of the twentieth century.

In the General Strike in 1926, Jean recalls that in the area "students who were 'blacklegging' on the trams were being dragged off their vehicles by angry strikers."

Jean witnessed a gang fight in Dalmarnock Road, between local gangs. To supplement their weaponry, the gangs made use of a load of bricks from a lorry, which happened to be passing at the time.

During her time at John Street School, in an era when Saint Patrick's Day, on March 17, was a holiday for the Roman Catholic Schools in the city, Jean recalls that when the pupils at John Street had finished lessons for the day on this holiday, they were sometimes confronted and intimidated at the school gates by youngsters from the Catholic schools.

Jean later lived in London Road and also Ruby Street. She remembers well the tram depot and the 'steamie'-cum-public baths in that street. Jean remembers when "we always kept our best shoes for Sunday." She concludes, "We were poor but happy."

Tommy Dunn was born in Heron Street in 1949. He now lives in Easterhouse but travels to Bridgeton three times a week to attend the Dalmarnock Centre in Lily Street. This centre, in part, is situated where part of Springfield Road Primary School once stood.

Tommy also lived in London Road, at number 867, close to where the present day police station is situated and across the road from where my grandmother lived. He recalls as a boy, watching from a window, seeing the number 9 tram going along London Road and also the horses and carts of the numerous coalmen in the area. From the window, which looked into the backcourt, Tommy could see Denholm's Bakery in the background and recalls seeing rolls being transported from here.

Tommy went to St. Anne's Primary School, which was then in Crownpoint Road. "I hated the long walk up Fielden Street and past all the factories and workshops there to get to school," he says. Tommy later attended St Mary's Secondary in Abercromby Street.

Tommy recalls going to the 'Olympia' picture house, with his mum, to the Saturday afternoon matinee, at Bridgeton Cross, where he saw such favourites as *Flash Gordon.* "It was always mobbed with kids," he recalls. On Saturdays too his mother would send him round to the Salvation Army Hall in nearby Summer Street, where he would get a free meal.

Tommy recalls going to Shawfield Stadium with his grandfather to see Clyde play and also to the greyhound racing there. "I have never been interested in football, but I remember that it was always crowded and that the seats in the stand were wooden. I think it was about a 'tanner' to get in," recalls Tommy. Sometimes he would get 'lifted over' the turnstile.

Tommy remembers the Coronation of Queen Elizabeth 11 in June 1953, when "London Road was crowded and there were parades going up the road and a lot of music too. My mother had taken me out on to the main road to see it," says Tommy. Tommy always liked the sound of 'big bands' and recalled how he liked to watch the Orange Walk parades going past his home.

Another interesting recall from Tommy is of seeing 'entertainers' coming round the backcourts.

This would usually occur on Sundays, he recalls; it was usually a few men who would sing a few songs and hope that people would throw them some coppers from their windows.

In another memory, Tommy relates how, when he lived in Heron Street, he would often see trucks loaded with pallets going in and out of Martin's Leather Works, which was located in Heron Street.

Like myself, Tommy never had any encounters with the gangs of the area. "I heard about the gangs, but never saw them," he tells me.

Among the local shops that Tommy recalls are Raleigh's Cycle Shop at the corner of Dunn Street and London Road, Cochrane's in London Road and a "candy ball " shop in Heron Street (or the part of it that was known as 'wee' Heron Street).

Tommy says that when he was growing up in the area "You could leave your door open." He recalls though, that sometimes rows would occur, between neighbours, over whose turn it was to clean the stairs.

"Most children were born at home in those days," says Tommy.

Eddie Fairman is a resident of Kerrvale Nursing Home in Bridgeton. Eddie was born in 1915 and lived in Walkinshaw Street and later at Tollcross.

Eddie tells me that he first worked as a milk delivery boy in the Calton District.

He recalls a cinema in Tobago Street called 'The Paragon', where he tells me, on occasion apples and oranges would be thrown by patrons (presumably when the picture was not up to expectations).

'Eddie's favourite pub was the 'Cottage Bar,' which still stands in present day Abercromby Street. He recalls too, a busy cobbler's shop in Abercromby Street.

A particularly interesting recall of Eddie's is that following a bombing raid during the Second World War, the landmark clock on the 'Umbrella' at Bridgeton Cross, stopped.

Another interesting recall is of there being a 'tossing school' (gambling), after football matches, in the precincts of Shawfield Stadium. "The police turned a blind eye to it," says Eddie. Eddie also remembers the well-known Jimmy Gilmour's Boxing Club in Olympia Street.

Donald Findlay is currently a resident of Kerrvale Nursing Home in Bridgeton. Born in 1923, he lived in Mordaunt Street. Donald tells me that he was associated with some of the gangs of the area when he was a young man. "The gangs fought amongst themselves. It was second nature in those days" he says. Donald adds "You would walk along the road, someone would shout and bawl at you, you would shout and bawl back and usually a fight would start." He says that there were a lot of "hard men" as he put it, in the area in those days. "You made your own pleasure, and your own fights." He mentioned a gang, the 'Redskins,' who would "cut the head off you."

Apparently, fights would also break out in local cinemas and dance halls. Donald recalls that in one of those makeshift dance halls, the 'Carl Hansen' (the dancing), as Donald described it,

Coronation Day in Nuneaton Street, 1936.

in Dalmarnock Road, people would throw shells and mussels at each other for their Saturday night 'entertainment.' Donald's favourite pub was the 'Dal Bar' (The Dalmarnock Bar). He relates a very interesting story, that in those days, if you turned your pint tumbler upside down, it was a sign that you were 'looking for a fight.' (I take it that was *after* the contents had been drunk.)

Donald also remembers the many local singsongs of those days round the backcourts. "Anyone who fancied themselves as a singer would give it a try, but if they didn't like your singing, they (the tenants) would throw bottles down at you." On my asking if this really happened a lot, Donald replied, "I know, I was one of the ones who threw the bottles."

Donald attended Damarnock Primary School in Albany Street and later John Street. He worked for a time in Sir William Arrol's works, as a rivet-heater and "knocking the rivets into shells."

Donald recalls the street bookies in Mordaunt Street, the "cream cookies" as he put it. Donald refers to times past in Bridgeton as "The good old days.

*Wilma Flavell was born in 1942 and lived in Newhall Street, Greenhead Street and finally Main Street, directly across from Crolla's (Café). She now lives in Canada.

"Although, when I grew up, Bridgeton was mainly a working class area, Greenhead Street was where the professional people lived. Mostly doctors, engineers etc, lived there. Around 1950 most of them left to buy homes in Burnside. Their children went to 'Wee John Street' (Hozier

Street) school until they qualified and left to go to Glasgow High or Hutchison Grammar. We had two elocution teachers in our early years and we were encouraged to speak properly. Nae ayes and naws, ha ha. I suppose they had to take care that the ones who would go on to fee paying schools didn't go with a local accent."

"I loved the atmosphere of Main Street of the Main Street on a Saturday. Everyone seemed to be so happy and busy. This was the day to shop and it seemed everyone bought luxuries like cakes, flowers and sweets as if it was a special day. There would be buskers playing music on the street and it seemed to be a stop and start affair with meeting everyone. The kids would be lined up outside the 'Wee Royal' (Picture hall) with their jeely jars in their hand waiting to watch the latest episode of Flash Gordon. Women would have scarves over their curlers and wavers, or sporting their new hairdo from the hairdresser, and their message bag in one hand and their tottie bag in the other. Potatoes at that time were bought at the fruit shop. They were bought usually by a quarter stone but they were dirty, so "the tottie bag." The men of course were leaving for the pubs to go to the football match at Shawfield. The Main Street was a real cheery and happy place at that time and it was wonderful to see the colours of the flowers and fruit outside awaiting to tempt the shoppers."

A few people Wilma recalls from the district at that time. "Going to work was fun. You seemed to know everyone. Sometimes when you waited for the bus Joe Williamson would be waiting. Poor Joe had no nose. I think he worked at the

White's Chemical work and the chemicals were the cause of his loss. It was a shame, he was a nice wee soul. I think many people suffered from the effects of the chemical work. There was Maggie wan eye, as kids we used tae look for her for some reason and then got scared from her and ran away. We used to have an old woman in an old tatty fur coat and she used to come around the backcourts and sing hymns. When nobody threw her money she used to curse and swear like a trooper."

"There used to be gangs, although I never saw any trouble with them. I used to pass the 'Norrie Conks' about eleven thirty pm at night and they didn't seem any different from any of the other boys who stood at the corners. They never bothered you. Norman Street was across the road from the gas works and they had a huge big shamrock painted in green with white around it. I remember when I was young, at the 'Twelth' (July 12 Orange Parades), Newhall Street would be decorated with flags. It seemed to me that everyone enjoyed the 'Walk.' Well it seemed everyone was there to see them coming back at night. There was an Orange hall in Olympia Street and I think they were quite a bunch. I couldn't believe it but it seemed everyone in their band had a massive scar on their face so I guess there must have been trouble although I never saw any."

"At the Coronation we had a party for the kids, with cakes and ginger and sweets. Balloons, decorations and hats made from crepe paper. At night, on Pentland Place they had a great street party. The McPhees supplied the band and everyone was dancing well into the night.

"Crolla's ice cream shop was a hub of activity in our area and they knew everyone. They were a great family and this was where we spent most of our free time if we weren't out dancing. I remember you used to take a big jug for a shillings worth of ice cream. I suppose at that time paper was scarce so there was no cartons. We would sit in summer and winter. Hot Orange or a cup of Bovril and crackers in the winter and a 'MaCallum' in the summer."

Another place recalled by Wilma is the 'Station Bar.' The Station Bar was on London Road, near Bridgeton Cross. This pub backed on to Olympia Street. It had a door front and back. The customers used to arrive in a taxi and ask the taxi to wait while they ran in for someone. Of course the taxi driver would get fed up waiting and go into the pub, only to find their customer had nicked out the back door. At that time the men from the Orange Lodge in Olympia Street frequented this pub. When the pub was closing they all insisted on standing to sing the [the National] Anthem. Sadly to say if you didn't stand for the anthem they would hit you with a pint tumbler."

Finally Wilma recalls that "the buskers on the Main Street used to play for the wee dances in the church halls or weddings, or even the wee YWCA that was in Tullis Street. Their hall was just past the Orange Halls towards the Green."

Marion Forte has lived in Australia for the last forty years. Margaret was born in Troon Street in 1939 and grew up there.

Marion recalls hard times, she says. "My mum struggled for money and I had to go to the pawn so many times and hide up closes so I wouldn't see any of my pals from school. I always remember my mum bought a quarter of pound of mince and made it into a soup to feed eight of us."

Marion recalls a family from nearby Lily Street, the Martins, "who used to sell fruit from a horse drawn cart at the 'Strathies' picture hoose, and when they were finished at night selling they would go home. I don't know what they done with the cart but they took the horse upstairs and kept it in a room, they lived one up."

"My dad was a bookie up the closes in Lily Street when I was at Springfield Road school. I remember standing in the (school) playground in lines and we marched up the stairs with someone thumping on the piano. I remember the wee bottles of milk would come frozen. I also remember the dinners [at school]: sago, yuk."

Marion recalls also the nurse coming to the school "and look through your head for lice." [I remember this well. Marion and our class regularly got our heads seen to at the same school.]

"The sirens would go off after the war broke out and I was upset as I got sent home to our shelter in the garden and others in my class could stay in the school shelter."

"My Aunty Mary lived facing the school and I would stand and call up Aunty Mary, throw me down a 'piece' and when she would go and make it I would stand in the street and sing. Aunty Mary would come round to the school on the cold days and bring tea and treckle scones for her daughter Jean and sometimes she would give me some, which was great."

Marion informs me that the man who sold me the wine gums all those years ago in the wee shop in Lily Street was a Jim Harver and the people who owned the shop, May and Tommy Craig.

William Fraser has lived in the Bridgeton and surrounding area since he was born in 1926. Now a resident of Carmichael House Care Home in Bridgeton, he worked as a labourer with a firm called Govan Croft Pottery. "

William says, "I liked Bridgeton." He especially remembers the pictures and the dancing and recalls visiting picture halls such as the 'Black Cat' in Springfield Road and the 'Olympia' at Bridgeton Cross. He went dancing at Bridgeton Public halls in Summer Street.

William went to London Road and Bernard Street schools, both of which he describes as "good schools." Interestingly, William adds, "I think Bridgeton has changed for the better."

*Paul Gunnion was born in 1943. He now lives in Kirkintilloch. Paul takes up the story of his early years. "My first home was in my gran's house. The tenement stood at the corner of Newhall Street, overlooking the Clyde, just before Newhall Street turned right into Greenhead Street. The tenement was like an ocean liner. One side of the building was in Newhall Street, then the building "turned the corner" into Clyde View Terrace. A few steps led off the pavement from Newhall Street and past the garden of the first main-door house to a little terrace that ran past three closes and three main-door houses each with its little garden; just like the tenements in Greenhead Street between James Street and Greenlodge Terrace."

"My first close, my Gran's, was at 2 Clyde View Terrace, later it became 289 Greenhead Street. My gran lived two stairs up; two-up right. I remember being in my cot in the main bedroom on the curve of the building, with the firelight playing on the ceiling. Another early memory is sitting in a basin on a kitchen chair being bathed in front my Gran's big black and brass Kitchen range. With my Uncle Pat, who was about ten years older than me, I was trying to stick Plasticine shapes on a plywood board which was upright against the back of the chair. The board was wet from the steam coming off my 'bath' and the shapes kept falling off, which made me shriek with laughter, as my uncle giggled."

"The neighbour below my Gran was Mrs Wardlaw. Like everyone else she had a pulley in the kitchen for drying her washing when she couldn't hang it out in the back green. As she raised her heavy laden pulley, the wheels made a sudden squealing sound, like a frightened cat. "It's ok. It's only Mrs Wardlaw's pulley," I was told as I got a fright."

"My Gran's house was on the corner of the tenement. The kitchen and two bedrooms overlooked Newhall Street. The main bedroom was at the 'corner,' and looked towards the Glasgow Green and down the Clyde. The two windows of the 'big room' as the sitting room was aptly known, were on the other side of the building and looked across the Clyde to the Richmond Park. The 'lobby' turned a slight dogleg corner to accommodate the shape of the building. All the rooms were on one side of the lobby and the bathroom was on the other side. A little high window onto the landing, near the front door, ventilated the bathroom. The 'check' key for the door was kept on this window ledge. In the winter, the wind off the Clyde would whistle up the big round stairwell of the close and moan through the front door. As a little boy, I didn't like the sound of that wind, and my uncles would torment me sometimes by blowing gently across the top of the hollow tube of the 'check' key to make that moaning sound."

"My gran had seven children; my mother was the oldest. Above my Gran lived her brother-in-law, Uncle Matha, and his equally big family. Across the landing were the Lavins, a family of adults, who had a lovely big Old English Sheepdog which gloried in the name Lochiel. When I lived there with my Gran, I seem to have been the only small child."

"To this day I don't know who lived in the main door at the house at the corner of the building, but in the house next to my Gran's close was an old lady who was bent almost double and walked very slowly with a stick. She may have looked frightening to some children, but to me, as I went in and out of my Gran's close, she was just Mrs Murphy, with the gentle smile and the soft voice."

"As I drive down Newhall Street now, with my grandson – at two-and-a-half, the same age I was when I lived there – I point to the empty space on the left, by the Clyde and say, "That's where my Gran lived," but only memories live there now."

*Mary Hall, now living in Kilsyth, was born in 1947 and lived at 299 Greenhead Street, "the wee terrace with three closes looking over to the Richmond Park."

"At the top of Newhall Street, where it met Main Street there was pub and a wee man used to stand on the corner frequently. When we had beer bottles, to get the money from, we were frightened to go near him and would wait until he went away. I'm sure he was a local character, and we were told not to stare at him. Near the Cross (Bridgeton Cross) I think, there was a Well, and there was a lady whose hands were all raw, my mother said she could not stop washing her hands, guess she had an obsessive neurosis. We lived next door to the Gilmours whose uncle was the one linked to the boxing, think it was Tommy Gilmour. We played with Jim and Mary, my brother and I."

"We used to go to the 'shows' (on Glasgow Green) in the morning when they were closed and get the beer bottle tops, as many colours as we could and take the centres out and replace them when they were on the front of our jumpers. We would get skelped for going there as we were wearing the evidence. It was great as we would find luckies and cash sometimes. We were scared of the dogs though. Wee Mrs Barrie of Newhall Street, she fed all the stray cats in the Green."

"Also there was what we called the triangular shaped garden, the cats' garden, you sometimes got the biddy drinkers sleeping in there."

How times have changed dramatically from then is demonstrated by Mary.

"Only two people had cars in the area, The

Farrells of Newhall Street and the Bruces, next close to us at 289."

"We used to fight with the kids from Madras Street."

Elizabeth Hunter was born in 1956 and grew up in Heron Street. She now lives in County Down. Elizabeth begins "My ma was a one parent family (divorced). As you know it was hard with a da never mind without. Anyway, we lived at 62 'Wee' Heron Street. Why 'wee' I don't know because to me 'big' Heron Street was the same size, ha." [more or less my thoughts too, Elizabeth]. Our wee single–end was on the top flat, with us in the middle and Missus Wilson on the left and Auld Aunty Jessie on the right, an auld spinster. It was always aunt or uncle or Mrs or else. I had more aunts and uncles than tongue can tell. Friday night was wash the close night, there was an auld wife washed them down for you for half a crown. If nothing else, the stairs were clean.

"My ma worked in a bedding factory, I think it was near Fielden Street, so our wee hoose was quite well aff looking for my ma would bring wee bits a cloth hame and make curtains and cushion to match, so we thought we were the bees' knees.

Then came Sunday night and the carbolic soap and the lorexine lotion for the nits appeared. I always thought it was my fault for getting nits. Every time my ma got one I got a big clout on the back of the heed, then I was put in the jaw box for a good wash wi the lifebuoy toilet soap. The best of it was the window was facing the leather work, and I was feared of anybody looking up at me, so I got a slap on the arse for jumping aboot in the jaw box, wit a night, I was glad to see the bed recess, wi my wee pottie at the side of the bed. No way was I going to the gludgie doon the stairs inn the night, it took me all my time going in the daytime. I was aye feared of something jumpin oot of yon pan at me. I used to think there wis snakes doon there, and because the auld wife next door wisnae well I got the nice job of taking her BIG POTTIE doon the stair, jist cause I was a wain and had to do wit I wis telt. Right enough my reading was all right. I got reading Oor Willie and The Broons [from *The Sunday Post*] depending how neatly the toilet paper was ripped."

"I used to take myself away roon the back wi my pals to play wee wee shops, broken gless was our money and dirt wis a nice chop wrapped up in a newspaper to take hame as your shopping. I used to love shouting up tae the window for a poke a chips or a piece and treacle, sometimes syrup if it was payday and my ma had got the rations in. Saturday wis the day though. I'm away to the ABC Minor's, sixpence to get in. Sometimes they took jeely jars and away in wi ma jubilee and a bar of Highland Toffee. By the time I came oot my lips were like two tyres, they'd swelled up sooking my jubilee. We used to get up on the stage and do a bit of dancin' and if you were lucky you got a wee tin badge or a ticket in to the afternoon matinee. I remember the first big film I seen, my ma took me to see *Imitation of Life* and *Madame X*.

Even the men were comin' oot greetin, awe wi hankies as big as table cloths."

"I went to Dalmarnock School, they used to bring in mobile showers, they put them in the school playground. Well there wis us, oot in the freezin' cold wi bathing costumes on, and them auld black rubber caps on us wi the snauters trippin' us and the lovely smell of carbolic. How we go through those days I'll never know but sometimes I wish I could turn the clock back, if only for a wee while. We had nothin' yet we had a lot if you know what I mean. I can still smell the mince and tatties and carmel cake and custard, what about the Sago? We all thought it was frog spawn. Ha Ha."

Les Jackson is currently residing at Kerrvale Nursing Home in Bridgeton. He was born at 984 London Road in 1940 and lived there as a youngster. He lived above 'The Ship Bar' where his father was the manager. Les recalls how, when he would be sweeping up on a Sunday morning following the usual busy Saturday night, he and his father would find pennies in the sawdust in the bar, left for them by some of the customers from the previous night. Apparently this was also the custom at the 'Gleniver' in London Road and also the 'Glengarry,' which was at the corner of French Street and Webster Street, both of which were managed by Les's uncle.

"A penny was a lot of money then," says Les. He tells me that 'The Ship Bar' was full of 'characters' and he remembers that a frequent topic of conversation amongst the clientele was how some of them had dodged the 'draft' during the Second World War.

Les's father was a Clyde supporter and he recalls how he was "dragged by the scruff of the neck" along to Shawfield. Tommy Ring [I remember him well, Les] was a big favourite of both father and son.

Les remembers the 'tossing schools' (gambling) near the turnstiles, to which the police "turned a blind eye."

Like myself, Les attended Riverside Secondary. He remembers 'MacLeod.'

"I was a bit of a fighter when I was young so I liked to give the 'Billy Boys' a 'hand'. It was just natural."

Les also remembers Mr "Gather in the books boys" Dunlop, the Science teacher. "A wee guy," he recalls. "Science was my favourite subject."

Les worked at Joseph Dunn's as an apprentice electrician, at both their Mordaunt Street and Blackfaulds Place premises.

Les has fond memories of my favourite 'flea pit,' 'The Plaza.' He recalls walking to here from his home and says, "The stalls had wooden seats but the balcony had leather padded seats." In the 'Geggy', he recollects that it was "Thruppence for the stalls and four-pence for the balcony." Les says that if you went to the 'Olympia' down at Bridgeton Cross, you were considered a 'toff.' Les also went to theatre shows, which were held at Bridgeton Public Halls in the appropriately named Summer Street, during the summer months.

A wartime memory of Les is of when the sirens went off, of being "rushed out of the house and a blanket thrown over you on the way to the air-raid shelter."

Les recalls that he lived as a child in a tiled close. "We were the toffs," he adds. "I loved Bridgeton," he concludes.

*Wilma Stirling Johnston lives in Australia. She was born in 1938 and lived "up the Pend" at 175 James Street. "There must have been about fifty families living there. The good thing about it was that we always had plenty pals to play with. I can remember the girls playing houses, great fun! There were also games of 'rounders,' never had any trouble getting enough people to play. Another thing I remember was climbing dykes. When I think about it now it's a wonder we survived. Some of those walls were quite high, my parents would have had a fit if they had seen me."

"We used to go to the Sunday School at the Ebeneezer Hall in Landressy Street. I think the boys came along for a cup of tea and a bun they gave after the service. In the evenings we used to go over to the Salvation Army and sing all the songs out in the street, at London Road, then it was back into the hall for more free food."

"I went to both the John Street Primary and Secondary Schools and can vividly remember our teacher in the qualifying class, she was a right old Tartar, her name was Mrs Brogan. I also remember wee Johnnny Potts, a Maths teacher at the high school, he was a bit scary."

Jack Kennedy was born in 1912 and lived in Swanston Street. He is now a resident of Kerrvale Nursing Home in Bridgeton. Bowie's Dry Cleaners owned the building in which he lived when growing up in Swanston Street.

Jack went to Strathclyde and Bernard Street schools. "School was never the love of my life," says Jack in a straightforward way. Also he says that Bernard Street was the only school that he knew that had 'spray baths'.

Jack worked as a driver with a motor hiring and engineering firm; William Rowan and Sons in Park Lane, which was near Broad Street.

Jack tells me that he remembers when the 'Olympia' picture house was a music hall. Also, there was a picture hall near Bridgeton Cross, which was later the 'Reveller's' dance hall. He also recalls 'social dancing' at a hall in Greenvale Street.

Playing football was one of Jack's pastimes as a youngster and he recalls playing football on open ground known as "the Roy" near his home. Also on football, he remembers that he could see from a window at his home, the crowds on their way to Shawfield on match days.

I asked Jack if he could remember any 'characters' from bygone Bridgeton. "They were *all* characters in Bridgeton," he replied.

Interestingly Jack, on speaking of the gangs in the area in days gone by, told me that the 'main man', in such situations, was called the 'leader off.' It was the 'leader off' who led the gang into battle.

Other memories were of the Sewage Works in Swanston Street and even more interestingly, of the horn which signalled the shift changes at Marshall's Tube Works in Swanston Street, that according to Jack "went off at all hours of the day," *and* the night to it seems.

Finally, Jack tells me that there were "bookies galore" in Bridgeton.

*John Kirkwood was born in 1951 and grew up in MacKeith Street. He now lives in Uddingston.

'The Dwellings' where I was brought up was like an old castle. It had a courtyard where we played, with the houses all around. At our back window was the graveyard, the 'Gravy' to us where we had a rope hanging from a branch and we would take turns swinging from the dyke. Backing on the courtyard was Guthrie's the butchers; in the summer they would open the windows during the day and pass out pieces of black pudding and sausage. Out in the street we played 'canny,' football, with a Tennant's lager can as the goal. You had to knock the can down with the ball to score. If you knocked it down with your foot it was a foul, if the defender done this it was a penalty."

"As for the area, I remember I had to go to a close in Mackeith Street to put my father's line on. The Bookie was halfway up the stairs. Leisure was the ABC Minors (The Olympia) at Bridgeton Cross). Then as I got older it was the Working Men's Club in Landressy Street. We used to dog school and go down to play snooker, misspent youth or what? In James Street we had our chippie, 'Reekie's' where you got a bag of batter, all the bits of the fish and such for threepence, or the fruit shop, a bag of chipped fruit. The grocer, Curley's, a bag of broken biscuits."

*Alice Maxwell was born in 1938 at 175B James Street and grew up there; she now lives in Cambuslang.

The Box Brownie camera provided millions of families with "snaps" in the middle of the Twentieth Century. These two show (above) Alice Maxwell, aged 2½, and big sister Dinah, aged 7½, taken around the early forties in the Daisy [Dassie] Park Greenhead Street, Bridgeton, with the statue of James Watt Statue in the background, and (below) Evelyn Day, age 14, in front of Templeton's Carpet Factory, Glasgow Green, in 1952.

"I was born and raised up the post office pend, as was my father, who lived and died up there at the age of fifty-five years. Our windows faced out to the 'Umbrella,' great view of the 'Orange Walk' etc for our other neighbours and relations too."

"We had a wonderful camaraderie up that pend that you would not believe. The games, plenty of children to play with and great neighbours to go to if you were locked out. In fact I still have the big old key for our tenement door, also the carpet-beater which my mammy would chase us with if making too much noise and "getting on her nerves." There were also the wonderful 'back court concerts' we had up the pend, where we would rehearse for weeks then invite all the neighbours down to see the show, refreshments served of course, and when one fattish girl would dance on the roof of the wash-house. One year she fell right through, thereby breaking her leg, which was in 'stookie for weeks afterwards."

Alice also recalls visits to the 'Daisy Park' and the bowling green, both at Glasgow Green. "My mother used to go to the 'Daisy Park' quite a lot, sitting chatting. My dad was a great bowler and won lots of prizes and his name was inscribed on the 'cup' a few times."

"We came from a mixed religion family so had no problems with the 'Orange Walk' and we loved to watch the Catholic procession through the streets in the summer."

Alice also recalls both Dr McKechnie and Dr McKay, our family doctors when we lived in Bridgeton.

Alistair May, now of Cambuslang, was born in 1947 and lived in Swanston Street as a youngster. He remembers a shop in the East End where when you paid for your goods purchased, on say a weekly basis and were given a payment book to bring with you. On every payment, this book would be returned to you downwards through a sort of 'chute.' (I remember this as being part of the set-up at the Glasgow Eastern Co-op Society at Westmuir Street, just along from Parkhead Cross.) Although Alistair could not remember the name of the shop, it was probably in the Co-op where he saw it. The Co-op was a general store with drapery and household good departments among others.

Bob May was born in 1916 and lived in East Kilbride from the 1960s. Bob was brought up in Bridgeton in Savoy Street and later lived in Swanston Street.

Bob was for many years the vice- president of the British Legion in Old Dalmarnock Road.

Bob remembered the nearby Savoy Arcade (or the 'pend' as it was locally referred to) that provided a shortcut into Main Street from Savoy Street and vice-versa. [I well remember this arcade] Bob interestingly, informed me that at one time there were shops on one side of the arcade. Bob's mother worked in one of these - a confectioners and he recalled how the 'peppermint creams' were sent from the shop up to Carson's chocolate works in French Street to be 'chocolated.' Also, Bob's grandparents owned premises where firewood was sold to the local people. He recalled as a boy, delivering firewood etc. to the homes around the area of Savoy Street – Main Street etc. and sometimes would receive a halfpenny from the grateful tenants for his troubles. Similarly, when a boy, Bob would sometimes deliver coal brickets to homes in the East End. He did this to help out his boyhood pals who worked as delivery boys, transporting the brickets to the homes in barrows. He told me that they would work their way all the way up Springfield Road to Parkhead and then on to such far-flung places as Shettleston. All the way along the route, the time honoured cry 'coal breek-ets' would be heard .

Bob recalled too the street bookmakers. Just as I recall Jimmy McKay whose 'patch' was in Barrowfield Street, Bob remembered one of the characters of the area who was a 'bookie.' This was Davie Leyton who worked down near the 'buggy lawn' buildings at the start of Bernard Street, just round from Heron Street. It was here that Davie the bookmaker 'lifted the lines' from the 'punters.' Bob informed me that the 'bookies' of that period were regular drinkers. Given their precarious existence in the days before betting became legal, this is not all that surprising really.

Bob's late wife lived at 9 Bernard Street, which was near the 'buggy lawn' houses, to the back of Bernard Street itself. He had many happy memories of their time together in Bridgeton, before moving to East Kilbride in the 1960s.

Bob in particular recalled the coronation of Queen Elizabeth II in 1953 and how he helped decorate the landmark Umbrella at Bridgeton

Cross. Bob recalled that at the time of the celebrations, red, white and blue lights decorated Bridgeton Cross.

The same year, he remembered the occasion of the funeral of Queen Mary (mother of King George VI) and that there was a big turnout from Bridgeton to pay their last respects.

Bob attended John Street school in Bridgeton and described it as "a wonderful school." He recalled, as a youngster, putting his pocket money into the Royal Bank of Scotland at 609 London Road, near Bridgeton Cross. He told me that he still had an account with that bank.

Bob also had fond memories of one of my favourite haunts, the 'Plaza' picture house in Nuneaton Street. He used to attend the matinees in the old 'Plaza' 'flea pit' as he called it. He also went to the old 'Olympia' at Bridgeton Cross and the 'Geggy' in Kirkpatrick Street, off London Road. He also mentioned a 'flea pit' that I don't remember. This was the 'Star' in Main Street, near the 'Wee Royal', also in Main Street. Bob informed me that when you went in here on a Saturday morning for the children's shows, the staff would give you a comic after you had paid the admission fee into the hall.

Bob also recalled the old boxing booths that used to be down near Bridgeton Cross. This would probably be the premises at 36 Olympia Street. Many famous names, or those who later became famous, including Benny Lynch, would go in here according to Bob.

Bob, showing me an old photograph taken in the early 1950s at Bridgeton Cross, helped me to (if somewhat vaguely) remember something that I had completely forgotten about. This was the weighing machine just across from the old Olympia cinema. It was here that coal, sand and all sorts of other materials would be weighed during the course of their being transported to various outlets from many of the local industries.

For many years Bob was involved in charity work in the East End and was generally well known throughout the area. "Everyone knew me," he said.

Bob recalled the distinction between 'wee' and 'big' Heron Street in local parlance. 'Wee' Heron Street was the part that led off London Road up to the junction with Bernard and Baltic Streets. 'Big' Heron Street was the part that continued from that junction, on into Dalmarnock Road.

(Sadly, Bob, a treasure chest of information on the Bridgeton area of Glasgow, died aged 88 in November 2004)

Elizabeth Miller was born in 1922 and lived in Gallowgate in a room and kitchen and with an outside toilet. Elizabeth now lives in Kerrvale Nursing Home Bridgeton.

Elizabeth went to Barrowfield and Bernard Street schools. "I liked school," she says.

She worked in the Bridgeton area, being employed as a bottle labeller in Dunn's bottle factory in Mordaunt Street and with a firm called McLellan and Rose in Arcadia Street where she worked for four and a half years. This firm was a cardboard box manufacturer. "I made up the boxes," says Elizabeth.

Always a keen cinema fan, she remembers such halls as the Orient in Gallowgate but also the 'Geggy', the 'Plaza' and the 'Olympia.'

On a darker note, Elizabeth recalls the gangs of the area and tells me how she sometimes witnessed gang fights at Bridgeton Cross, when chains and bottles would be just some of the weapons used by the combatants. Apparently these fights occurred mainly at weekends and were a regular 'event' in the 1940s.

Much has been said of the fact that the gangs of that period would only fight their rivals and people going about their daily business would be safe. Elizabeth offers evidence of this. She recalls that one day when out with her mother near Bridgeton Cross, on her way to her grandmother's home, they were both 'tipped off' that a battle was about to 'go off' as we would now say and that they should get out of the way quickly.

Elizabeth has some memories of the Second World War in the area and that "we were up and down from the air-raid shelters all the time." She remembers too that a 'Doodle–Bug' V1 rocket hit a building in a cul-de-sac close to where she lived. Sadly, children were amongst the victims.

Elizabeth recalls. as a child, the 'sawny-pond' (sandy pond) at Glasgow Green, and also tells me that when the Orange Walk came round the area when she was a child, the children would give pennies to the band.

Tam McArthur was born in 1943 and grew up in Bridgeton. He still lives in the area.

Tam went to the same secondary school as myself, Riverside, (Rivi). He went there in the mid 1950s and remembers the bane of my schooldays - Mr Macleod, the PT instructor. He also recalled Mr Galloway, the other PT instructor, as well as Mr Brown, a woodwork teacher and dear old Miss Dewar, the Geography teacher. He says too that he liked Miss Dewar. So I wasn't the only one after all.

Tam also remembers going to the 'Geggy' picture hall as well as the 'Strathies' and that old haunt of mine, the 'Plaza', which he remembers going to on Saturday afternoons.

Tam recalls Gus, the 'bouncer' in the 'Plaza', as "the bane of my life." Tam tells me that Gus was "five feet nothing and used to throw me out for making too much noise."

On Bridgeton, Tam sums up; "It was all we knew. We didnae know any better or any worse."

William ('Wull') McArthur was born at 80 Reid Street on Boxing Day 1953, and now lives in Cambuslang.

"Whilst still very young the family moved to single-end in the close at 202 Baltic Street. This was a tenement one apartment house in the close with an outside toilet. Early memories of this toilet is been taken out by my Da by candlelight and using torn up squares of newspaper for you know what."

"My sister Linda was born and the four of us slept in the bed recess which housed the family double bed. Curtains were used to hide the bed during the day. Being the oldest, I got the 'feet' end of the bed. The single-end also had a walk-in cupboard called a scullery which housed the cooker, and we had a sink at the window. Being young children we thought nothing of it and my memories are fond ones."

403

"We then flitted and moved round the corner to number 74 Fairbairn Street, two-up, two houses to a landing. Number 74 was the end close between two shops, one a newsagent on the corner, the other a dairy. This house had an inside toilet, two bedrooms but no bath. My sister and I got a room each, the living room was the family area and housed a bed recess for my Ma and Da. (There was) a scullery, and a sink at the window which had a gas geiser for hot water. My second sister, Janice was born in this house in July 1963 and I remember her taking her first steps from the living room right into the lobby.

"Every Friday was chippie night, a feast from our local chippie Adam's (Adam De Rosa's, in Baltic Street). Saturday mornings were special, a walk along Dalmarnock Road to the ABC Minors at the Olympia Picture house, pure magic."

"I attended Queen Mary Street School, then Dalmarnock Primary School which I enjoyed very much before completing my education at John Street Secondary School. The church, and the Boys Brigade were a big part of my life and I joined the Boys Brigade 'shipmates' in the Congregational Church in Fairbairn Street when I was five, before moving into the 'Lifeboys,' then finally the Boys Brigade. I remained a member of the BB, boy and man for over thirty years."

"I spent many an evening hinging oot the windae watching the local gangs kicking lumps oot each other, glad to say the only trouble I got into was for playing fitba in the street."

"Every Saturday I went the messages and remember being trailed round all the shops in Main Street, Curley's – slabs of butter, ham haughs

404

and biscuits. City Bakers for fancy cakes, Eiffel towers, fern cakes, meringues. Newsagents for the paper, butchers, fruit shop etc. By the end of the afternoon your arms were breaking, carrying all the messages in leather shopping bags. Other shops frequented were Logies, Timpsons, Galls and Vernon Bros. Sunday was the weekly visit to the Barras, always stopping off at Peter's café for ice cream drinks, hot peas and 'MaCallums.'"

"My Brigton memories are good ones, my one big regret is that the city fathers decided to renovate the tenements after they had demolished my neighbourhood, destroyed the community and more importantly in my case, ruined friendships that had been nurtured throughout childhood and teenage years."

Nan McConnell is from Newton Mearns. She was born in 1939 and originally lived in Dennistoun. Nan has indirect connections only with the Bridgeton area but she relates the interesting story of her grandmother having a shop, a small sort of general store, at 25 Queen Mary Street, off London Road. Nan tells me that her Gran had this shop from 1912 to 1965. As this was virtually just around the corner from where my own grandmother lived, it is quite possible that I was in the shop at some time for sweets or whatever.

Nan tells me her Gran told her, that during the years of the depression in the 1930s, people with little money to spare would come in to the shop and buy a single woodbine cigarette, as they were unable to afford a full packet.

When her Gran went to the public baths in Ruby Street, she recalled there was a ten minute 'maximum' on the time allowed for each individual bath here. This was of course, at a time when few people in the entire district would have bathing facilities in their home. The demand would be overwhelming.

Nan's father was a cyclist and she recalls that he used to train at Westhorn Park, a favourite haunt of mine in years gone by.

Bill McGillivary, now living in East Kilbride, was born in 1930 and as a youngster lived with his parents and his sister, in a 'single-end' in Arcadia Street, Bridgeton, sharing an outside toilet among three families. Later Bill lived in what is now called 'Merchant City.' Bill remembers local shops like Drummond's dairy in Arcadia Street and the paper shop next door.

Bill was a regular visitor to the nearby People Palace Museum on Glasgow Green and also recalls playing putting on the nearby green. He also has fond recall of going along the River Clyde on a rowing boat from Glasgow Green, which he tells me cost "about a shilling."

A good wartime memory of Bridgeton from Bill concerns his memory of the sirens going off to signal a Luftwaffe air raid. On hearing the sirens, Bill tells me that people would make their way to the air-raid shelters at Glasgow Green, or the 'trenches' as they were sometimes called, reached by going down a wooden ladder. The context of the times is fully captured when Bill says that when the sirens went "you grabbed what you could and stuffed it into a bag, because you never knew when you were going to come back to your home," adding ominously "you might not come back at all."

Bill also remembers the water-tanks on the streets of Bridgeton during that period. He tells me that, as a youngster, he and his friends would sometimes throw empty matchboxes into the water tanks to use as 'boats.' Apparently this was a regular pastime for the local children, but sadly some fatalities resulted from children falling into the tanks.

Bill tells me that the only evidence of gang-fights that he saw in the area was "a few skirmishes in the street. But you could walk the streets safely at night" he adds. "There were some 'hard cases' though, especially in the dole queues at nearby Megan Street where there were sometimes a few fights," Bill says.

Myra McGuigan (nee Rankin), now of East Kilbride, was born in the 1930s and grew up in Queen Mary Street, Bridgeton.

Myra remembers a 'well' or fountain, which was situated in Queen Mary Street and was apparently a well-known local 'landmark.' She tells me that it was known as the 'Black Well' and that children would splash about in the water from it. It was situated opposite the 'Cot Bar', at the corner with London Road.

Another memory from Myra is of roller-skating as a child in Baltic Street. Apparently the surface here was perfect for such a pastime. Then there was the tram depot in Ruby Street and like myself, Myra enjoyed watching the trams come and go from here. She tells me that "I used to watch them going in for the night."

One particularly interesting recall of Myra's is of performing as a child of about ten years old, with the Muriel Daly dance troupe at the old 'King's' Cinema in James Street. This would be during the interval, probably between the 'big picture' and the 'wee picture' as they were called in those days. Apparently, this dancing on the stage was a daily event. These days Myra performs as an artist, with some of her work on display at East Kilbride Arts Centre.

Myra also recalls the 'Wee Royal' in Main Street, which she says she did not like, as it was a 'flea pit'. (Weren't they all? But we loved them). Myra tells me that she much preferred the 'Geggy' ('Premiere') in Kirkpatrick Street but also, the 'Olympia' down at Bridgeton Cross. As her mother worked as an usherette there, she used to get complimentary tickets for the films.

In the mid 1950s Myra worked as a colourist with Templeton's Carpets, at their factory in Tullis Street.

Myra went to John Street Elementary School in Hozier Street but also, she tells me the interesting story of her cousins who went to Sacred Heart School in Old Dalmarnock Road. In those days, the children had apparently to go to mass every morning. When they attended, they would be given "a card" to let the schoolteacher know that they had attended mass. If they could not produce this card, they would get 'the strap.'

A somewhat darkly amusing recall of an undertakers, by the in some ways appropriate name of Matthew Bones, was related to me by Myra. Apparently these premises were in Muslin Street (or possibly Landressy Street) and Myra would pass them on her way to school.

On a somewhat lighter note again Myra recalls how as a youngster out with her pals, they would stand outside McBride's bakers shop at the corner of Queen Mary Street, pressing their noses against the window while eyeing the pancakes and crumpets on display.

Frank McKenna was born in 1939. Now living in Shettleston, Frank grew up in French Street, Bridgeton. "There were five of us in a single–end" he says. There were twelve families in the tenement building where he lived, with common "landings."

Frank went to Sacred Heart School in Old Dalmarnock Road and tells me that he "hated every single day at school."

Like myself, Frank was a film fan. He says, "The pictures were marvellous" and recalls halls such as the 'Plaza,' 'The Kings' in James Street and the 'Royal' (or the 'Wee Royal' as it seems to have been better known by most people), in Main Street. Frank in particular, has some good memories of the Plaza and tells me that the usherette would often come around, shine the torch and ask people when they came in. This was of course, to try to prevent people watching the picture for a second time. Frank says, that in order to get round this, "you would try and remember a bit of the film from later on and say that you came in at that bit, so you'd get to stay for a while longer."

Like myself, Frank remembers the posters advertising the films on the billboards in the street. It seems that they had a similar effect on him as they did me as, he says, "The posters made the films attractive to us." Interestingly, Frank recalls that some of the local shops would get free passes to the films on at the 'Plaza' through advertising the programmes at the shop. I don't remember this advertising, but Frank mentions Milne's fish shop right next door to the 'Plaza', which I remember well. This would presumably be one of the shops where the programme was advertised. Frank remembers too, that the 'Plaza' changed their programmes twice a week, while down in Main Street, at the 'Wee Royal', there was a change three times a week.

Frank remembers seeing a well-known jazz band of the period, (1950s-1960s) - the 'Clyde Valley Stompers', playing at Tollcross Park. One of the members of this band, Bill Bain (who had lived in Bridgeton) was a friend of my father; since he lived near us, I recall, he visited us once or twice when we first moved out to East Kilbride.

Frank recalls queuing for 'char' down at the old Dalmarnock Gasworks in Old Dalmarnock Road.

He also remembers the old public baths in Ruby Street which doubled up as the local 'steamie' and which I remember well. Just around the corner from here, in Dalmarnock Road, he remembers Collie's billiard hall.

Of the baths Frank recalls, "It was always mobbed on Friday. When you came out that was the dirt off ye for a week."

Like myself, Frank remembers that home life was very different in the past from what it is in the present day and recalls home-centred entertainment like playing cards. Frank adds the comment that "television killed the art of conversation. It was the worst invention of the twentieth century."

Like myself too, Frank was something of a 'tramspotter'. He remembers especially, the "yellow car" - the number 7 tram which went along James Street and Kings Drive, all the way to 'far off' Bellahouston. Frank also remembers the East Kilbride Dairies, which used to be in Silvergrove Street and near to the East End Dental Laboratory, my very first place of employment.

John McLaughlin was born in 1939 In College Street Townhead but grew up in Dalserf Street, Barrowfield; he now lives in America. Here he reminisces about his time at Riverside School, Springfield Road which he attended 1951-1954.

"Riverside was a great experience for me; the teachers were all characters, besides knowing their stuff. The one who stands out was big 'John McKay, from the Isle of Skye.' He was a British Israelite and had a chart in his room that showed the lineage of the British Royal family all the way back to King David. He was very patriotic, very Scots, he saw no conflict there. Tall man, with a red face, white hair, wore a blue sports jacket, the right colors. Used to tell us he didn't care if we learned History or English, his subjects, as long as we turned out Christian gentlemen. Oh well."

"Once we had a young Music teacher, a Miss Munroe, and a bunch of us wanted her to do 'High Noon' the big song that year, in class, and she was trying to stay with the lesson, whatever that was. So we all started running our fingers along our combs, hidden beneath the desk, this weird, rippling noise, all across the room. So she was going around confiscating combs, and we'd put out our back up combs, keep going. A real cheeky lot. Finally she burst into tears , sat down at her desk and sent the class captain for Big John, who was our home room teacher. He came down with his belt, excused her, still in tears and went round the entire class, grim faced, six times without stopping for a rest. We all deserved it too."

"I remember they took us all up to a movie house up at Parkhead Cross to see Sir Edmund Hilary on top of Everest, as a school outing. And, there was a bus trip, final year, somewhere or other where the other kids tried to hook me up with Jean Morton, a nice black–haired lassie, because she and I were the top of our classes but I was smitten by Cathy Swisher, a girl with straw-yellow blonde hair that had a green streak right down the middle of it, and we kissed all the way home, making a total exhibition of ourselves. I was just a nutcase."

"The Maths teacher was wee Eddie Palmer, who used to go to sleep in class, then wake up with a start and jump to his feet and start writing the solutions to the problems that he'd set us on the blackboard."

Janette McLean is now resident in Cumbernauld, Janette was born in 1945 and grew up at 811 Dalmarnock Road (A tenement block still in existence present day, unlike nearly all others from the past).

Janette recalls a special celebration concert held in the backcourt of number 811 at the time of the Coronation in 1953, when each child was supplied with a bottle of milk by East Kilbride Dairies. "There were big log tables out, I can't remember if we had anything to eat but I do remember getting a whole bottle of milk to ourselves, which was a complete luxury then. We used to have concerts quite a lot at 811, they were normally organised by a girl called Marion Mackintosh who stayed in the bottom flat in the close. We used to make up costumes with crepe paper and they were usually attended by adults as well. The weans used to sit on the dykes and listen to us either singing or saying a poem or whatever their particular party piece was. I don't remember being in the house for any great length of time in the summer. We were out from morning until we got dragged in for our tea, sometimes we would shout up for to get a jeely piece thrown over, from the third storey in my case."

"Jim, my late hubby told me about the penny tossing which he took part in and was probably a very important event at the time. He worked in Stevenson's Dairy in Baltic Street, next to the 'Strathies' picture house, before leaving school."

"There were shops all the way along Dalmarnock Road as you know, and I often wonder when I go back how so much was packed into such a small area."

"I went to Springfield Road Primary School and found it pretty uneventful. Always remember having to attend church, which was just around the corner from the school, every Wednesday. The Minister was a Reverend Wilson, and he was your typical old time Minister in appearance, tall, thin and grim looking. He used to ramble on every week in his sermon, don't remember anyone carrying on or anything, we were all too feart."

*Jane McMullen was born in 1946 and lived in Nuneaton Street. She now lives in America.

"Yes, I came from Brigton, and it was the happiest days of my life. I remember in Nuneaton Street my ma live facing Gorman's butcher shop in a low down house. There was a guy who worked in there fancied ma big sis, so he would come oor way butcher meat every night tae my ma for us. I got sick looking at butchers! haaaaaaaa! and the pubs on a Saturday night, it was better than goin oot anywhere, all the drunks singing and dancing in the street and not to forget the wee fight to top off their night. A drunk fell through oor bedroom windae, haaaaaaaa!, got up and continued singing the 'Sash.'"

"My da also worked in the 'Plaza Bar' pub doon the other end of Nuneaton Street. I would go to the pub door and tap my da for money as I was always skint. Efter the Friday I could get roon my da but never ask my ma, haaaaaaaa! Then, come a Monday [John's?] bakery doon at the close where we lived tae get the rools [rolls] for school on the tick book, ha!, as my ma had the six weans, and she always paid on a Friday then back oon the Monday."

"Aye, a lot of great memories from Brigton, it was the kind of street ya never had to go oot the street as they hid all the wee café fur yer ice cream and the fish and chip shop. My granny lived doon there too so it was one big happy family. Money wasn't the issue, as they made their own fun. All the wifes had a wee party oon the Saturday, wae the cakes and tea while the men at the pub then came up and [had] a wee sing song. I love listening to them when we were all in bed and if any cakes were left my da wid share them all with the weans. So, nothing to beat the good auld days."

Elizabeth McNeill grew up in Dennistoun. Now living in Newton Mearns, she recalls a visit in the late 1950s to one of my old childhood haunts - Shawfield Stadium. It was here she met her future husband, at a jazz concert, where the band the Clyde Valley Stompers, were performing.

John Oliver from East Kilbride lived in Dennistoun as a youngster. His main memory of the Bridgeton area is being called up on September the first 1939 to the Territorial Army (7th HL) hall in Main Street, on the outbreak of war. He tells me "pandemonium reigned" on that first morning. This hall was right at the corner with Muslin Street. (I remember it well. It existed till the 1970s at least). John recalls that on the morning he was called up, he and his fellow soldiers were given £5 "embodiment money."

John recalls marching down Main Street, every year to Bridgeton Station, on the way to Boroughead in Wigtonshire, which was the place where the regiment went for their annual fair camp.

John also remembers the "points boys" changing the tramcar points at Bridgeton Cross.

Finally, John remembers visits to the Bird Market in Sword Street, which runs between Duke Street and Gallowgate. The prices were three old pennies for men and a penny for boys. But if you got your hand stamped when you went in at first, you could go in and out all day at your leisure.

Helen Orr was born in 1930 and has lived in Bridgeton all her life - formerly in 'wee' Heron Street and Mordaunt Street and now in Main Street.

Helen attended Queen Mary Street Primary School and later went to Bernard Street Secondary. She recalls that at Bernard Street boys and girls would go to the 'dunny close' to smoke. She remembers that there was a Mathematics teacher at this school who was "very strict." His name was Mr Boyd, though his nickname was 'Pinty.'

Helen has fond memories of going to the picture-houses as a young girl. In particular, she remembers walking from her home in 'wee' Heron Street to the Plaza in Nuneaton Street and seeing "all the nice curtains in the windows of houses and the nice closes," in the streets along the way. "Everyone took their turn to keep the closes clean," she tells me. In the Plaza, Helen would feast on chocolate ices and sweets.

Helen also went to the Barrowland dancing at weekends, "looking for boyfriends," she says. During the week, usually on a Wednesday, she would go to the dancing at the Bridgeton Public Halls in Summer Street. "It was cheaper there," she says.

Helen provides a particularly interesting recall of the 'street bookies'. A bookie called Willie Flannagan often stood at her mother's window in 'wee' Heron Street. He would also use the close for 'taking lines' and would give Helen's Mum some money for the privilege of using the close for this. Helen recalls that when the closes were raided by the police, Willie Flannagan would throw his book through the window of Helen's mum's house, while the men – 'the punters,' – would all run away. Interestingly, Helen remembers the bookie Jimmy McKay, to whom I refer.

Helen recalls her aunt being an "illegal money lender" who would lend people who were down on their luck five pounds which would be paid back at the rate of five shilling a week, with an extra half-crown 'interest.' Helen recalls that in those days (1940s-1950s), neighbours were very supportive of one another. "Everyone helped each other out," she says.

Among the local shops recalled by Helen, are Cook's grocers opposite Blair's the butchers in Main Street, Gall's clothing shop, and Russell's electrical stores, both in Main Street too.

Helen recalls childhood games such as "kick the door and run fast" where you would kick one of the tenement doors and run away before the tenant opened it. She also remembers tying ropes to the doors of houses opposite each other on a stair 'landing.' Then there was peever, and rounders too, "I was a 'tom boy' as a child," explains Helen.

An amusing story is also told by Helen of how, on Saturday mornings when she was supposed to be looking after her brothers and sisters while her mother was at the 'steamie' in Barrowfield Street, she would be out playing round the backcourt. "I would get hell when my mother came home," she recalls.

Helen worked in a printer's - Clarke's in Cotton Street, as a machine worker, manufacturing envelopes and also at Moore's ginger factory in Mordaunt Street.

*Linda Pinnock was born in 1956 and lived at 14, then 24 Colvend Street. She now lives in Jersey.

"My father's side all came from the Bridgeton area and I was brought up in Colvend Street till age nine-ten when we move to the country, i.e. Cranhill.

"We lived in a tenement where my granny and granda lived on the first floor, my aunty and her family on the second, and us on the top."

"I went to Strathclyde Primary with my brother and I remember there was a small sweet shop around the corner where I once found two bob and thought I was a millionaire. "

" There were plenty of local characters around, one old Italian man I recall, Joe Maloosey, whose house always smelled of cooking and onions."

"I remember putting on backcourt concerts for my mother and her pals and charging a penny to watch us perform. My mother worked at Lairds box factory around the corner. Sometimes we would go to the baths at Ruby Street or sometimes accompany her to the Steamie. In those days all of our family went on holiday *en masse* and I have wonderful memories of those times."

Eddie Reid was born in 1962 and lived in 27 Beechgrove Street. He is now a police officer in Scarborough, Yorkshire.

"The bottom flat, a single end, was right beside the power station. It is no longer there [neither is the power station, Eddie]. Also, there was Penman's factory, at the top end of the street.

I remember walking over the bray to get to school. I went to Strathclyde Primary School. We used to sneak through the Lairds factory as a shortcut to school, often getting told off for it but we were very daring in those days.

"My next door neighbours were called the Redmonds. I think the boy of my age was called George, a right little tearaway. I remember Alex Ramsay as he blamed me for smashing a window and I remember the police coming round to my house and me not having a clue what they were talking about, but would anyone believe me? However the truth did come out in the end. I also remember the fire brigade at my house because my father came home drunk and decided he wanted to make chips on the old fat fryer; of course he went to sleep. However not a lot of damage was done but the neighbours weren't best pleased. This all happened in the late sixties, early seventies.

"I remember football was the be-all-and-end-all and we used to play every day and night. I remember that we were always skint but happy in those days playing football and the days lasting forever."

"The school I went to was brill. My teacher was a Miss McNaught, who used to take us poor wee souls away for a holiday at Rosneath, where her dad's caravan was. Such innocent days, bet you couldn't do that now."

I last visited the old place around three years ago and it was sad to see that the streets were all gone. I also remember the pub I used to get sent to by my ma to try and get my da out of it for his tea, without much success. It was called the 'White Horse,' on Dalmarnock Road, near the old power station.

"I remember a couple of names from my street, they were Jim Boyle and Pat Kelly, then there were the Redmonds and the Ramsays. I remember there was a wee sweetie shop at the bottom of Beechgrove Street where we used to get our sweeties. There was also a wee lassie who was a friend of mine, whose house I used to visit, I think her name was Agnes. The opposite street was Ashgrove Street. I remember the Grays from that street."

*David Reilly was born in the Gorbals in 1948 but grew up in Gretna Street, Parkhead, he now live in Leicestershire. The following extract is from pages 32-33 of his book *Oot The Windae,* (Glasgow: Lindsay Publications, 2000) in which he poetically evokes aspects of everyday life in the district. The piece is titled *The Ragman.*

> He gave you fair warning whenever he came
> though the tune he played was never the same
> in a neighbouring street a bugler played
> and it wasn't the lifeboys or the boy's brigade
> all the young mothers gripped with fear
> as this dreaded bugler came ever near
> tis the ragman playing a chordless tune
> the bedraggled Pied Piper of Glesga toon
> Came into our street pushing his cart

didn't need a horse he played that part
his old brown case was full of toys
like Santa's grotto to the girls and boys
paint sets and crayons and coloured chalk
to create a design on your whipping top
spud guns and peashooters and catapult slings
the toys of war the ragman brings
Took out a Woodbine the last of his fags
*then he bellowed **toys for rags***
last blast on the bugle and then he'd hush
lit up and waited the expected rush
the kids in the street would all go mad
looking for rags from their mum and dad
in all the cupboards through the rooms
a handful of rags for a couple of balloons
With great anticipation they stood in line
eyes fixes on the ragman all of the time
no pounds or ounces of imperial measure
just a bundle of rags for unlimited treasure
though I could only stand and stare
we never seemed to have rags to spare
now looking back and assessing the facts
all of our rags were on our backs

*Peter Scott was born in 1925 and grew up in Fairbairn Street. Later (1955) on marrying, he "bought a single-end at 16 Ardenlea Street for two hundred pounds." He has lived in Canada since 1965.

Peter attended Dalmarnock Primary School, 1930-37. "My class mate George Storie and I were forever curious about where our teachers lived, imagining addresses in Hyndland, Bearsden, Mount Florida and, to us, far away places. Much to our astonishment, Mr Campbell, 1934-35, lived at 525 Gallowgate. The Gallygate, for heaven's sake, our aunties lived there , which to our small minds was about as classy an address as Fairbairn Street."

"Anyway, one Friday at four o'clock, George and I set off in search of the truth. To our surprise, 525 Gallowgate wasn't some run–down tenement, instead it was a posh, red sandstone two storey building with stained glass windows. While I stood guard at the closemouth, George ran upstairs to check out the name plates. Suddenly I spotted Mr Campbell heading straight for the close. I yelled "George, he's coming" and bolted. George, in a flash of genius, pulled his jersey over his head and calmly walked right past Mr Campbell on the stairs. Talk about a close encounter."

"Mr Wright, 1935-36 was nearing retirement and was what today would be described as a 'laid back' type of guy. George, again was teachers pet, clean the blackboard, tidy the cupboards, etc. Mr Wright lived in East Kilbride, and every Friday George would wait for Mr Wright and offer to carry his case to the bus stop in Dalmarnock Road, where George would be awarded with a thrupenny bit. On this particular Friday, they reached the bus stop, but no thrupenny bit. George was in a panic, as he saw the bus fast approaching, Heron Street, Hozier Street, Ruby Street and George kept seeing his pocket money disappear with every turn of the wheels. Just as Mr Wright moved forward to board the bus, George, never one to miss a trick, said " Mr Wright d'ye know what I did wi' the thruppence you gave me last week?" Mr Wright must have given a wry smile as he dipped into his pocket and produced the precious coin for his helper.

Peter went to Bernard Street Secondary School. Here he relates what it was like in the 1930s.

"Bernard Street School is in the very heart of Bridgeton, and in the tenements overlooking the school, on most days you'd find the housewives engaged in their favourite pastime of "hingin' out the windae" and on the street below, the usual greeting was not "How are you?" but that almost imperceptible shake of the head known as the 'Glesga nod.'"

An outsider observing such behaviour might think that the inhabitants were persons of low quality and inferior intellect, but he'd be wrong, dead wrong. For in spite of the extreme poverty and the hardship they endured in the Depression, the average Brigtonian was a bright, considerate individual who would give you the shirt off his back, it cannot be said any plainer than that. And in education the student in Bridgeton enjoyed the benefits of an education system that in its day was among the best in the world, no question." [Excellent stuff Peter].

Amongst the people Peter remembers from 11 Fairbairn Street, 1927-1939, are "Joe Welsh whose mother lived at No.45. The McIntyres, third storey, the McKnights, the McGhees, the Provans, first storey. In the close was the Smiths, later to be occupies by my family, the house on the right was the Gormans."

Claire Tedeschi was born in 1936 at 31 Rockcliffe Street; she now lives in Australia.

"Many of the things I remember most about my childhood in Bridgeton are to do with food, things like h'penny tumshies from Kate McGowan's fruit shop in French Street, ice cream cones from Crolla's in Main Street. The ones that stick in my mind most are as follows: Saturday morning, going to Carruther's bakers in Main Street for seven scotch pies and just as we were about to start our meal the Provident Insurance man, whose name was Peter McKay, would come in. Every Saturday he said the same thing. 'There will be pie in the sky when you die for McKay, Hooch Aye' and each time we laughed as if we had never heard it before."

"Friday night about six o'clock being sent to the chip shop at the corner of Martin and French Streets for eightpence worth of hot chips for the tea, and if you went at the right time and the man was in a good mood he would make a little poke and give us the hot scraps from the chip pan with plenty of vinegar; food never tasted better."

"In Martin Street there was a bakery called Maggie Black's who made cream cakes and we would stand watching the baker with his piping bag of cream, fill all of the little jam tarts. They cost twopence h'penny each and we though they were magic. In Peter Hart's shop in Poplin Street where we got our Sunday paper and the 'Beano' and the 'Dandy' comics week about, there was the most wonderful red drink available for a penny a glass. I hated school milk especially when they heated it on the pipes, so when it had to be paid for (until about 1944 I think it was, it cost a h'penny) I would keep my money for two days and then buy a red drink. I was told many times not to do this so it made that drink so much nicer knowing it was forbidden."

Claire was evacuated to Strathaven during the Second World War and attended St. Patrick's School there, 1940-43 her first school. She then attended Sacred Heart Primary, and later Our Lady and St. Francis (Charlotte Street) Girls Senior Secondary School. She first worked in J.P. Harrington's warehouse in Hanover Street, Glasgow, and then in the House of Fraser in Argyle Street, and finally went to work in Gall's shop in the Gallowagate, before getting married in 1959.

Margaret Thomson, born in 1936, is now a resident of Bishopbriggs, but originally from Bridgeton.

Margaret recalls, as a child, going along with her grandfather to the Gas Works in Old Dalmarnock Road, for 'char.' She tells me that there was always a long queue and that people would bring along anything that they could push along the street to take the char back to their home in, things like prams.

Like myself, Margaret has fond memories of the carnival or the 'shows' at Glasgow Green. She says further, "Money or not, we must have spent many happy days there watching the side-shows etc."

Margaret also recalls a backcourt game, called 'moshie.' She says that this was a boy's game, played with whatever money you had. She also has fond recall of games like peever and skipping-ropes.

Margaret recalls one day hearing, from a childhood pal, that there was a tree round a backcourt in Playfair Street and that it was "the only tree in Brigton."

Margaret attended Dalmarnock Primary School in Albany Street and later Bernard Street. She recalls that during her time at Bernard Street, she received the punishment of 'the strap' after she was spotted throwing snowballs in the school playground. While at school, she remembers too, getting an old halfpenny from someone at school for her tramcar fare up London Road to "huts near Celtic Park", where, at the time, the schoolchildren were served their lunch.

Margaret too remembers many of the local 'flea pit' cinemas that are so familiar to me. Margaret adds, "You never went to the toilet at the pictures. The place was always stinking."

Margaret remembers that her mother worked as a 'clippie' on the tramcars and was based at Dalmarnock Depot, in Ruby Street.

Yet another memory from Margaret is of being screened during the TB (Tuberculosis) campaigns of the 1950s down at Bridgeton Public Halls in Summer Street, off London Road. I myself recall, in the late 1950s, seeing the Mass X-Ray units at Tollcross Park. They also visited Riverside School.

Thomas M Waugh, born about 1920, has lived all his life in the same street in Shettleston. Thomas recalls starting work in Arrol's in Bridgeton, as an office boy in 1937. He eventually became transport manager with the company and remained with the firm until his retirement in 1985. His first wage was two pounds ten shillings.

Thomas tells me that in his early days with the company, he would take a tram from his home in

Shettleston, get off in the Gallowgate and walk down Fielden Street to his work. Thomas says that in those days most people walked to their work. There were many fewer cars on the road than there are in the present day.

According to Thomas, about three hundred people worked in Arrol's, most of them from the local area. He recalls how, during the Second World War, the company employed women to do some of the jobs normally done by men who had been conscripted into the armed forces – e.g. working on lathes. They had, Thomas recalls, the strict dress code in those days. "You had to wear a suit," he says.

Thomas recalls that the workers would go to shops in nearby Nuneaton Street for snacks. He also remembers going along during his lunch break to Capaldi's café in London Road.

*'**Wee Meg'** was born in 1937, and has lived in Bridgeton all her life. Here are some of her memories of the area. "I remember go'n' te pey the rent fur ma ma tae a hoose in Reid Street. It's on the corner o' Rumford Street."

"Due to TB being in the family we were given free malt, cod liver oil and orange juice. This was a fun part of the household as no one seemed pleased at hivin to take this stuff but a loved the malt on a piece. We also got emulsion that was either pink or white, God it was rotten but you had to take it."

"Ma da was a jack of all trades, he could put his hauns tey ony thing, he wid go oot an paint ma aunty's hoose and de them delved doors, an paint fancy designs on thur ceiling so they gave us stuff for oor Xmas, plus they wid bring up fruit and veg, and other things like mince, stew, sausage, liver. We didny always get sweeties, as ma mither could swop they coupons for others like butter and things mer useful so she got a few bob for that. Some times if there wisney enough money for the 'Wee Royal' (Picture House in Main Street) we wid get the jeely jaurs te take as they let u in for a wee wan and if ye wur lucky enough te get a big wan, ye got an ice cream or something else, like a carmel. Boy it was rer, the kids of today don't know how te live."

"There were five lassies in oor hoose and three boys, so aw the auld coats came in haundie for the winter, an if ma da wis short oh money he wid gie ye a letter to go te the parish for money oot his savings an the parish man wid say te ye "whit dis he need the money fur?" So a wid say "cause we hiv tae share a bed an some oh them pea the bed." Ha ha. Ma ma hid te go te the parish te get us claise, the jumpers were ded jaggie, an ye did nothing bit scratch when ye hid it on. An the shoes they gave ye were took back te be repaired when they were wearing doon. The first time we got a hale egg on a piece we thought it wis oor birthday an Christmas aw in wan, an ma brither John wis shoutin te his pal "Hey Peter we got a hale fried egg fur wur breakfast."

"There wis a shelter in Madras Place thit we used to play in, and we wid sit innit an sing songs for hours, an we would kid on wee wur great it sports an we wid run roon the outside o' this shelter. I remember aw the mothers sitting it the close te efter twelve at night, singing. God it wid be rer te get they days back, an the weans wid be better the day."

"We used tae sit it the windaes on a Saturday night and watch the 'Norman Conks' and the 'Billy Boys' fight, bit they never hurt women or kids, no like noo, they don't care who they hurt.

"When you were skint yur ma would say "Go roon te 'Mrs X' an tell her a need her mans suit for the pawn." Whit wid we hiv done athoot the pawn?

"Ah mind wan day me and ma mither went te Blair's the Butchers in main Street and she said "will ye gie me a bone for the dug?" So, me being rent a mooth said "ma we don't hiv a dug." The man said, "well ye hiv noo and you're the dug." That wis te make soup wie."

"When we started work we thought we were rich cause we got five bob pocket money, bit that hid te de ye aw week, then yur ma wid gie ye pieces on spam or something like that fur yur break."

Carl Wilson was born in 1942, "in a three storey tenement at 157 Springfield Road." Carl now lives in Leicstershire.

"My mother fought to have an air-raid shelter built in Sorn Street, just around the corner. The funny thing was, when the sirens went off during the war by the time we got down three flights of stairs there was no room left for us. I spent all my young life at the same address until I got married (in) '63 then moved to Penilee and lived with my parents, and moved to Priesthill to have a place of our own."

Carl begins, "I can remember when the two gangs, ('The Baltic Fleet' and 'The Norman

Conks') used to have some real tough fights. They used to meet in Baltic Street at the railway bridge and they laid into each other something awful. My brother who used to work in a pub at the corner of Lily Street and Springfield Road used to go over to the banks of the River Clyde on a Sunday morning at 10 am to sort out the punters he had a "set to" with in the bar the night before. He used to come back in some states but never did anybody in them days use a 'chib.'"

"I left Pirn Street School and went to work in the slaughter house on the Gallowgate. That was in 1959. I served my apprenticeship as a slaughterman. Can always remember getting thrown off the tramcar because we stunk from the high heaven and had to walk home from work and that included my mum as she worked in the gut-work there."

Carl reveals that his sister was the singer 'Nancy Whiskey' who had a hit record called 'Freight Train' in 1957.

Carl concludes, "I remember sitting in my car one day watching them pull down my old building. That made me cry I will admit."

St Columba's Episcopal Church (now demolished), Baltic Street, in 1966. Park of the swing-park where I played is visible on the left; the tenements are in Lily Street.

Source references.

Most of this book is written through personal recollection of places, people dates etc. In part though, at various points throughout the book, I have supplemented this with reference to various sources. The main ones consulted were as follows...

Kelly's Directories 1952-1974.

Glasgow Post Office Directories 1952-1974.

Electoral Registers (Glasgow) 1940-1974.

Register of Births, Deaths and Marriages at the Strathclyde Genealogy Centre, 22 Park Circus, Glasgow.

Various school Admission and Logbooks relating to the 1950s and early 1960s.

Also, various national newspapers but most especially...

Evening Times 15 September 1947.
Sunday Mail 15 December 1957.
Daily Record 22 March 1961.
Glasgow Herald 27 August 1973.

Printed in the United Kingdom
by Lightning Source UK Ltd.
118991UK00001B/58-66